# A LITTLE MADNESS

*Ciarán de Baróid*

**Ogham Press Belfast**

Published 2013 by Ogham Press
5-7 Conway Street
Belfast BT13 2DE

Copyright © Ciarán de Baróid 2013

The right of Ciarán de Baróid to be identified as the author of this work has been asserted by him according to the Copyright, Designs and Patents Act 1988.

All rights reserved. This book is sold subject to the condition that it shall not, by way of trade or otherwise, be lent, resold, hired out, or otherwise circulated without the prior consent of the author/publisher in any form or binding or cover other than that in which it is published and without a similar condition including this condition being imposed on the subsequent publisher.

ISBN    978-0-9566166-1-6

Typeset from disk by Leslie Stannage Design, 71-75 Donegall Pass, Belfast BT7 1DR. Artwork by Leslie Stannage Design.

Printed by W&G Baird, Greystone Press, Caulside Drive, Antrim BT41 2RS.

Cover Photo: Gujars on the move in central Afghanistan. © Jerome Starkey 2013.

Back Cover, top to bottom: the author's partner, Cora, in Kandahar, December 1971; the author aboard the roof box of a truck on his way into Pakistan December 1971; Tony O'Connor, leaving Ameyugo, Spain, January 1970; Berber woman from Morocco's Rif Mountains.

**Contents** **Page**

1. The Innisfallen .................................................................... 3
2. The Smoke ........................................................................ 11
3. France ............................................................................... 17
4. Mañana ............................................................................. 24
5. The Sandeman .................................................................. 42
6. The Coast of the Sun ........................................................ 49
7. 'The Only Hope…' ............................................................ 56
8. Long Way to Rome .......................................................... 78
9. Petruccia's Folly ............................................................... 93
10. No Dough, No Show ........................................................ 99
11. The Pudding Shop .......................................................... 113
12. The Erzurum Express ..................................................... 125
13. Viktor .............................................................................. 137
14. Ashura ............................................................................ 144
15. The Land of The Great Hashish ..................................... 151
16. The Fall ........................................................................... 163
17. Carted Off ....................................................................... 168
18. Lorna .............................................................................. 178
19. Munich ............................................................................ 190
20. The End Of The Beginning ............................................ 198
21. 'Gone to Afghanistan' ..................................................... 205
22. Yener and The Golden Rules ......................................... 211
23. Run to Kabul .................................................................. 217
24. The Bicycle Ride ............................................................ 232
25. Desert of Death ............................................................... 239
26. Mr. John and Baden-Powell's Cousin ............................ 249
27. Christmas ........................................................................ 259
28. Qeshm ............................................................................. 265
29. Return to Tehran ............................................................. 274
30. Minus Forty .................................................................... 285
31. Later ................................................................................ 297

# Acknowledgements

I owe much of this book to the two principal people who shared the journeys described. Had they not agreed to join me when others thought it folly, the tone of the travels would undoubtedly have been different, and the details would have been preserved to a far lesser extent. Although I kept a diary while on the road and managed to retain photographs, it was the constant reminiscing down the years in the company of my two companions - one remaining a lifelong friend, the other becoming a lifelong partner - that kept the people and places so alive. In addition, Tony Lee, on regular visits from Sydney, would jog my memory around some forgotten note from the wilds of Asia or the Munich abode of Viktor Strommler. I was also able to return to some of the places in the book - London, Morocco, The Netherlands, France, Spain, Turkey and Germany - to check on half-remembered details.

The rest of the book I owe to all those idealists, hedonists, adventurers and lunatics who made the journeys what they were. You remain close to my heart. I would have loved to have given you all your full and proper names, but who knows who you are now? Where I couldn't check if you were OK about appearing in person, I have changed your names to avoid prosecution, persecution or an untimely end.

Finally, a very special thanks to Paddy Kelly and Áine, my first readers who provided valuable comments and suggestions and spurred me on to completing a task long on the back burner.

Ciarán de Baróid
Belfast
June 2013

For Tríona and Áine.

And my old friend
Tony O'Connor.

# THE ROAD TO ISTANBUL

*'No matter which reasons took them on the trail, they have one thing in common: few of them remained the same persons after their return.'*

Erik Pontoppidan from Denmark who travelled overland to India in the spring of 1969.

Greek-Turkish border March 1970

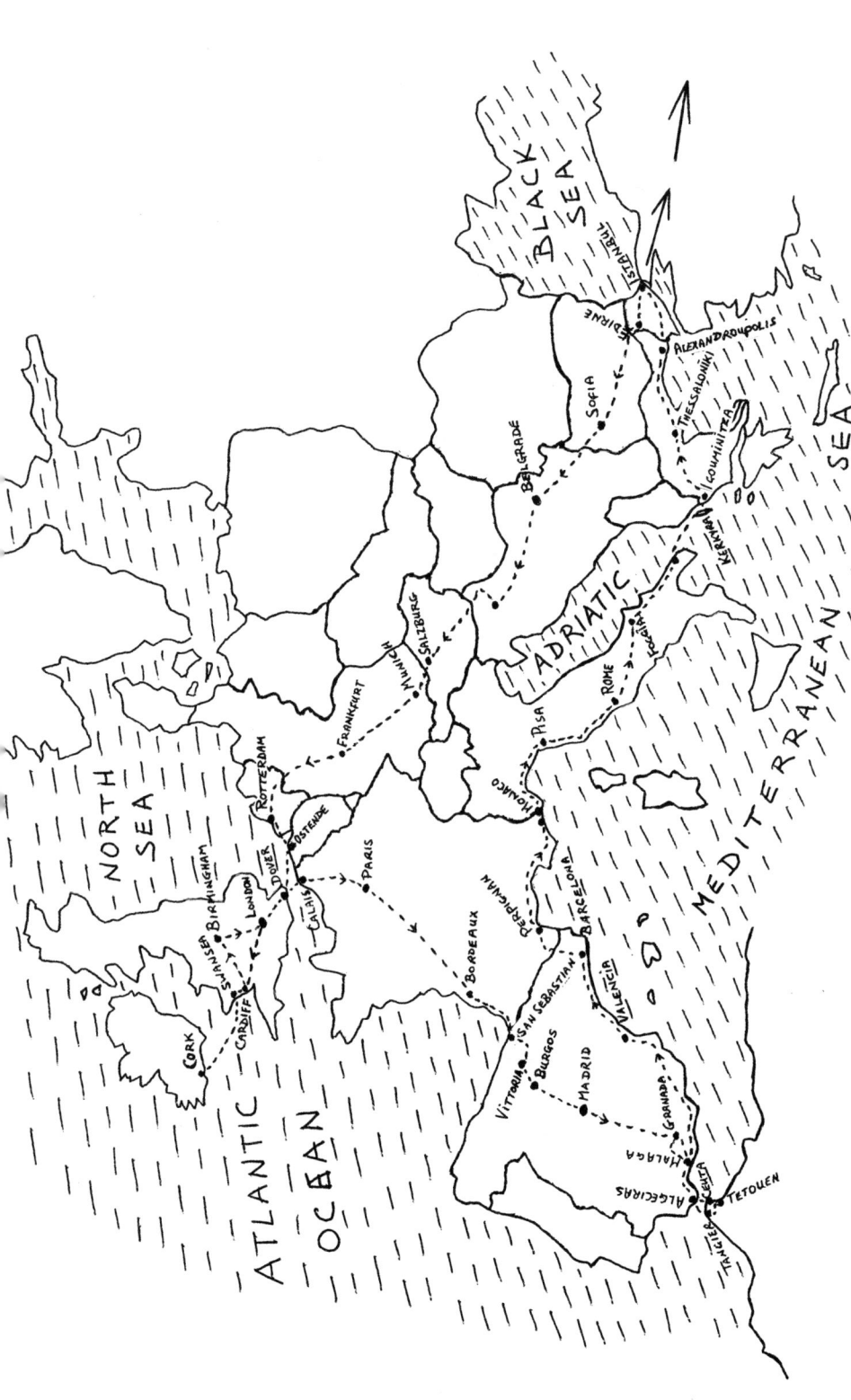

# Chapter 1
## The Innisfallen

*'A man needs a little madness, or else he never dares cut the rope and be free.'*
Nikos Kazantzakis (Zorba the Greek)

Monday January 5th 1970 was a day like any other. But for the fact that, at eight o'clock that evening, with the cloak of night tight on our town, Tony O'Connor and I climbed the ramp of the Innisfallen. We were both eighteen and bound for the Welsh port of Swansea.

The Innisfallen of 1970 was not the only one of its line. Ever since 1896 they'd been heaving them into the sea. The first, operated by the Cork Steam Packet Company, had linked Cork to Fishguard until it became a 1918 statistic of World War I. The second was lost to Hitler's magnetic mines off the British coast in December 1940 after the owners had switched the service to the Dublin-Liverpool route. The third - the only real one as far as our generation was concerned - set sail again from Cork in 1948. With its black hull, white superstructure and black and white funnel, it left Penrose Quay three nights a week for Fishguard, carrying passengers, livestock and cargo. On winter nights you could watch it sail down the River Lee in a fairy-tale of lights and a shrill roll of whistle-blasts that cut the cold air long after the ship was lost to sight.

In 1967, this third Innisfallen was sold to the Greeks and Penrose Quay was abandoned. Work began on a proper terminal downriver at Tivoli and two years later a modern car ferry, running a new route to Swansea, set off on its maiden voyage. When it entered service, the fourth Innisfallen, with a speed of 24.5 knots, was the fastest ferry in the world. It brought to its passengers class, distinction and something called a cafeteria. But to us of the *real* Innisfallen, it always seemed a swaggering imposter. Nevertheless, it maintained the primary role of its predecessors as the emigrant ship that funnelled the southern columns of the Irish Diaspora to the shores of Britain. 'Never worry, never fear,' they said in Cork. 'The Innisfallen's always near.'

Given that four years earlier it was reported that a million Irish-born economic refugees were now living in Britain, it was likely that the majority of people on board the ship on that January

## Chapter 1

night in 1970 were emigrants returning from the Christmas break. It was also likely that anyone who noticed the two of us trudging up the gangway in our combat jackets, jeans, walking boots and black berets, with rucksacks on our backs, would have chalked us up as a couple more lads off to London for a start. The small Irish tricolours on the packs might have extracted a second glance, but the conclusion would've still been the same. And wrong.

Far from being our saviour from the brittle economy left behind by centuries of colonialism and the aftermath of World War II, the Innisfallen was our getaway. After three years of hitchhiking around Ireland and lowland Scotland, learning the dark arts of sleeping rough, jumping trucks, cooking on fires and living on our wits, we had launched on the great emprise. We were hitchhiking to India.

Now, let me slide this into its historical slot.

It's unlikely that anyone then living in our little city on the Lee had ever met anyone who'd hitchhiked to India or gone to India by boat, donkey or bus. True, we had our share of heroes. You could go back to Séamus Hearney and the winter of 1962-63 when Cork had the biggest freeze in living memory. Snow, frost and gales that began at Christmas lasted clear through to the end of January and left the country under a sheet of ice. On January 1st the staff at the transmitter station on Mullaghanish in West Cork, found themselves cut off from the world and running out of food. A helicopter drop was abandoned due to the ferocity of the gales.

'I know what we can do,' rigger-driver Séamus said. 'We can ski down the mountain.'

Séamus cobbled together a pair of skis from old planks and managed to get down to Ballyvourney - with another man on his back. He then traipsed back up with 40lbs of food and repeated the journey several times - presumably without the man on his back, although this was never clarified.

Then there was Joey Kerrigan who died on January 9th 2008 at the ripe old age of 96. A teacher in Crawford Tech, Joey was a living legend. Back in the forties, he'd gone up Carrauntoohil, Ireland's highest mountain, on a bicycle. He'd crawled through every cave he could find in Ireland, canoed through the streets when the Lee burst its banks, and skied down Vernon Mount to the horror of a farmer out looking for his cow, as Joey didn't know how to stop.

We had another man whose name eludes me, who tore up telephone books with his bare hands outside the Golden Bowl on

Merchants Quay (the new public toilet so named by the people of Cork owing to the luxury of its fixtures and fittings). And we had men of iron who, when the annual floods swamped the inner city, sat on high bar stools and refused to budge as empty beer-kegs floated past and mullet swam through low-lying streets. Photographic evidence of these happenings can still be found in the pages of *The Cork Examiner* and *Evening Echo* of those times.

Yet, I can probably assert without fear of contradiction that there had never been two lads who had left our town half broke to hitchhike 5,000-odd miles to India and 5,000 back. Not to mention another thousand if you threw in North Africa. We were, in that respect, pioneers, luminaries of our little town, although this was yet to be recognised.

Sixteen months earlier I'd had an Einstein moment. One minute I was perched in front of a black-and-white TV documentary on slum life in Calcutta. The next, I was catapulting for the family Atlas to see if any major seas stood between Cork and Calcutta.

There was no rational explanation for this. However, many years later, a theory was proffered.

On a day back in 1953, Mrs. Hardy who lived around the corner in Summerhill South was staring out her bedroom window. Not easily stirred to the irrational, the good woman first assumed that the sight assailing her eyes either constituted a joke of the morning light or an apparition of the baby Jesus come to roost on the roof of a two-storey house - 3 *Ard na Gréine* to be exact - around the corner in Evergreen Road. There could even have been an element of prescience in it, she thought. *Ard na Gréine* translates into Height/Hill of the Sun as indeed that roof might well have seemed on that bright and alarming morning, particularly if the baby Jesus was up top. However, after severe rubbing of the eyes failed to dispel any trick of the light, or bring to focus a baby Jesus halo, Mrs. Hardy considered the one remaining option - indeed an awful conclusion - and despatched her son Liam at a gallop. A loud banging brought my mother to the front door.

'Mrs. de Baróid,' Liam panted. 'Do you know that your son is on the roof?'

Followed by Liam, the poor woman raced to the back of the house to find that this was indeed the case. Her two-year-old was closing in on the ridge tiles, having climbed by way of a ladder and cat-ladder left in place during renovations. Theory goes that, having

## Chapter 1

survived the climb back down, the panorama from the roof was the catalyst.

Anyway, as the most rudimentary knowledge of geography will establish, there are no major seas between Cork and India. Once confirmed, I struck out for the Pavilion cinema where Tony O'Connor, the sole likely companion for the journey forming inside my head, might be found.

We'd been friends since meeting at the age of eight at the misnamed Model School where, in one single week, pupils set fire to the school shed, drove a tractor into an outer wall and peppered the trilby of one of the teachers with a .22 air pistol. Two famous brothers from Anglesea Street also took it upon themselves to save the imperilled soul of a Jewish lad in a sink in the outdoor toilets. 'I baptise thee in the name of the Father ...' could be heard from over the toilet wall.

From the classrooms of the Model, we progressed to the dockside mills where cigarettes and chocolate, scrounged from dark sailors smelling of rum, tar and Valparaiso, were consumed in camps up among the sacks of flour when we should have been at school. In the years since, Tony had grown to six feet, was deft with the mitts in a tight corner, and had an unsinkable sense of humour that appreciated the vagaries of the human spirit and the absurdities of the likes of tapioca. In his teens, he'd been stabbed, almost annihilated by the spray of a submachine gun in the careless hands of another and, more recently, mauled by half the Irish population of earwigs while sleeping on a roadside verge south of Belfast, of which there will be further mention. Never a lad to dodge a challenge, or bow to a tyrant, or deny that you only failed if you didn't try, Tony would say yes or I'd be on my own.

His job at the cinema was that of projectionist and he hated it. So between reel-changes he could be found on the flat roof, keeping an eye on Patrick Street. (If the celluloid film split and had to be spliced, he used to explain, he'd know by the howls and stomping of the punters.) He was up there, sitting on the balustrade, when the yell came from street level.

'Do you want to go to India?'

'What!' he howled. 'Are you shaggin' *serious*?'

'We could go by North Africa.' This was a thought from half way across the South Gate Bridge.

Some years earlier, Tony had had a similar proposal. The Atlas had just come into our house, and on the basis of its pages being glossy and giving the impression of looking down on Earth from a hundred miles out in space, I had a vision.

'When I grow up,' I said, 'I'm going to cycle around the World.'

This took no account of minefields, the Iron Curtain, swamps, jungles, wars, revolutions, the Darién Gap or the practicalities of riding a bike across the Bering Strait in winter. I could cross the ice from the Chukotskiy Poluostrov Peninsula of the then Soviet Union to Alaska.

All is possible when you're eight years old.

If my father, recipient of the vision, harboured doubts, he never said. Encouraged, I took off for High Street, half a mile away, where Tony lived.

'That's a great idea, boy,' Tony said, secretly putting it down to the fact that I'd fallen nine feet from the top of a pig-lorry to a double fracture of the skull two years earlier, while decisively winning the street game of who could jump from the highest of the lorry's slats.

This time, the response was more positive.

'Hang on,' he yelled. 'I'll be right down.' He disappeared from sight, then reappeared five seconds later. 'Saddle me the grey, boy,' he roared, hopping about the roof like a blue-footed boobie. 'Saddle me the grey.'

Passers-by stared at the madman on the roof of the Pavilion. 'Look,' some respectable-looking old duffer in a tweed overcoat muttered to his wife, 'It's Quasi-fuckin'-modo.' I gave him a dirty look.

When Tony went back inside and told the others, the Pavilion rocked with howls of ridicule. When I told the ones at school, the school rocked. My father thought a stay in France might be a good idea: I could learn the language. Tony's father, Con, thought he'd taken a turn.

'If that eejit jumped into the river,' he said, 'you'd jump in after him.' (This would later unfortunately prove true in our very own River Lee.) 'Some day,' he concluded, 'there'll be a bad end to that fella and if you're around there'll be a bad end to you too.'

My girlfriend, Cora, couldn't make head nor tail of it. 'Not to mention the fact,' she said, 'that you're going in the wrong direction.' (The North Africa bit.)

Bernard Cronin who sat beside me in school tried to get one of the teachers to outline for me the fine line between illusion and delusion.

# Chapter 1

In June 1969 I finished secondary school and Tony quit the Pavilion. For the next six months, we could be seen with our sandwiches and shovels on the building site of the new science block at Cork University where labouring paid a half decent wage. Meanwhile some support began to filter through. The Pakistani Embassy in London sent us a lovely letter of encouragement. The Iranians sent us a map of Turkey, Iran and Pakistan. Tom Barry, legendary leader of the IRA's West Cork Flying Column during the War of Independence, gave us a letter of introduction, pronouncing us sound of character and mind. 'It might come in handy,' he explained, 'if you run into any revolutionaries.' The Soviets, however, told us that 'due to the vastness of our country we do not allow hitchhiking'.

The Mir of Hunza, we read somewhere, loved to welcome strangers. He lived in Pakistan.

'Chalk the lucky man in for a visit,' Tony said. 'We'll only be passing the once.'

By Christmas, we were ready. Two cheap packs held a change of clothes, some washing gear, cooking equipment, and the sleeping bags and long johns meant to insulate us at night from frozen winter ground. Sewn to the inside of our combat jackets, we each had a hunting knife to ward off bandits. In the pockets we had our passports and travellers' cheques. (I had £160. Tony had £120. Light pockets even in those times.) We'd pick up any necessary visas along the way. Deep in my pack, I also carried *The Oxford Book of English Verse* and a substantial travel diary tucked into an aluminium sleeve that I'd rivetted together on the university building site. Deep in his, Tony carried an orange shirt and a brown tie for when we'd meet the Mir of Hunza. We tried for travel insurance but were told that nobody wanted the business of anyone hitchhiking to India. Then we bought our tickets for the Innisfallen.

Ten years after Tony had so spurned my first offer, he and I were on the freezing deck of the emigrants' hope, the wind howling through the masts, the future as opaque as the night beyond. Looking behind, we watched the small city in which we'd grown up fade to a pale glow in the winter sky and had no doubt that we were the only people in the world taking such a step. If all went well, we didn't expect to see those who'd waved us off from the Tivoli quayside for another six months. Some of them didn't expect to see us ever again. As we passed the lighthouse at Roche's Point, exiting the outer harbour and thumping into the black swell of St. George's Channel, I was hit by a mighty gush of pride and responsibility. Not a body on board could've guessed the stature of the personae in their midst. We were carrying on our backs the flag for Ireland. We were the unofficial first Irish overland expedition to India.

'Ciarán boy,' Tony said, staring down into the white horses being churned up by the ship's bow, 'how could you bate this?'

Away out beyond, the lights of another ship bobbed in the heaving swell. My heart did a somersault. If there is an Everest of happiness, that moment on the wind-scoured deck of the Innisfallen must have been pretty close.

In the morning we stood again on the wet deck, berets pulled down over our ears, as the ferry berthed and the first snows of winter swirled like confetti around the dockside lamps. Shivering with the cold, snow melting on our faces, we stared out at the lights of Swansea and neither of us said a thing. Compared to all that travelling in Ireland and Scotland, all that sleeping in blankets in frost-encrusted fields, all that living off loaves of bread and pints of milk lifted from unsuspecting windowsills, this was taking your raft out of the paddling pool and launching it into the ocean. In a time before Discovery Channels, *Lonely Planet* and the Internet, much of the world was still a place of there-be-dragons. Who could tell what lay down there, where the Swansea quay met the gangway of the Innisfallen?

Raw-eyed from fitful sleep on the cafeteria seats, we left the port and picked our way through dark empty streets to the edge of town for the long haul to Calcutta. At a sign pointing to Cardiff, we dropped our packs in the snow and stuck our thumbs in the skinning air. Unknown to the people of Swansea, this was where the road to India began.

To stop my teeth rattling I shared an India-related thought.

'Tony,' I said, 'did you ever consider that if Columbus had gone looking for China instead of India when he stumbled on America, the red Indians would've ended up being called the red Chinese...'

'Ciarán,' Tony advised. 'Get a grip...'

## Chapter 1

*The 'unofficial first Irish overland expedition to India': the author (left) and Tony O'Connor. Photos taken in Istanbul, March 1970.*

## Chapter 2
### The Smoke

We stood two hours in the snow before a blue Volkswagon Beetle screeched to a halt fifty yards down the road. It reversed at speed and screeched to a second halt at our feet. The passenger door opened and a small chubby man of about fifty, whose distinguishing features were a bushy beard, a small red nose and a feathered felt hat, leaned across.

'Cardiff,' he said, 'if that's any good. Only thing is you'll have to squeeze one of you and the rucksacks into what's left of the back seat. The boot is full.'

Looking in, we saw that a set of drawers occupied most of what would normally constitute a back seat. With some difficulty, Tony managed to work himself and the packs in while I sat into the front passenger seat.

'Where are you for?' the driver asked.

'India,' I said. 'Well, London first, then India.' The man gaped.

'You can't be serious. India is thousands of miles away.'

'I know,' I said. 'We're giving ourselves about six months for the round trip. Down to Morocco, then over to Istanbul, then across Turkey, Iran and Pakistan to India. Overland. Hitchhiking.'

'Are you out of your minds!' he said in what sounded like a mouse squeak. 'What about bandits? You get bandits in all those Asian countries. You could get kidnapped by bandits.'

'It's his idea,' Tony laughed from the back. 'He told me to buy a knife for the bandits.' The driver looked at me and then turned to Tony.

'Maybe he should sign himself in somewhere,' he suggested.

Having consigned us to the margins of sanity, the driver then admitted to being a vermin-exterminator by trade and an amateur magician by hobby. His name was Eddie, he told us, and he was on his way to do a show at a children's party in Cardiff.

'I'll drop you off on the Bristol side,' he said.

It took about an hour of Eddie trying to convince us to go back home before we reached the east end of Cardiff.

'This is as far as I'm going,' he said. 'But, let me show you a trick before you go. First we need to get out of the car.'

## Chapter 2

Tony and I exited and retrieved the rucksacks, by which time Eddie was standing in front of us.

'Ready?' he asked.

'Yeah,' we both said.

At that Eddie pulled a golf ball and pen from his pocket. 'Here,' he said, handing them to me. 'Write something on the ball.'

Although never keen on being a magician's assistant, I wrote *Cork* on the ball. Then, right before our eyes, Eddie popped it in his mouth. I watched him like a hawk. I saw it go in. I saw the shape of it go down his throat. When it reached the bottom of his throat, he made great show of a final forced gulp. 'Look,' he said, showing both hands and opening his mouth, 'no ball.' He then took a handkerchief from his pocket and waved it around the top of my head. 'Now,' he said, 'take a look in your right jacket pocket.' I reached in and there it was.

'Eddie, boy,' Tony said, 'You got us with that one.'

Personally, things like that annoy me.

We were now thirty miles from Swansea. Two hours later we were still thirty miles from Swansea. At first it was OK. After more than a year of planning, and the occasional pang of doubt, we were finally on our way, feet firmly on Welsh soil. The snow and black skies could do their worst. But two hours is a long time. As the snow melted the cold into our clothes, we both began to shiver uncontrollably. We took turns to hop over a wall into someone's garden to pull on our long johns, but the cold seeped through the long johns too and spirits began to sag. We and our hefty packs were going nowhere fast. Silently I did the maths.

'Tony,' I said. 'At an average rate of seven miles an hour it'll take us about four days at eight hours a day to cover the 240 miles from Swansea to Dover plus another half day to get through London.'

Tony looked at me as if I'd grown spikes.

'And if we're here another hour,' I added, 'the average will be down to six miles an hour. We'll be the guts of a week crossing England.'

'Begod, boy,' Tony said, 'that's the nightmare sums.'

Faced with such an appalling calculation we had no choice but to split up. We'd flip a coin for who went first, and meet at the ferry terminal in Dover. This was a blow. The whole point of leaving together was to travel together - to watch one another's backs and share the ups and downs of wherever the journey would go. There was also the small question of one set of cooking gear. Who would get to carry it? However, before the latter could fester, we resolved it in a novel way. Tony took the pots. I took the stove. That's equality for you: we were now equally unable to cook. There would be days of bread and cheese, days of bread and salami and days of nothing at all. On the peripheries of scurvy, hot food became the stuff of hallucination. I often think there could've been another way.

Once I'd lost the toss, I hid in the bushes until Tony was away. In a great wrench of separation, abandonment even, I watched him disappear in the direction of the great heathen lair of London, of which more later in the manner of explanation.

Five minutes later, a massive truck juddered to a halt and a beer-bellied bear called Harold offered me a lift. Stubble-chinned, hook-nosed, aged about sixty and wrapped like a teapot, he looked not unlike a Toby Jug.

'I'm goin' to Baymingham,' he said. 'Any good t'ya lad?'

'Is it near London?' I asked.

'Aye lad,' he said. 'Hop in.'

I assumed this to be true. But as anyone who's ever been there will vouch, it wasn't. After hours of howling blizzards, and me (who'd never driven) taking turns on steering the skidding truck while Harold rolled cigarettes, I arrived a nervous wreck in central Birmingham. As far away from London as when in Cardiff, my sentiments were with Harold. *Harold*, I thought, *you geographical gobshite. You drivelling rantipole. You gobemouche of the highest order.* Abandoned, I trudged through sleet and gathering dusk to the edge of the city.

An off-duty soldier brought me the short distance to Coventry and I called it a day. I was tired, wet, miserable and hungry. Not quite fit for a night outdoors. Although out of line with the financial considerations, I hopped on a train to London. I knew this would mean paying for a bed in the city but the finances would have to carry that as well. It was a good move. On board, a university student explained that I would most likely not be murdered that night.

To understand my concern, you need to go back to the Cork of the 1960s. Television, restricted to one channel prone to 'snow' and reception collapse, had only arrived in the middle of the decade: there was not yet a great window on the world. At the same time, the city would see huge annual Eucharist processions of 50,000 marching men and boys. Led by the Garda Síochána[1], the Irish army

---
[1] Irish Police

## Chapter 2

and Bishop Cornelius Lucey, the great column would wind its way through streets lined with another 50,000 women and girls to hear the bishop deliver to the entire population of Cork. Reading between the lines of the latest update, it was clear that London was where Irish people came to a bad end. If they weren't murdered by body snatchers or people wanting to turn them into wax exhibits, they were corrupted beyond redemption. The English capital was a place devoid of morals and hope, populated in short by Pagans. It was in fact the last Pagan stronghold in the world. Although I'd been several times to Dublin, and six times to Glasgow, London – 'the Big Smoke' - was Beelzebub's den. The city of Soho and Jack the Ripper.

I was therefore grateful for my friend's comforting words.

'That,' he said of my Cork understanding of London, 'is a load of old bollix.'

Nevertheless, as we travelled into the city through mile after mile of suburb and high-rise, the lights and the size of London filled me with a new trepidation. I wished I'd arrived in daylight. It was a feeling magnified a thousand times when I stepped from the train in Euston Station to be confronted by the entire allotropy of humankind wrapped in overcoats, saris, turbans, kaftans, keffiyehs, hijabs, kangas, dashikis and shalwar-kameezes. Many people who looked like me were speaking in tongues. I thought I recognised German, Spanish, French. There was also an Englishman whom I recognised from his bowler hat.

'If I was you,' my student friend advised, 'I'd plant myself somewhere and catch a breath.' He gave me directions to Ken's Guest House which was close to the station and skipped off into the crowd with the sang-froid of a Ghandi. I sped off into the rain.

At Ken's Guest House, Ken wasn't at home but his wife was. As it happened, she turned out to be a homely woman of about forty from West Cork, her accent an article of great rejoice in that heart of Pagan London. She had, apparently, been a long time in the city and looked like nobody had murdered her yet.

'Look at the cut of you!' she howled when she heard my own accent. 'You're like a drowned rat. Does your mother know where you are?' I ignored that last bit.

After showing me to my room, she sat me down to a mug of tea and a ham sandwich and hung my jacket to dry. 'Are you here to work?' she wanted to know. 'If you're for the building sites, be careful. Lots of Irish lads are killed stone dead on them building sites.'

'Actually,' I said, 'I'm going to India.'
'You can't be serious.'
'I am.'
'Don't be doing anything daft now,' she advised. 'If you'd just like to see Indian people you could go to Southall.'
'Where's Southall?' I asked.
'We're not getting anywhere fast,' she said and the conversation went on in that general vein.

The one thing that drove me back outside that night was the possibility of solving the mystery of Seáinín Jack. Seáinín came from a village on the Dingle Peninsula, close to where our family used to holiday. Although he was a few years older than me, we'd been friends since I was nine. When he was seventeen he fell out with his father on the grounds of unreasonableness. The father had refused to sign a licence application for a .22 rifle for Seáinín. This was shortly after Seáinín had crashed his motorbike while navigating the narrow lanes of west Kerry while reading *The Beano*. Seáinín had stormed off, swearing never to return. Now, he was five years missing. As rumour had it that he was in London, it struck me that it might just be my destiny to find him. It was a long shot, but you never knew.

It was four tube stops from Euston to Trafalgar Square, a logical place to start the search. It took a while to figure out the system; but once I did, I spent a good hour whizzing up and down the dark tunnels, and getting off at random stations to join the throng battling their way back in the other direction. Eventually, long in the tooth on tubes, I arrived in Charing Cross and climbed endless steps to surface at one corner of Trafalger Square. It was a sight to behold: the floodlit buildings of Empire adding to the festive lights of an enormous fir tree that vied with Nelson's Column for dominance. Sitting by one of two fountains in the square, I contemplated the straggler pigeons still hoping to be fed by anyone who turned up, and the big black lions that guarded the base of Nelson's Column, and finally old Horatio himself. Spotlit and staring down on London, he looked imperiously unassailable. I just couldn't resist. *Well*, I said into his smug back, *you weren't so smart in Dublin, were you?* We both knew what that was about. We used to have him in Dublin - smack in the middle of O'Connell Street on a much bigger pillar, a gloating symbol of a brutal colonial past - until the IRA came along with a bomb one night in 1966 and turned him into an astronaut.

## Chapter 2

'*Poor oul' Admiral Nelson is no longer in the air,*' went one of two subsequent chart-topping Irish songs, '*Tooraloooraloooralooraloo...*'

Putting Horatio aside, I scanned the passing faces for Seáinín, but no luck. I decided to switch tack and moved a few blocks to Piccadilly Circus (bigger crowds) where I sat on the rim of an eagle-topped fountain under a neon sign for *Cinzano* and imagined what it would be like to find my curly-headed friend. But the bewildering crowds and the cold and rain got to me.

I gave up and went back to Ken's and never saw Seáinín again. None the less, that night set a pattern. Every time I passed through London in the years to come, I'd sit at that fountain in Piccadilly and watch the races of the Earth pass by, and wish we had it at home.

But Perfidious Albion got wind of that and they took the fountain away.

\* \* \*

Dame Freya Stark, who lived to be a hundred and was said to have been the first Westerner to journey through much of the Middle East, once said that: 'To awaken quite alone in a strange town is one of the pleasantest sensations in the world.'

When I woke up in my warm bed in Ken's I was overcome by whatever Freya Stark had meant. The apprehensions of the night before were gone. Listening to the traffic and the sound of people going to work, I felt settled and fully alive. No work for me today lads. Tweedle-dum, tweedle-dee.

I got up, showered, packed my gear and went downstairs. Outside, morning was breaking over London with the metallic early-morning smell of cities.

'How does your family feel about you heading off to India?' Ken's wife wanted to know as she loaded a double fry onto my plate. 'Won't it be dangerous?'

'Naw,' I said. 'But I couldn't get insurance.'

'Imagine that,' she said.

But, to guide me on my way, she gave me the B&B for £1 instead of £1.50 which helped counter the next blow to the financial considerations - the train fare to Dover.

'I have a cousin around the corner from you in Cork,' Ken's wife said, 'Sheila Cahane who lives in Capwell Road. If you get a chance when you get back, tell her I was asking for her.'

'I will,' I said and wrote down her name. Sheila Cahane became the first of many people I one day mean to visit.

# Chaper 3
## France

---

It was mid-day in Dover. There was snow on the ground and Tony was a jangle of nerves.

'I've been here since last night,' he said. 'I had no idea what to do if for any reason you didn't turn up today. Or supposing you didn't come tomorrow either? We didn't think about that, did we? With no phones in either of our houses back in Cork, we've no base.'

'What about this?' I said after mulling it over. 'Every time we split up, we give one another two days after the agreed meeting time. Then whoever is running late gets a bus or train to make the deadline.'

'And if he doesn't turn up?'

'The other one goes on. We're either there or dead.'

'Begod,' Tony laughed. 'That's a great plan. I bet nobody else ever thought of a plan like that.'

We pulled out the stove and pots, boiled up a billy of milky coffee to accompany a loaf of bread and a tin of sardines, and tried to think of a better plan.

'Tony,' I said in the end, 'there isn't one.'

Replete and satisfied that we'd done our best we sailed out that afternoon from the chalk cliffs of Kent and crossed the English Channel to Calais. We made landfall on mainland Europe in late afternoon to find more snow and a freezing mist that drifted in, wet and sticky, from the North Sea.

'If we had a flag to plant,' Tony said, 'we could claim this place right now for Ireland, the way the British claimed New Zealand and Australia.'

Sorry that we hadn't thought of this in England so we could've claimed that as well, we disembarked, crossed the canal that separated the port and old town from the rest of Calais and began to hitchhike. But it was late in the day; and once darkness mixed with the fog, hitchhiking became impossible. After a hopeless search for a dry place to sleep we were forced back into town to punch another sad hole in the finances. We checked in to The Corner House where I pointed out to Tony that we were now living like millionaires, and it had to stop. Tony, sodden and blue with the cold, pointed out that

## Chapter 3

he'd like to meet the millionaires I knew. On the plus side, we were able to buy bread and cheese, boil up coffee in the room, and put something warm in our stomachs.

Outside in the corridor, happenstance cut across our trajectory. We ran smack into the solid block of John Hussey in his big Aran sweater and jeans.

John was an American student, returning to Spain from an Irish break from his studies in Madrid. Two nights earlier, as Tony and I were walking (by choice) to the Innisfallen, my father and my brother Niall were driving down to see us off. Spotting John and his pack heading for the ferry terminal, they offered him a lift. Consequently, Tony, John and I had stood together on deck as we sailed down the River Lee, Tony and myself pointing out the landmarks. The heights of Montennote where we believed the posh to live. The coal-fired electricity generating station at the Marina where we used to strokehaul mullet. The lights of Cobh where the Titanic picked up many a person 'who later wished to fuck' - as Tony put it - that it hadn't. Now here was John again. We invited him in for coffee and later adjourned to the nearest pub to celebrate coincidence.

'When you get to Madrid,' John offered, 'come and stay.' He scribbled his address on a piece of paper. 'I live in a brothel,' he added without a trace of shame, 'but don't let that put you off.'

'Nothing like that would put us off,' Tony said, 'after a few nights sleeping out in weather like this.'

'Exactly,' John encouraged. 'That's the spirit of the road.'

In the morning John took some civilised form of transport to Madrid. Tony and I again walked to the edge of town, split up and agreed to meet in Paris at a Franciscan monastery on Rue Marie Rose where Dermy O'Sullivan from West Cork was a student monk. The monastery was one of several addresses donated by friends of friends before we left home, each a guaranteed feed and a night indoors. Deep in my pocket, as I hitchhiked south through picturesque French villages and towns with pan-tiled roofs and cobbled squares, the list was the insurance policy we'd been officially denied.

After a rush-hour battle that evening with the Paris metro, I arrived in pelting rain and rapped at the door of the red-bricked monastery. Hollow footfalls on the far side preceded the drawing of a bolt, and the door slid open.

'*Bonsoir*,' a tall monk in brown robes said.

'I'm here to see Dermy O'Sullivan,' I explained in Martian French. 'He is a student here.'

The monk ushered me in to a tiled hall, then held up his right hand in a hang-on-a-minute gesture before disappearing back the way he'd come. A few minutes later he reappeared with another monk who introduced himself as John Crio. John, who came from India, was a friend of Dermy's and had been summoned to assist with translations.

'Is Dermy expecting you?' he asked.

'I think so,' I said although that was the first time the thought had crossed my mind. But surely those who'd supplied the list would've wired off the hosts?

'H-m-m-m,' John said. 'He's not at home. He will be sorry not to be here to greet you in person. However, you will be most welcome until he arrives.'

I was introduced to an older, benign-looking monk who was the monastery Guardian, given a fine dinner and lodged in a small sparsely furnished room for the night. *What you might call*, I said to myself, *a monk's cell*. All new experiences now had to be catalogued. Outside it was bucketing down and I pitied poor Tony, sleeping under God-knows-what bush as I curled up in my blankets and drifted off to a deep and dreamless sleep.

In the morning the phone in the room rang.

'Good morning.' It was John Crio's pleasant voice. 'Breakfast will be ready shortly. I will come for you in ten minutes.'

I showered and shaved and was escorted to the dining room where I was introduced to everyone while enjoying another great feed. Over cereal, I pointed out to the gathered monks that the milk tasted different from the milk at home. Needless to say, they were very interested in facts such as this. John pointed out that a plaque at number 4 Rue Marie Rose marked the spot in which Vladimir Lenin had lived from 1909 to 1912. Regaling in this exchange of facts, I pointed out that Che Guevara's grandmother was the daughter of Patrick Lynch from Galway.

To cap the morning, Tony turned up at eleven o'clock and, just to please the monks, I had a second breakfast.

'Begod boy,' Tony said, 'things appear to be going well.'

After swapping stories of our journeys from Calais (Tony had spent the night in the sheltered doorway of a workers' café and had the workers stepping over him when he woke up in the morning)

## Chapter 3

we spent the rest of the day traipsing the streets of Paris. We walked the Champs-Elysées and posed at the Arc de Triomphe for a photo. We braved the unisex toilets, although the 'barrel' toilets on the footpath that shielded a standing chap from knees to chest was a step too far for an Irish upbringing. We called at Notre Dame Cathedral and the Louvre and stood under the puddle-iron mass of the Eiffel Tower where, on February 4th 1912, Austrian tailor Franz Reichelt came to a mushy end after testing his home-made parachute from sixty metres up; and where in 1925 an enterprising conman named Victor Lustig twice sold the whole shebang to some very gullible scrap men.

Satisfied with our day, we went back in a squall of rain to Rue Marie Rose, looking forward to our meeting with Dermy and the evening feed.

'Maybe horse and chips,' Tony joked.

But as soon as we walked through the monastery door, we knew that laughing was over: instead of a smiling Dermy, we were met by a flint and frosty Guardian.

'I do be feeling it in the bones,' Tony prophesised. 'No horse, no chips.' Tony was the man for the bones.

The Guardian handed me a note from Dermy who'd been and gone. 'I don't know you from Adam...' the note went, the Guardian is having a canary. '...and *bon voyage*'. We were evicted onto the wet streets of Paris.

Checking the underground for sleep possibilities and finding Paris's other down-and-outs already in possession, we had no choice but to book into one of the city's two youth hostels, run - my notes of the time reliably inform me - 'by a pig of a man'. We spent the next evening in Versailles, taking a long look at the palace of Sun King, Louis XIV, and shuffling idly through the damp streets where we were befriended by a raving tramp who clearly saw in us his foreign cousins. In my travel entries for that fifth day on the road I noted that '...*all they seem to do in Versailles at night is drink wine and eat sandwiches*'. But never mind.

When the town turned in for the night, we spread our sleeping bags on the concrete floor of a derelict shed on the southbound road, cooked some porridge and finally felt grounded in proper travel.

'This,' I said to Tony, 'is what life is all about.'

'Don't let anyone hear you say that,' Tony counselled, 'or they'll lock ya away for keeps.'

Turning periodically throughout that night to avoid petrification from the seeping cold, I heard Tony snort repeatedly in his sleep as if trying to make sense of something. In the end it came.

'Snakes,' he mumbled. 'They have poisonous ones in France.'

Lying there with bloodless toes, I wished he'd kept that to himself.

\* \* \*

Spurred on by atrocious weather, we travelled hell-for-leather down through the rest of France, a dull journey of flat landscapes, lowering skies, leafless trees and mucky winter fields. Despite being apart again, lifts were slow. This meant walking long hours during short days with little to eat, and standing at night on dark empty roads in howling wind and drenching rain, or trudging on, scanning the shadows for a place to sleep. Every now and again the oncoming lights of a vehicle would raise the hope that pity still lived, only to have it mercilessly dashed as the lights swept past in slicing spears of rain to disappear in all-consuming darkness. But there was solace in the knowledge that we were moving south towards the sun, feeling the new warmth of the days.

I slept the first night on an empty trailer in a farm shed, thinking of home, Cora and my young brother Cathal, whose eyes had brimmed red on the night I left. There and then I was the last lonely lad on an incessantly forlorn planet. On the second night I recovered in the youth hostel in Bordeaux (there was only one), my bed paid for by an old man who drove me straight to its door. Any attempt to sleep outside in my soaked condition, he insisted, would end in 'tooberculossus'.

The hostel warden was surprised to see me. I was the only guest.

\* \* \*

I left Bordeaux in tip-top form. Showered, shaved, fed and admiring the beginnings of a curved moustache, I waved goodbye to the unvisited cathedrals, museums, theatres and esplanades of the world's wine capital and headed for Biarritz, 170 kms to the south. It was an auspicious morning. The rain had gone and the sky was blue with a hint of cirrus running in narrow bands, promising to soon go away. The sun was a yellow ball of flame. It was warm as a summer's day at home. Less than 800 kilometres south of Calais and a silver wand had swept away the wicked climate of the north. Palm trees, vineyards and banana plants confirmed that I was now somewhere near the Tropics. Time was no longer important and was in fact being stretched. The events of yesterday seemed a week

# Chapter 3

past. Routine was drifting away. With no watch as tyrant, it was eat when hungry (if possible), sleep when tired, move when the day broke through.

I wallowed in the triumph of it all.

By mid afternoon, I was down to shirt and jeans and swinging jauntily along through vast rolling forests of pine, a verdant infinity planted in the 19th century to prevent sea erosion of the sandy soils of the Landes region. I sang out loud. I thought of how much my old schoolmates, now mostly at university, were missing. I shouted.

But a note of caution was on the way.

An hour before dark, I got a lift on the back of a small backfiring motorbike from a heavy man of middle years. With a Gauloise hanging from his mouth, a beret pulled down to his eyebrows and a huge curling moustache hiding what remained of his face, he looked quite the madman.

'*Bonjour!*' he roared and nodded towards the third of the saddle still available. Even as I hopped on I knew it was a mistake due to the hum of wine.

There's nothing more terrifying than a small motorbike and a drunk fat man going too fast, while a heavy rucksack and *The Oxford Book of English Verse* try to flip you off backwards.

'Wau-u-gh!' I howled, grabbing the shoulders in front.

'*Vous êtes bien* [You are OK?]?' the drunk in front called through his Gauloise.

'*Oui! Oui!*' I stammered, trying not to sound a wimp, or hang on too tight in case he got the wrong idea. Twenty minutes later the snowpeaks of the Pyrenées loomed up, marching east into a purpling sky like a wall of glistening threat. Then we hit a bomb-crater of a hole and I was flung into the air. When I came back down I missed my third of the saddle and landed hard on the carrier. The impact caused the bike to slew off to the right and plough into a ditch in a great splash of muddy water. The driver went over the handlebars. I went over the driver, my short life passing before my eyes, its imminent end a real shame. Then, an apparent miracle. Somersaulting a full 180 degrees and narrowly missing the stout bole of an old pine, I landed on my pack, punching a hole in the main compartment. As I lay there, tentatively checking for breaks, I heard myself laughing.

I don't know if anything untoward had happened to cause the laughing - a bang maybe or some chemical discharge squirting the brain. It didn't seem so. We dragged ourselves upright and could find only minor cuts and a nosebleed of the driver's that made him look like a crazed vampire. Even the bike suffered nothing worse than a broken mudguard and a footrest that pointed doggedly at Australia. But there I was, laughing. I studied the hole in my pack and noticed that the seams were also beginning to unravel in several places but this had more to do with quality than the accident.

When the driver kick-started the bike back to life and nodded, I returned the nod and climbed on board.

'Boom! Boom! Boom!' the lunatic roared and we charged off into the gathering dusk in a terrible shindy of racket, smoke and atrocious driving that ran all the way to Biarritz. By the time I stumbled into the railway station for a night on a bench, my legs were lactic acid. But I felt good. Like a rock climber who has pulled himself up to the overhang of a precipice.

Verily was I on the road.

# Chapter 4
Mañana

A morning train brought me to the Spanish border town of Irun. I passed through Imigration and Customs in the railway station, then boarded a second train for San Sebastian. The difference, for having crossed nothing more than an imaginary line, was striking.

First, the sudden change of language. On one side, the people spoke French; on the other they spoke Spanish. There was no clear reason for this. Then in between, there coexisted the Basque language of Euskadi. Nobody knew where that came from.

Of course, this kind of thing happened right across Europe. On the far side of France, you went a hundred metres down the road and everyone suddenly spoke German. In Switzerland, within internal imaginary lines, they spoke three separate languages. Then there were the physical differences: on the French side the horse and cart was in its final days, the train was spotlessly new and the passengers sat sedately, looking out the window or reading the papers. On the Spanish side horses and carts outnumbered cars, the train was a rickety wreck and half the passengers in my carriage seemed to have staggered from a riotous all-nighter that I was sorry to have missed. Although it was early morning, they were singing, yelling, and topping up on bottles of red wine. A woman with castanets and a rose in her hair danced along the aisle to rapturous rounds of applause. At one of the stops, a man hauled a goat onto the train and everyone cheered.

The good humour baffled me. I had expected gloom and doom south of the Pyrenées. This was Franco's Spain, ruled by the dictator who'd taken power at the end of the civil war. After the half million deaths of the war, the flight into exile of another half million, the mass killings that followed, and Franco's tacit support for Hitler, the dictatorship had been a bit of a social pariah to the rest of Europe. The consequences for the ordinary people were an economy that had lain stagnant for most of the period since 1939. Despite a burst of economic growth in the sixties, much of the country was undeveloped. And there had been the continued death-squad killings since the civil war. Yet, here were happy people who'd been to a party. *How come?* wondered I.

To avoid staring, I looked out at the passing Basque countryside. Small whitewashed farms surrounded by sheep, cattle and goats. A farmer riding by on a mule. A man in a sloping field with a horse-drawn plough. Wooded hills. A string of drab towns. Rundown blocks of flats with wrought iron balconies. The port of Pasaia with its small ships and fishing fleet. And the mountains to the east pushing clear to the coast and forcing the train through a couple of tunnels. Twenty minutes after leaving Irun, I was in San Sebastian's North Station.

When we split up in Versailles, Tony and I decided to meet again in Bilbao. There was probably something in the decision but it eludes me now. Bilbao didn't sit on any direct route between Versailles and John Hussey's flat in Madrid. Nevertheless, my clear purpose when I traipsed down the steps of North Station was to hitchhike the 100 kilometres to Bilbao.

Outside the station, I set off across the Maria Cristina Bridge, the most elegant bridge in San Sebastian. Said to be a copy of the Alexander III Bridge in Paris, both ends were flanked by 18-metre white obelisks topped by sculptures of rearing horses and their riders, while cast iron lanterns and railings spanned the length of its three arches. Down below, the Rio Urumea coursed through to its choppy collision with the Bay of Biscay.

On the far side of the bridge I turned left hoping that this was the Bilbao road. However, realising that guessing could cost a lot of walking I turned back to ask a cop on point duty if I had it right. It was a fortuitous move. Otherwise I would've missed Tony who was at that moment on his way across the bridge, planning to catch a train to Bilbao. Consequently, neither of us went to Bilbao. Instead we decided to have a look around town and treat ourselves to our first restaurant meal since leaving home. The latter was based on the fact that neither of us had eaten in twenty-eight hours and that Spain was cheap beyond our dreams.

The Basque city of San Sebastian sits on the northwest Atlantic coast of Spain. It's an old city steeped in history and rimmed by a spectacular half-moon beach that separates it from the waters of the Bay of la Concha, itself shielded from the Bay of Biscay by the island of Santa Clara. In 1970 it was still a small city, encircled by the rolling hills and distant mountains of 'green' Spain, and backed at its northern end by the wooded ramparts of Mount Urgull whose cannons once protected the city from attack. The Parte Vieja (Old

## Chapter 4

Quarter), surrounded by walls until 1863, was the traditional heart of the city.

A short walk down the left hand bank of the river, and we found ourslves in this maze of narrow alleys, tall sandstone buildings and overhanging balconies. It was a relatively small area, twenty or so streets, but its architectural gems included the massive Gothic church of San Vicente, the Renaissance-Baroque Santa María del Coro and the porticoed Plaza de la Constitución. On the port side we found a track that led to the slopes of Mount Urgull. Following it upwards, enjoying the sunshine and the views of the bay, we stumbled on the 'English cemetery', a rough overgrown enclosure, backed by a low cliff and the rising, tree-covered slope of the hill itself. We went inside and, stumbling over roots and broken steps, came on a statue carved from the rock, depicting living and dead men around what may have been a cannon wheel. It had long ago been vandalised. Above it, a stone eagle crumbled among the shrubbery. Reminders of the forgotten of war.

Back in 1835, the British Auxiliary Legion was set up in support of Spain's Queen Regent, María Cristina de Borbón, in the civil war that engulfed the country between 1833 and 1839. The First Carlist War was fought between the 'Cristino' followers of the Queen Regent and the opposing followers of Prince Carlos María Isidro of Borbón, who were known as 'Carlists'. Queen Maria Cristina had persuaded her husband, King Ferdinand VII, to change the Salic Law (which prevented female accession) to allow their daughter, Princess Isabella, to inherit the throne. When Ferdinand died, Maria Cristina became Regent as Isabella was only three years old. This led the supporters of Ferdinand's brother Carlos, who had expected to inherit the throne as male heir, to embark on the civil war.

Britain, pursuing its own strategic interests weighed in on the Cristino side. Those who flocked to the banner and the promise of food and a pension were the poor of London, Manchester, Glasgow and Dublin. According to the records many of the Irish brought along wives and children, around 700 in total, who accompanied the Legion throughout its mission.

Towards the end of the summer of 1836, the 10,000 British and Irish, under the command of Lieutenant Colonel George de Lacy Evans, gathered on the outskirts of San Sebastian to do battle with the Carlists. In one of the fiercest engagements of the war they managed to hold the free port of San Sebastian and the fort on Mount Urgull where they were now remembered in the rough and rocky cemetery. Some lay under low stones swallowed by moss. One, an officer, merited an upright tomb with an inscription that could still be read. He was Whiliam (William?) I M Tupper, Colonel of the 6th Scotch (sic) Battalion and late of the 23rd RWE who, 'at the head of his regiment, at the taking of Ayete on the 5th of May 1836, fell mortally wounded at 32 years of age'. But most of the poor who died on Urgull and at San Sebastian were buried in a mass unmarked grave deserving of their station. Carved on a rock face that presumably sat above that grave were the words: 'Honour to the heroes known only to God'. The occasional bird and the distant scour of the sea served only to amplify the silence of the forgotten.

Ironically, the Basques supported the Carlists in the war.

\* \* \*

Our promise to ourselves of a decent meal was fulfilled in a small pub in the new town. Wooden tables and chairs, sawdust on the floor, and legs of fossilised ham hanging above the bar had the look of our kind of place. We sat at an outside table and were shortly approached by a smiling young woman with red lips that could've stuck her to a windowpane.

'*Buenos dias*,' she said and handed us the menu. It was in Spanish, of which we spoke not a word. But never let it be said...

'Do-you-speak-English?' Tony asked. She shook her head and pursed her lips.

'*Parlez-vous Francais?*' I asked. Same response (just as well), all of which left us in a bit of a stew. Nevertheless, we scanned the menu with an air of gourmet authority.

'Look!' I said to Tony. '*Sopa*. That has to be soup.'

'Yeah,' Tony said. 'Or soap.'

'What about this?' I said, ignoring the facetious quip. '*Chipirones en su tinta*. That'll be chips.' I was delighted: such an innate grasp of the language. 'Chips with something or other, but definitely chips.' After a further fruitless search for anything more familiar, we ordered.

'Bob's yer uncle,' Tony said.

The soup arrived: fish, and good. We dived in, wiping the bowls clean with the bread that came with the meal. The waitress took away the bowls and sashayed back a few minutes later with the main dish. Two plates were planted down before us. The smiling waitress departed.

## Chapter 4

'What in the name of Jaysus is that?' Tony squawked like a hen being choked.

I looked hard at mine and had to admit that he had a point. What sat there was a greyish white lump unlike anything I'd ever seen on a plate. I checked shape and size and concluded that it was possibly the stomach of a dog in what looked like a bed of melted duck-droppings. To compound the sorry affair, there wasn't a chip in sight.

'No way am I eating *that*,' Tony spluttered.

'It must be edible,' I reasoned. 'Otherwise they wouldn't be selling it in a restaurant. Would they?' I began to prod the grey matter, feeling guilty at having unearthed the obvious flaw in the local dialect. But Tony was resolute.

'I'd rather have a plate of cat-sick. Wonder if they sell any cat-sick? You wouldn't ask in that Spanish of yours, would you?'

Determined not to be beaten, I forced mine down.

'It's not bad,' I said, not mentioning rubbery, dog-like texture. 'Try it.'

'All yours, boy,' Tony said.

I forced half of Tony's down before conceding defeat. In consolation we ate more bread and washed it down with a bottle of that wine they call bull's blood. We sat a while in silence contemplating possible future food disasters.

'Right,' Tony said in the end. 'We need to get us some proper food. Spuds.'

We went to the market, stocked up with potatoes, milk, cheese and bread, and walked a kilometre down the Tolosa road. Soon, a mound of spuds could be seen boiling on the side of the road. Soon after that, us two could be seen wolfing them down with the cheese and two litres of milk coffee. Overcome by a state of *fou rire* we flopped into the ditch, howling like hyenas. After a day of starvation we were drunk on the massive intake of food. Finally, we dozed off in the sun. When we came to, it was late afternoon and we decided to stay the night in the city's youth hostel, a short distance from where we'd slept. The warden welcomed us. He didn't get many people from Ireland. Right now, it being winter, he didn't get many at all. Apart from one thirty-odd Australian sleazebag who took a shine to Tony 'darling', and was on his way to Morocco 'for the darling little Arab boys' we had the place to ourselves.

'I'm a peace-loving mouse of a man,' Tony said, imitating Captain Hercules Hurricane from the *Valiant* just before the famous captain

went into one of his raging furies and tore tanks apart with his bare hands. 'But if that bastard comes near me during the night, I'll give him "the darling little Arab boys". I'll slit his fuckin' gizzard.'
I was myself of the same mind.
Hunting knives went under pillows.

* * *

We left San Sebastian as soon as daylight began to show itself and walked most of the way to the town of Tolosa before finally succumbing to the afternoon bus. Next morning we went south again in the company of a French woman not much older than ourselves who spoke fluent English and Spanish, looked like the quintessential Parisian model and went by the name of Aurélie.

Aurélie was deranged. To prove it, she set off from Tolosa on a narrow secondary road so she could drive across the mountains like Stirling Moss. Flanked on both sides by forests stripped bare by winter gales, we screeched around reckless bends on that side of the road notionally reserved by Franco for oncoming traffic, with Aurélie's professed belief in God's benevolence the only thing between us and the testing of Aurélie's belief in an afterlife. In Basque villages with streets so narrow that only one vehicle at a time could pass, we gave no quarter to donkeys or old men on carts. In the town of Etxarri Aranatz, we skidded to a halt outside a pub so we could throw in a quick hot coffee and Aurélie could top up her spirits with a cognac and introduce myself and Tony.

'These people are Basque nationalists,' she explained. 'They like the Irish because they make war with the English.'

She then proceeded to tell the half dozen other people in the bar that Tony and I were Irish *revolutionaries*!

'Here, Aurélie,' I said, 'this is getting a bit out of hand.'

'You could get us shot,' Tony added.

But, try as we might, we couldn't dampen her enthusiasm as she sprayed the bar with an imaginary hip-held rifle. This, she later admitted, had the desired effect: all three of us were feted like visiting royalty and the coffees and cognac were on the house. Meanwhile, Aurélie's eyes did a remarkable thing: as she bullshitted the people in the bar, they changed colour. One minute they were green and the next they were ice-blue. While I considered this an even worse omen than the fact that she had picked us up in the first place, Tony was wondering if there was any way we could escape without losing face.

# Chapter 4

'Maybe one of us could top himself,' he suggested. 'The confusion might save the other.'

However, as we turned west for the city of Vitoria the road improved, restricting Aurélie's suicidal tendencies to the manageable.

'You know,' she said as we closed in on the city, 'this is where Napoleon's brother, Joseph Bonaparte, was defeated during the wars with Spain in the early 19th century. On 21st June 1813 an army of British, Spanish and Portuguese soldiers fought the French army along the Zadorra River and more than 10,000 men on both sides were killed. Soon after, it was the end of Napoleon's occupation of Spain.'

Driving through the city, Aurélie added another little snippet. The inhabitants, she claimed, were known locally as *Babazorros*.

'That' she said, 'is the Basque word for 'bean eaters'.'

Forty kilometres further south, Aurélie dropped us off in Miranda de Ebro.

'May the Virgin of San Sebastian de Garabandal go with you,' she said.

'May all the virgins of this place stop you from ever picking us up again!' Tony shouted after her when she'd gone.

A walk of eleven kilometres through mountain country and we arrived in Ameyugo, an impoverished village of red-roofed stone houses. Built against an outcrop of rock, it straddled a narrow dirt street off the main road. Stares followed us to the cantina where we bought some food, sat to a table and ordered glasses of vino tinto. The vino heated our hearts. The cantina's wood stove reddened the windburn on our faces. We were joined at our table by two local men, big unshaven farmers with Popeye arms, who tried to talk to us and plied us with more glasses of vino tinto.

'A sing-song,' Tony said after the third glass. We treated the lads to *Mrs McGrath*, *The Louse House in Kilkenny* and *The Ragman's Ball*. They treated us to some god-awful raucous screech.

After dark we made our way to the church porch, threw down our sleeping bags and set about cooking a meal. The local padre, attracted by the flame of the stove, came to check that we weren't pyromaniac anarchists left over from the civil war. After a brief and futile attempt at communication he blessed us and departed as we looked forward to a cold night on the stone tiles.

In the morning the padre came again to ring the bells, say mass to a congregation of one, and bring Ameyugo to life. As we stuffed our sleeping bags into our gradually disintegrating packs, women came to the village fuenta for drinking water; a shepherd with a brightly coloured blanket over his shoulders rode past on a donkey, herding a dozen sheep before him; children went to school; and an old man came down from the hills with a basket of firewood strapped to his back. Shivering, we splashed cold water from the fuenta on our blue faces and Tony jerked upright from the shock of it.

'My oul' man was right,' he declared. 'This shit would give you piles or kidney trouble.'

We then shouldered our packs on an empty stomach, walked out of the village in the long morning shadows, and continued on down the road to India.

\* \* \*

We covered several kilometres of a long rocky canyon before entering a tunnel that opened out onto what we assumed to be La Meseta, the plateau that occupies much of central Spain. After a further hour or so, in terrain that was now much drier, we stumbled on the day's first event: a deserted Spaghetti-Western ghost town a little off the road.

'Clint Eastwood,' Tony yelled. 'Eat yer heart out!'

We diverted. We donned our six-guns and loped the boardwalks of the main street. We swaggered into the swing-door saloon, shouting 'Draw!' I was Billy the Kid. Tony was Bat Masterson. For a full ten minutes we shot our way up and down that town, smoking the unlucky Earps, the James Gang and the Murphy-Dolan faction of the Lincoln County War.

'That shower won't bother us again,' Tony said, blowing smoke from the barrel of his Buntline Special.

Not long after this encounter, the real thing showed up. Two horsemen in long green cloaks and shiny black tricorne hats pulled out from behind some trees. Looking down the barrels of submachine guns, they demanded our passports. Franco's Guardia Civil were still protecting the flanks of the regime.

'Speak in Irish,' I said in Irish to Tony.

In memory of the Irish James Connolly Unit who fought with the International Brigades on the republican side during the Spanish civil war we pretended not to understand a word.

'*Cad tá á rá agat?*' [What are you saying?] I asked.

'*An labhrann sibh Gaeilge?*' [Do you speak Irish?] Tony asked.

## Chapter 4

'*Passaportes!*' both of them shouted. Tony and I looked at one another.

'*Passaportes!*' they shouted again and one of them cocked his gun.

'*Ah,*' I said to Tony. '*Na pasanna.*'

'*Ah,*' Tony said. '*Na pasanna.*'

Down the road we got a lift from Mantzio, a young bearded Basque nationalist who chain-smoked through the side of his mouth and was on his way to Madrid. Mantzio was a joiner by trade and came from a small village in the Sierra de Aralar, the great karstic massif that straddles Navarre and Guipúzcoa states to the south of Tolosa. He'd also been stopped by the two horsemen and was fuming.

'You saw them?' he said in Americanised English. 'They killed more people *after* the civil war than were killed during the war. In the Basque Country alone, more than 20,000.' He then expounded on the poverty of Spain, and how it would never end under Franco's regime.

'They are fucking, fucking fascists,' he said.

Tony told him the passport story and he nearly fell out the door of the car.

'You must be very careful,' he warned. 'When they ask you for your *passeportes*, you must show. Or maybe they will kill you too. It is dangerous with these people.'

Clearly Mantzio didn't rate our intelligence very highly as he went on to outline the most basic of Spanish and Basque customs and how to avoid offending the general populace.

'If you have an appointment, you must be patient,' he said. To emphasise the point he blew smoke rings over the windscreen. 'The person will not be on time. But also you must not be more than fifteen minutes late. If you are meeting a lady she will give her cheek for you to kiss. You must not kiss her mouth like in England. Only her cheek. If you go to eat in some house and you have the vino, you must wait for the toast. In Spanish it is *Salud*. When no more drinks are coming you must leave. In the day there is the siesta from two o'clock until four-thirty o'clock. Everbody is eating and sleeping. Shops, they are closed. You must also eat and sleep. In every town and village, there is a saint for that place and there is some day every year a fiesta. If you are lucky, you will see many fiesta. And very, very special for you: the girls. All the girls, they must be home for ten o'clock in the night. That is the time for dinner. And if you are very, very lucky and you will marry a Spanish girl, she will wear a black silk dress for her wedding and a black veil. Not white like in your country. And the last thing I must tell you is *mañana*. You must know what means *mañana*.'

'Tomorrow?' I said, sure I had it right this time.

'Yes, and maybe no. Sometimes it means tomorrow. Or maybe tomorrow tomorrow. Or maybe tomorrow tomorrow tomorrow. Or maybe never. You must understand this.'

We well understood the ideology of anything less definite than tomorrow. We came from a country that had a story about a Spaniard who turned up one day looking for the translation of mañana. 'Sorry,' he was told. 'We have no word to express such urgency.'

Happy that we were clear on all critical points of local culture, Matzio reverted to his Basque roots.

'Do you know the Basque language? It is the only language in Western Europe that does not come from the Indo-Aryan. It is very old, from before the Romans came to the Iberian Peninsula. Nobody can tell how old or where it has come from.'

'The Irish language is a bit like that,' I said although I didn't know for sure. It was more of a gut feeling.

After a contemplative silence, Matzio asked some questions about the brewing conflict in Ireland. What was happening? Who were the good guys? Who were the IRA?

'You know ETA?' he asked. 'Maybe the same as the IRA.'

No, we said, never heard of ETA.

'ETA is *Euskadi Ta Askatasuna*. This means 'Basque Homeland and Freedom'. ETA is fighting for the Basque people since 1959. They rob many banks and one and a half years ago, in June 1968, they killed one of those men you saw, one Guardia Civil. He was shot by Txabi Etxebarrieta from ETA at a road check like the one you saw. Then Txabi Etxebarrieta was killed by the Guardia Civil and his friend, Iñaki Sarasqueta, was wounded. Two months after this, ETA went to the home in Irun of Melitón Manzanas, chief of the secret police in Donostia [San Sebastian], and they shot him dead. Manzanas was responsible for many tortures against prisoners. Also he helped the Gestapo during World War II. He gave them the Jewish people who were escaping from France. He was from the Basque Country but he was with Franco.' The Franco bit came out in a snort.

Chewing on the culture and history of the land under our feet while Mantzio kept changing the music on his portable tape-recorder,

## Chapter 4

we barrelled on south through the vineyards and wheat fields and semi-desert of Castilla La Vieja. We crossed the snowcapped Sierra de Guadarrama on narrow twisting roads scented by forests of pine that were home to ibex, deer, wild boar, weasel and the European wild cat as well as the more familiar fox, badger and hare. Some time after nightfall the sky to the south blazed orange over Madrid.

'Madrid is a beautiful city,' Mantzio said as he dropped us off at the junction of Calle de Alcalá, a broad busy boulevard of trees and classical buildings that was the longest (ten kilometres) street in the city, and Gran Via, a brightly lit upmarket shopping street. The junction was dominated by the landmark triangular building that is now known as the Edificio Metrópolis (Metropolis Building). Three storeys of glaring white were topped by a black onion dome that supported a statue of the mythological Phoenix, with Ganymede, the Greek divine hero from Troy, sitting on its right wing.

'You know this bird?' Matzio said. 'It is like Madrid. This city, it has a rich history, beautiful museums, beautiful churches, *very* beautiful senoritas; but it has bastard Franco too. This makes it die like this bird in the fire. But, some day Spain will be free again. It will rise like this bird. The Basque Country too. You will see.'

Tony and I felt sorry for him as he drove away.

\* \* \*

Rush hour on the Madrid metro was horrendous. Once we'd entered, we were swept along as if caught in the current of a river, and had some difficulty in reaching a train that would take us to Calle O'Donnell, in the Barrio de Salamanca, the station closest to where John Hussey lived. When we reached the train, we and our packs had to be shoe-horned on board by a burly cop who seemed to be standing there for this very purpose.

As the train rocked its way through subterranean Madrid, we wondered how a street in the Spanish capital could bear the name O'Donnell. There had to be an Irish connection. There was. And it wasn't a good one although the Spanish seemed to have no problem honouring the tyrant after whom Calle O'Donnell had been named. But then, former colonial powers and the victors of war seldom have a problem with their own despots.

Don Leopoldo O'Donnell was a descendant of the O'Donnell princes of Tirconnell. Born in 1809 in the Canary Islands, he'd become a divisional commander in the Spanish Army when the First Carlist War broke out in 1833, the same war that had left those 'known only to God' on that forlorn hill behind San Sebastian. Fighting on the winning side of Queen Regent, Maria Cristina, he subsequently became Spanish Minister of War in the government of Baldomero Espartero, Duke of Vittoria. However when Maria Cristina, who was to become an increasingly autocratic figure, was forced into exile by Espartero in 1840, O'Donnell also fled.

He then staged a counter coup in 1843, after which Maria Cristina's daughter, Isabella, now thirteen years old, was declared Queen of Spain. In 1844 O'Donnell was rewarded with the Governorship of Cuba, where he achieved enduring notoriety when credited with the massacre known as the repression of La Escalera, the Spanish response to an alleged plot to overthrow colonial rule on the island. Thousands of slaves and 'free people of colour' were dragged off to dark dungeons to be savagely tortured and executed in what became known in Cuban history as 'the year of the lash'. *La Escalera* (the ladder) referred to the practice of tying slave suspects to ladders and whipping them during interrogation.

Across the path that Tony and I were taking, O'Donnell's dark shadow would fall again.

\* \* \*

John Hussey, square, stocky, with short fair hair and the clean-shaven jaw of a scholar, didn't quite live in a brothel. But there was a connection that would allow for poetic licence. Of the fourteen flats in the block in which he lived on Calle Fundadores, five were occupied by smiling senoritas de la noche who plied their trade to foreign men in the Bar Americanos. We met some of their number shortly after arriving.

John had just returned from the nearby University of Santa Cristina where he was studying Spanish and hadn't recognised us coming up the dark street. When the penny dropped, he was almost overcome by his own yelps and handshakes and the generosity he carried as securely as Tony and I carried our packs.

'But,' he added as we set foot on the stairs, 'a word of caution. We're two floors up and you might have to perform some aerobatics to get there.'

At the top of the second set of stairs, we discovered why. Three young women of nulli secundus proportions were spread across the landing, engaged in jocular colloquy. All lipstick, perfume, kohl and shining hair, they lay with mini-skirted legs stretched up the banister and stairwell wall like guardians of the Hesperides. This, I

## Chapter 4

suspected, was the kind of thing that led all those Irish lads astray back in London. But John was nonplussed.

'*Buenas noches,*' he said and joked with the legs in Spanish. He then led the assault. Scrambling over the nut-brown tangle was clearly a regular stairwell challenge. The women laughed and raised the boom higher. By the time we'd safely crossed we were ready for a cold shower. Mind you, that house trapped heat.

'Sorry about that little impediment,' John said. 'Saturday night is a big night. The ladies are out in style.'

'Not to worry,' Tony said. 'At home, we have to hop over puddles and this beats the hell outta that.'

We stayed three nights with John, sleeping on the tiled floor of his living room, reorganising our gear, battling the legs on the stairs and eating strange foods. With a friendly roof over our heads, we caught up on sleep, washed clothes, dumped the long johns, aired our sleeping bags, offloaded unnecessary junk (but not the hefty *Oxford Book of English Verse*) and came to the sorry conclusion that our cheap rucksacks were finished. Ever since leaving home, both had been slowly parting at the seams and shedding their exterior frames, on top of which the hole punched in my own pack by the motorbike accident was now saucer-sized, needing my towel as a liner to keep everything in.

Having to buy new packs was a blow but we had no choice. On Sunday morning, we traipsed down to the market stalls of El Rastro, the biggest open-air market in the world, and steeled ourselves for the parting of significant cash. When we managed to bargain down the price of two grey canvas packs endowed with an entirely new innovation - *inbuilt* steel frames - Tony was suspicious.

'At that price,' he said, 'we could have crap again. Remember the old Irish saying: *if you buy a dear thing you have a cheap thing; if you buy a cheap thing you have bugger-all.*'

However, we did OK. The pack I bought that morning would see out the journeys of the next twenty years, until the frame finally sliced through the canvas on a sad day in the spring of 1990.

The eating of strange foods began on the night of our arrival when John dumped half a bottle of red wine into an Irish stew. Then to our horror, he served it with rice. Whatever about the wine, rice had only ever come to our tables back home with 'pudding' attached. Stew had only ever come with spuds. Over this blasphemy dinner, however, John was able to enlighten us on what we'd eaten in San Sebastian.

'*Chipirones en su tinta*,' he told us, 'is squid in its own ink. Not quite dog after all.'

On the Sunday we continued the experimentation. At El Rastro we ate fistfuls of chufas (brown tubers from the root of the nut-sedge plant) and olives, initially mistaken by myself and Tony for grapes. We then retreated to a small tapas bar with a stone floor covered in sawdust and the type of detritus you'd expect to find in a family bin. Sitting at a metal table, we drank cheap Spanish brandy with prawns and clams. As was custom, we threw the shells on the floor, adding to the midden that was piling up.

At lunchtime, we met with John's girlfriend, dark statuesque 20-year-old Mercedes of the long black hair, olive skin and deep brown eyes. Mercedes suggested we have paella. This dish, from the city of Valencia, combined rice with vegetables, shellfish and their shells (more tossing onto the floor), and pieces of chicken and rabbit. I was unimpressed to find in mine a chicken foot, used I pointed out, by the chicken for everyday running about in chicken plop. Lunch was followed by a return to John's flat for the traditional siesta, followed by a return to the city centre for the bars of the Plaza Mayor. In a tavern that had walls dating back to Columbas, we drank vino tinto with octupus. In another, barmen in medieval dress served us vino tinto with hard-boiled eggs. Shells again to be tossed over shoulders. In the neighbouring back streets yet more bars with Spanish potato omelette and deep-fried squid rings.

Back at Calle Fundadores, as the bells chimed 1.00am, we discovered a final Spanish custom.

'The *sereno*,' John said. 'It goes back to antiquity when the cities were surrounded by walls. Inside the walls, each sereno had the responsibility of guarding a number of streets. He locked the outer doors at night and unlocked them again in the morning and the custom has persisted to the present day. Watch this. We clap our hands a few times and you'll hear the sereno tapping his staff on the street before he comes running to unlock the front door.'

John clapped his hands. The staff tapping followed from around the corner and a middle-aged man with a peaked cap and paunch came running to open our door and collect a few pesetas. Upstairs, we noted that the earlier barrier was gone. The senoritas de la noche were nowhere to be seen. However, as we settled down to a cup of tea a terrible din, accompanied by drunken laughter and frightful yodelling, erupted from the flat next door. A senorita had returned

## Chapter 4

with an hombre. We assumed he was Swiss.

John wished aloud that the beautiful Mercedes - who had long gone home - would fall from a kitchen cupboard.

\* \* \*

Greatly refreshed and conscious of the old maxim that fish and guests stink after three days, we left John on Tuesday, January 20th, and headed south towards Granada. Barely outside the city it started to rain and we were stopped by a cop on a motorbike.

'Now, remember the advice from that Basque guy,' Tony warned.

At first the cop was officious and aggressive; but when he realised we were Irish, everything changed. He shook our hands and joked about the weather in Ireland.

'Irlanda, pooh-pooh! Mucho rine!' he said, pointing at the stuff falling from the sky. He then got back on his bike and swept off in a flourish of smoke and a big salute.

'He must've taken us for English,' I said to Tony. 'Probably thought we were going to work in Gibraltar.' (Gibraltar had been cut off from Spanish labour by Franco's sealing of the border in 1969.)

'Nobody likes the English,' Tony said, whether true or not.

In the rain that lasted the rest of the day we walked twenty-one kilometres to the town of Pinto, arriving to unpaved streets that were ankle-deep in mud. Wet and miserable, we made our way to the railway station with the intention of cooking a meal on a platform bench. Instead, we were taken in hand by one of the workers. He led us into the waiting room where the stationmaster, a smiling grandfatherly man with swept-back steel-grey hair, was seated to a blazing fire. He rose, said something in Spanish, and slapped me on the back. Both men laughed. The stationmaster then shook his head as if he wished he was us, and gave us the waiting room for the night.

Next morning the rain stopped and we split separately from Pinto, arranging to meet again at the youth hostel in Granada. Over the next few hours I covered the 150 kilometres to Daimiel where my fortunes crossed those of a fat man with a bandido moustache who wore a straw hat and drove like he was taking a day off from wanting to live. He was on his way to Seville but his car broke down after a few kilometres and had to be towed away. After three close misses (two with mules) on the narrow winding road, this came as a great relief.

That night, the rats chased me out of the town of Bailén. I had bedded down on its outskirts in an avenue of palms and was enjoying my first full moon when it came to light that I had stumbled on the venue of a major rat convention. First I noticed one. Then two. Then millions. On the ground, on the palm-trunks, on the overhead wires and in the fronds above, the scurrying hordes were thick as the leaves of Milton's Vallombrosa. Engulfed by a condition known as crawlus hideous, I grabbed pack and sleeping bag and fled into the night. Behind, I imagined a pestilential wave in full pursuit: any minute now I would burst out onto the main road like a man with a pipe from Hamelin, towing in his wake a seething plague of scaly tails and fetid fur. In that instant I came to understand why delerium tremens is so often known as 'the rats'. Seven kilometres down the road I dared put my head down again, this time under an olive tree where bats, skimming through the fruiting moonlit branches, provided far more convivial company.

In the morning I crossed the Guadalquivir River on a horse and cart. I felt like Caesar. A car then dropped me in the town of Jaén shortly before ten o'clock. Sitting in the foothills of the Santa Catalina Mountains, the town looked stunning in the morning light, its steep narrow streets crowned by a massive three-domed Rennaisance cathedral. Beyond the town, olive groves ran across the red hills in every direction, culminating to the south and south-east in the peaks and forests of the Jabalcuz Mountains where the European lynx still found refuge, albeit in numbers of terminal decline.

Sitting in the Plaza Santa María in front of the cathedral to a lunch of bread, cheese and milk, I was joined by a local student, well-dressed, about sixteen, with collar-length curly hair and a flat nose. First he circled predator-like. Then he walked right over and asked if I was a mercenery.

'You go fight in Africa?'

'No,' I said. 'I just like wearing this jacket when I travel.'

'You travel where?'

'Morocco.'

'Ah!' he said. 'You *are* mercenery.'

He then told me that I was sitting in a 'very famous place'.

'Jaén is olive-oil capital of whole world. All America, they use olive oil from this place. This cathedral very famous too. Only here you will find 'Relic of Holy Face'. This is veil used by Santa Veronica to wash face of Jesús.'

My eyes must have boggled.

## Chapter 4

'You not believe?' he said, squinting at me. 'You can see every Friday.' [Unfortunately for me this was Thursday.] 'This very famous Christian place. In 1492, Christian army come here in Jaén, then attack Arab people in Granada. After this, no more Arab in Spain. You will read if you go Granada.'

He then practiced his English on me for ten minutes while I explained how the definite article worked. '*El toro,*' I said, using one of the few Spanish words in my lexicon, '*the* bull'. Finally I thanked him for all the earlier information and got up to go.

'Mercenery no good!' he shouted as I walked away.

South of the town, families were harvesting the olive crop. The women would first move in under each tree with canvas sacks to gather the fruit that had already fallen. The men would follow, placing a large net under the tree and whacking the branches with long poles after which the women again collected the fallen fruit. The full sacks were packed onto mules and taken to the nearby village to be deposited in small farmyards alongside carpets of drying corn.

Meanwhile, farmers rode to and from town on horses and mules, each strung with large wicker saddlebags weighed down with groceries and entire haystacks.

'*Hey Inglés,*' one of the younger women called from under an olive tree. '*Trabajo?*' I was being invited to join the harvesting. I don't know which was the more shocking: the offer of work or being mistaken for an Englishman.

'Going to India,' I shouted back. They hadn't a clue.

Eventually, around four in the afternoon I got a lift to Granada from yet another madman who took terrifying chances on the narrow road. Seventy if he was a day, with a cloth cap down to his eyes and tufts of fuzzy grey hair sticking out in all directions, he cursed the world as it swerved to avoid him and his pickup.

'I haf lucky strike!' he roared when we narrowly missed being embedded in the aftermath of an accident. But his madness was redeemed: he'd fought on the republican side in the civil war and had consequently spent ten years in jail. When he heard that I was from Ireland and knew two men who'd gone to Spain with the International Brigades, he began to fire away in broken English.

It turned out that he'd fought alongside former IRA officer, Frank Ryan, at the Battle of Jarama in February 1937 when men of the Connolly Column of the 15th International Brigade, along with Jock Cunningham of the British Battalion, had led a counter attack against Franco's troops at San Martin de la Vega. I sat like a mouse as we wound our way through sun-drenched valleys and across the mountains of the Sierra Harana to a firsthand account of the initial defeat and the rallying call that came from the Irish side.

'I am with Battalion *Espagnol*. We follow Battalion *Irlandés*. I go Senor Ryan. I say, "You have plan?" "*Si*," he say, "I have big plan: we sing." Irish, they sing; then everybody sing and we go.'

He went on to explain that despite their exhaustion, 140 men had marched back to try and retake the positions lost earlier in the battle. Franco's troops, believing them to be fresh reinforcements, retreated and ceded the ground. The republicans held it for the remainder of the war, protecting the Madrid-Valencia road.

'We win,' he concluded, 'before night finish.'

I tried to explain that singing was big in Ireland.

Finally we swung down the fertile valley of the Genil River, curving around the waters of Lake Cubillas where the sunlight danced like a million silver spangles. In the distance, the snow-shrouded peaks of the Sierra Nevada stood where they'd been since the great continental plates of Africa and Eurasia ground together away back in the Tertiary Period of geological time.

'*Mañana* you will visit Alhambra,' the old warrior said as he dropped me off in the centre of Granada.

'*Si, mañana*,' I agreed but had no idea what he was talking about. Then I let him go. To my eternal regret, I never got his name.

# Chapter 5
## The Sandeman

When I found Tony he was the guy sitting on the wall outside the city's backpackers' hostel.

'Guess what?' he said. 'We're out of season. The hostel is closed for winter. They don't expect anyone in January. But the good news is that I'm after booking us a room in the Pension Tanger a few blocks away - 50 pesetas [about 25 pence] for both of us for the night.'

'Which way?' I said.

'That's the bad news,' he said. 'I forget.'

'You're fuckin' havin' me on,' I said as politely as I could.

For the next hour we asked everyone in sight if they knew where the Pension Tanger might be found. Nobody did. We asked a cop who quickly corralled himself a crowd of advisors. Still, nobody ever heard of the Pension Tanger.

'Tony', I asked, 'didja by any chance bang yer head?'

Eventually a scholarly man with wire glasses broke the impasse. He pulled a pen and small notebook from his inside pocket and beckoned to Tony - write.

'A-a-a-ah!' the cop and all his advisors went. '*Pension Tanque!*' We were chided for our pronounciation.

'Know-alls who know fuck-all.' Tony growled.

Nowadays people flock to Granada. They go for the nightlife, the flamenco, the Moorish palace-fortress of the Alhambra and the old quarter of the Albaicín. We went because it was on the way to Málaga. The lack of money would have kept us away from any significant nightlife, and we'd never heard of the Alhambra or the Albaicín. Besides, when we were on the move we weren't city people. They tended to be expensive and full of museums and cathedrals in which we had little interest. Despite Granada's spectacular setting, a white city at the foot of the Sierra Nevada's ice-blue tops, we might ever have only stayed the one night had it not been for the parting command of the veteran of Jarama. Then we would have missed the jewel of Andalucía and the strange enigmatic figure waiting there.

Traipsing along pavements lined with palms and bitter-fruiting orange trees, and dodging tramcars that snaked the rails of the cobbled streets, I filled Tony in on the Battle of Jarama. The rattle of machine guns. The retreat. The march back up to San Martin de la Vega. The singing of *The Internationale*. I wondered if my father's old friend, Jim O'Regan, had been there. When we were kids, Jim was our second Santa Claus. On Christmas Eve, this quiet-spoken, chain-smoking man in trench coat and trilby would arrive on his bicycle to bring us presents. But even as kids, we knew that a shadow walked with Jim: he was one of the eighty men who'd gone to Spain with Frank Ryan. (He had also been jailed for his part in the IRA's London bombing campaign of 1939.)

I finished with the Jarama man's command: '*Mañana* you will visit Alhambra.'

'What's Alhambra?' Tony asked.

'Haven't a bulls, boy,' I said.

Tony raised himself to his full six feet and tugged thoughtfully at his nose. 'More of the mañana stuff.'

At the Pension Tanger, we cooked a meal, washed, shaved and went to the desk.

'What-is-Alhambra?' I asked the pension owner, spacing out the words as an alternative to speaking Spanish.

'*Alhambra bueno! Mucho! Mucho!*' he shouted.

On the strength of this we booked our room for a second night. When darkness fell we made our way to the nearest park. Huddled on a bench from the night winds of the sierra, we lit two cigarettes to warm our hands and looked for shooting stars. Up through some overhead palm fronds we located the Plough. By drawing an imaginary line from the constellation's Merak (79 light years away) to Dubhe (124 light years away), then multiplying it by five, we arrived at that great pointer of all travellers worth their salt - Polaris. The North Star.

'You know what,' Tony said. 'If that fell on top of you, you'd be stone dead.'

\* \* \*

Occupying the entire crown of the wooded hill of the Assabica on the southern side of the Darro River ravine, an enormous fortress palace of massive walls, towers and battlements rises above the south eastern flank of Granada. When floodlit at night, it is possibly the most captivating sight in all of Spain. As the most perfectly preserved relic of Moorish rule on the Iberian Peninsula, it symbolises an era that began in 711 when the Berber general, Tariq ibn Ziyad, led an Islamic invasion from Morocco. It was to

## Chapter 5

last until the Alhambra fell to the 'Catholic Monarchs', Ferdinand V and Isabella I, in 1492. The last Battle of Granada was the final act of the Christian reconquest of Iberia.

Al-Qalat al-hamrā' (the red fortress), to give it its original Arabic name, was built during the mid 14th century by the Nasrid dynasty of the Moorish Emirate of Granada. Over time it was extended by successive Muslim rulers who lived in the complex, but each maintained the consistent theme of 'Paradise on Earth' with column arcades, arabesques, calligraphy, reflecting pools, streams, fountains and elaborate gardens of cypress, pomegranate, palm, rose, orange and myrtle, all enclosed by thirteen massive towers. Once upon a time the towers defended a settlement of 2,000 Muslims who lived within the Alhambra walls.

After the reconquest, parts of the complex were used by the Christian rulers; and in 1527 the Palace of Charles V was built inside the Nasrid fortifications. Gradually the Alhambra fell into ruin until it was 'discovered' by European scholars and travellers in the 19th century. It was discovered by myself and Tony on the morning of January 23rd 1970.

We did the full tour, visiting the halls and palaces and gardens and standing in the tile and stucco décor of the Hall of the Ambassadors, where Baobdil, the last Moorish ruler of Granada, had surrendered the city after a seven-month siege and Ferdinand V met Columbas to discuss the idea of going west to search for India.

In the Hall of the Abencerrajes in the Royal Harem we stood under magnificent stalactite vaulting and heard of the sixteen princes who were murdered there by Baobdil's father, Sultan Muley Abul Hassan.

Story was that in his youthful days, the Sultan had married his cousin, Princess Ayxa la Horra. The couple had two sons, including Baobdil. When the years began to catch up he married again, choosing a young and beautiful Christian captive named Isabella de Solis, better know by her Moorish appellation, Zoraya. Together, they also had two sons. With each wife anxious to secure the succession of the throne for her own offspring, a civil war broke out in the harem.

Zoraya was supported by the Royal Vizier and the powerful Venegas family to whom the Vizier was connected. The Abbencerrages rallied around Ayxa, partly because of their long-standing opposition to the Venegas family and partly to protect the daughter of Mohammad Alhayzari, the ancient benefactor of their line. To sort out the mess, the Sultan invited the princes of the Abencerrajes to a banquet and massacre. The subsequent feud and its weakening of Granada signalled an opportunity to the united kingdoms of Aragón and Castile. In 1491 Ferndinand and Isabella marched on Granada with 150,000 soldiers. The city fell seven months later on January 2nd 1492.

At a fountain in the floor of the hall, reddish stains were said to be the indelible traces of the blood of the Abbencerrages.

'Not to appear too sceptical,' Tony said, 'but it looks like rust to me.'

As we made our way from this scene of treachery and massacre towards the Alcabaza, the Alhambra's fortified outer defences, a rare cut of a man stepped from nowhere.

'Sufferin' Jaysus,' Tony said. 'It's the Sandeman. That's all we're short.'

The first thing that struck you was the face: pure scrunched parchment, protruding cheekbones, and huge dark eyes framed in lank collar-length hair that streamed grey from a brimmed hat of the type worn by flamenco dancers. A ragged canvas bag hung from one shoulder while a black cape, like something from London's Carnaby Street, draped a tall frame, so thin that half a nose and one eye would've done the job.

Comfortably into his fifties, he could've passed for the quintessential Tolkein wraith. However, as he stepped our way on long spidery legs, a kind of sideways hop softened the image. This, he later claimed, was the result of being 'hit in the leg by a bomb' in the Philippines during World War II. Having most likely heard us speaking English he'd decided that we were the audience he'd left behind in the obscure part of Liverpool in which he normally drew his breath. After checking on where in Ireland we'd come from and where on Earth we were going, he introduced himself.

'I'm a poet,' he said.

That was it. No name. But to unkennel his bardic credentials, he stepped in front of us, stood to attention, closed his eyes and rhymed off with vigour the opening stanza of one of 'his' poems:

'There's a one-eyed yellow idol to the north of Kathmandu,
There's a little marble cross below the town;
There's a broken-hearted woman tends the grave of Mad Carew,
And the Yellow God forever gazes down.'

# Chapter 5

'Oh gawd...' Tony groaned. 'Why does this have to happen to us?'

Unfortunately for the poet, his was a plagiarism too far. *The Green Eye of the Little Yellow God*, written in 1910 by John Milton Hayes, was too well known to be claimed. But we drew this not to his attention.

'My friends,' he said when he'd finished, 'that was for you, for two intrepid explorers in whose esteemed company I am privileged to have found myself on this auspicious day. Tonight is not quite the night of the full moon. But by jove it will be a night to remember when the towers of the Alhambra gaze down on the city of Federico del Sagrado Corazón de Jesús García Lorca and my good self. This is a secret my friends: I have come to find the grave of Federico García Lorca.'

Tony and I looked at one another. This was teetering on the wire between eccentric and off the wall.

'Who's Federico García Lorca?' I asked.

'Who *was* he!' his nibs screeched, suddenly wired to the verge of overload and causing a passing family to jump to one side. 'He was Spain's greatest poet. A genius! A man for all seasons! A libertarian! A great man who, alas, was murdered not far from here by Franco's fascist forces back in 1936.'

'Maybe we should keep the voices down,' I said. 'You know, like, we're in Spain and all that?' But you might as well try and reason with a bat. Climbing now to the highest point of the Alcabaza, with its sensational panorama of Granada, it was clear that a grip would not be lost on Federico García Lorca.

'He was Spain's one man avant-garde. He was a champion of the free-roaming gypsies and their fiesty loving and living. His greatest collection - *Romancero Gitano* - means 'Gipsy Balladeer'. One of his famous poems, the 'Ballad of the Spanish Civil Guard', tells of a raid on a gipsy community, how the houses were burned and the people murdered. He was a friend of Salvador Dalí who did the stage settings in Barcelona for one of his plays. And he was born in Fuente Vaqueros, a few miles west of here and had his summer house in Granada. Right up until he was MURDERED.'

He then lowered his voice when it wasn't really necessary.

'He wrote his best works here,' he whispered, leaning in my direction. But the lowered voice didn't last.

'"HOW DID HE DIE?" you ask me?' [I had done nothing of the

sort.] 'He was a target for the fascists from the start of the civil war when they began to murder anyone they thought to be from the left. García Lorca wasn't political but he had a conscience and his sister was married to Granada's republican mayor and that was enough my friends. He died with 30,000 other people from Granada for supporting democracy and the peasants of Andalucía. He was taken by the fascists to a place called Fuente Grande, on the road between Viznar and Alfacar, where he was murdered. To this day his burial place is a mystery, so I've come to find it. I've got a small plaque here to plant on his grave.'

He pulled a crude home-made wooden cross from his bag. It read: 'Federico García Lorca, murdered by Bastard Franco, 19th August 1936'.

'Isn't that a bit dangerous?' I said. 'What about the Guardia Civil? They mightn't take too kindly to someone like you poking around for a grave of someone like that…'

'My friend,' the poet scowled, 'when Lord Cardigan led the Light Brigade at Balaclava, did he think of danger?'

'No,' Tony said, 'But maybe he should have…'

By now we had an audience and I was beginning to wonder if we weren't about to join Federico García Lorca on the Viznar-Alfacar road if that was indeed where he lay.

But as suddenly as the conversation had begun, it switched. The poet pointed down below, beyond where the Darro River cut through its narrow ravine.

'That hill you see on the far side of the river is the old Moorish Medina of Granada, the Albaicín. A labyrinth of alleys and steps and whitewashed houses typical of the Arab world. Over there you'll find the gitanos, the gipsy people of García Lorca. They call themselves the 'ancient people'. The descendants of people who came from India more than a thousand years ago.

'Do you know my friends, they brought the roots of flamenco to Andalucía. Have you seen the way the women dance in flamenco? They use the posture, the arm movements, of Indian dance. You'll find those people in houses dug into the rock. You'll find them in the caves in the Sacromonte Hills behind the Albaicín. Go there my friends. Go there.'

He then turned and strode off in a swish of cape, leaving behind an immortal enigma. To this day I don't know if he was genius or imbecile. Or if he ever found that grave or lived to tell the tale of his odd and reckless quest.[2]

'And if a bomb hit him anywhere,' Tony said as the cloaked figure limped down the steps of the Alcabaza, 'it hit him in the shaggin' head.'

*The Alhambra, Granada.*

---

[2] In October 2009, a team of archaeologists from the University of Granada began to excavate at a site outside Alfácar identified in the late 1970s by a man who claimed to have helped dig García Lorca's grave. But by mid December the justice minister of Andalucía, had announced that 'not one bone, item of clothing or bullet shell' was found, and that 'the soil was only 40cm deep, making it too shallow for a grave'.

## Chapter 6

### The Coast of the Sun

———————————

From Granada we travelled separately along the western road to Antequera.

It was a bright morning, with long shadows thrown across the foothills of the sierras by lines of olive and almond, and vines that undulated like advancing armies along their slopes. In the valleys between the ranges, the farmers were burning off the stalks of the corn harvest, filling the air with a sweet-smelling smoke and attracting scores of raptors to trawl for casualties. Where the corn was still being cut, mules ridden by men and women in straw hats carried the harvest home on a road bordered by clumps of prickly pear and agave. Here and there small wall lizards basked in the sun's rays to warm up and increase their metabolism in preparation for the day's bug hunt.

After five h*** *** ***intermittent lifts I arrived in Antequera, a small *** *** *** *** ***rlooked by the spires of its twenty churches and th*** *** *** *** of its own Alcazaba. East of town La Peña de los *** *** *** Lovers' Rock) leaned 880 metres into the sky *** *** *** flaky causes. Local legend told of a love affair bet*** *** *** ***istian shepherd from Antequera and a beautiful *** *** *** *** ***rom nearby Archidona. Driven to the top of the l*** *** *** ***oorish soldiers in an attempt to force them to ren*** *** *** ***hey chose instead to hurl themselves to their deat***

The road n*** *** *** ***inding dangerously upwards into the Sierra del T*** *** *** deep valleys with tumbling rivers, and finally risi*** *** *** ***ests of the Málaga Mountains. Throughout this *** *** *** Pumphrey was the man at the wheel. A retired *** *** *** a white handlebar moustache, a bald head and *** *** *** ohn Lennon's, Garnoc was a man who separate*** *** *** he wood. In his hands the most nondescript b*** *** *** ***en would become a tapestry of the outlandish. In the M***aga Mountains, he was in his element and mixing me up with Charles Darwin.

'Most of the trees you see are Aleppo Pines,' he said with a sweep of his arms that left the wheel disturbingly free. 'These were planted

## Chapter 6

in great numbers in the early 20th century to combat the flooding that had plagued Málaga for hundreds of years. They're the ones with the orange-red bark. In Greece, they use the resin of these trees to flavour a wine they call Retsina. They're native trees but wouldn't have been this abundant had it not been for the destruction of earlier times. Deforestation of the original forests began back in the 15th century after the reconquest of Málaga. When the Catholic Monarchs reallocated the land, the new owners stripped out the native trees and replaced them with olive groves and vineyards. This brought about massive erosion and catastrophic floods that first hit Málaga in 1544 and continued well into the 20th century, effectively until the new forests had taken hold. Mess with nature and that's what you get.'

'It is indeed,' I said.

This gush of interest sent Garnoc into a vortical spin. He began to pick out remnants of older Mediterranean species in positive bursts of glee.

'There you have the once abundant, evergreen Holm oak. This is often used in the establishment of truffle 'orchards' which do well in association with the tree's roots. The Holm Oak also gives us edible acorns which are fed to the free-ranging pigs that provide Spain's Ibérico ham. And look! Cork Oaks. You can see the thick bark that can be harvested in two-metre columns for up to a hundred years to provide the bungs of wine bottles and the floats of life jackets. And there's the Mastic Tree. Its resin has been used as chewing gum for more than 2,000 years. And over there, St John's Bread! That's a shrub of the pea family, which you'll often find cultivated in gardens for its edible legumes. And that umbrella-shaped pine is Stone Pine. It yields the pine-nuts used in cooking...' And on it went into ever-increasing obscurity.

The Kermes oak formed the food of the Kermes scale insect, from which a red dye was obtained in former times. The Gall oak, native to Morocco, Portugal and Spain was the source of nutgalls, produced by a gall-wasp infection and also used in dyeing. The Strawberry Tree was an evergreen shrub that didn't actually grow strawberries. Its red fruits were in fact nowhere near as edible as the name might suggest.

'The botanical name,' Garnoc told me, 'is *arbutus unedo, un edo* being the Latin for "I eat (but) one".'

*Garnoc*, I said to myself, *you're a shaggin' walking encyclopaedia.* I would've been an expert on the trees of southern Spain had the whole thing not become irrelevant on a bend on that mountain road. Two happenings made it so. The first was a big black monster with enormous curved tusks that erupted across the road in front of us. Springing from a clump of bushes, it caused Garnoc to swerve wildly and utter the unbotanical words, 'Where did that fuckin' boar come from?' The second was a burst of sparkling aquamarine that opened out into a full view of distant Málaga and the long sunbaked sweep of the Costa del Sol.

'If you could get high enough,' Garnoc said, 'you could probably see the coast of Africa from here.'

I often wondered afterwards if he'd been to Morocco and was tipping me some kind of cryptic wink.

Garnoc dropped me on the outskirts of Málaga in the shank of the evening. With night deepening around me, I walked in cricket-chirruping darkness to Torremolinos.

* * *

Until the end of the 1950s Torremolinos was a poor fishing village some fifteen kilometres south west of Málaga. But its location in the sunny climes on a seven-kilometre stretch of beach was to bring unimaginable change. When international tourism hit Spain, Torremolinos became the pioneer resort of the Costa del Sol. The opening of the village's Pez Espada Hotel in 1959 marked the arrival of luxury hotels on the coast. By January 1970, when I landed there, the resort had grown to several hotels and nightclubs and a flagged square that catered to the British love of fish and chips.

Close to this square I sat on the balcony of a small pension that night and strongly disapproved. Such was my angst that myself and a jug of self-made Sangria mulled over the draft of a letter of grave portent. As I could contemplate no truck with Franco and his ilk, I resolved to send it to the king, whom I believed to be somewhere in the political background or possibly in exile. *Here*, my letter would begin, *you need to rein this in. You don't want a whole load of Killarneys dotted along the coast of Spain, do you?* But I left it too long. Consequently, much of coastal Spain was obliterated in an orgy of rapacious environmental plunder. When I went back fourteen years later I found that the Torremolinos of 1970 had been small potatoes. The beautiful Andalucían coastline from Málaga to the far side of Estepona was now buried under tiers of villas, apartment blocks, high-rise hotels and restaurants that ran clear to the surf, a sacrifice on the altar of Mammon.

# Chapter 6

In the morning I set off early, as I was to meet Tony at two o'clock at Algeciras railway station. We would then catch an afternoon boat to Morocco. The narrow road proved slow for hitchhiking, but between lifts the landscape made good the shortfall. To the north and west, wooded valleys snaked into the folds of the mountains, broken by patches of white where villages sat among vineyards and fruiting citrus groves. To the south the Mediterranean, weaving by in a coastline of rocky outcrops and sandy coves, brimmed with sunlight and seagulls. Prickly pear, stands of eucalyptus and pine, and sweet-scented shrubs full of birds and insects lined the road.

Occasionally, the magnificent Spanish fighting bulls would appear in roadside fields, close enough to touch if you were that stupid. Large posters, meanwhile, would proclaim when El Cordobés, would next be in town to despatch a few for the baying mob in the slaughter ring of some local Plaza del Toros. Descended from wild bulls of the Iberian Peninsula and selected on the basis of aggression, strength, stamina and just enough intelligence to prevent them from distinguishing a matador from his cape, these bulls had been subjected to appalling cruelty since the days of the Roman games. El Cordobés (Manuel Benítez Pérez from Córdoba) drew huge crowds to his own special stunts which included cutting his barbed banderillas down to 'pencil length' and standing with his back to the bull as it charged. He would then swivel away at the last moment, causing the bull to swerve and allowing him to drive home the banderillas from behind. This dashing idol of female Spain was gored several times, but by the time of my passage down the Costa del Sol he had become the highest-paid matador in history.

At Fuengirola, Marbella and Estepona, razor-backed peaks towered above the towns, pressing them to the shore. Streets were shaded by palms, and buildings were cloaked in cascades of Bougainvillia's magenta. East of Estepona billboards began to advertise ferry tickets to Ceuta and Tangier, bringing home the fact that I was heading for Africa and confirming Cora's belief that the path from Cork to India was unknown to me and my kind.

Algeciras appeared on the skyline at the exact point at which a recently completed oil refinery belched smoke and flames from a series of tall funnels over the town of San Roque. The Rock of Gibraltar, sealed off by Franco, loomed up through the fumes, its British colonial status a reminder of why San Roque existed at all.

On August 1st 1704, during the War of the Spanish Succession, an Anglo-Dutch naval force laid siege to Gibraltar. They demanded that the inhabitants surrender unconditionally and swear loyalty to the Archduke Carlos of Austria, whose claim to the Spanish throne was being supported by the British. Gibraltar City Council defied the ultimatum and two days of heavy shelling followed, during which the castle and town were bombarded. On August 4th the Spaniards surrendered and fled as their homes and churches were looted. They had expected to return within months but the British stayed. The displaced refugees established San Roque.

\* \* \*

For a small town, Algeciras had a lot of railway stations. Two may not seem like a lot; but when you spend five and a half hours in one and the person you're supposed to meet spends over six hours in the other, it's at least one too many.

I arrived half an hour ahead of time to find no sign of Tony. At seven o'clock with the air growing thin and cold I gave up and turned for the port area of town. In the meantime I had spent two hours on a platform bench in the company of Gilberto of the Servicio Especial de Vigilancia Fiscal (Special Service of Fiscal Surveillance), in other words the customs police. Gilberto, a well-fed man of about forty, had spotted me looking grim some time around three o'clock and decided to liven up my day. I think he was being paid by Franco's government to do something else entirely. Or, perish the thought, did he see in me a national threat?

Either way, my saviour spoke no English. Apart from a handful of single words that I'd picked up since arriving in Irun, I spoke no Spanish. This allowed not for any grand flow of intellectual exchange. However, we did manage a form of communication. By drawing sketches, and using sign language and a calendar, we covered my travel plans, our families, the brewing Irish conflict and Gilberto's work which appeared to centre around the protection of Spain from some kind of tobacco. He also explained that a big flood had hit town on January 13th, as evidenced in the silt on the station's sleepers, and the grasses and weeds entangled in the wheels of stationary wagons. Eventually, however, we ran out of steam. Gilberto got bored and left. But I felt a great warmth for our time together: he an older man in a cop uniform; me an 18-year-old budding lefty in a combat jacket. *How easy to make friends*, I thought, *if you're open to the world*. But, down the road, Gilberto would rain ruin on the likes of that.

## Chapter 6

By seven o'clock all hope of sailing to Morocco was lost. It would be at least tomorrow, provided I could find Tony. I was worried. This rendezvous was of the 'there or dead' calibre. We had agreed that, no matter what, we'd both be in Algeciras station for two o'clock.

I walked the short distance to the portside Avenida de la Hispanidad, the location of several small travel companies that had been busy earlier in the day. There was a chance that somebody there might have seen a tall wandering Irishman with a combat jacket and a rucksack just like mine. It didn't take long. One of two Canadians I met had run into him over at the ferry terminal. He'd been there, at the small port railway station, since one o'clock.

When I found him he looked sick but it was a great relief to both of us. 'There or dead' had been an awful prospect. To celebrate, we bought food and went back to the main railway station to cook dinner on the bench I'd shared with Gilberto. We then returned to the waterfront where Avenida de la Hispanidad tingled with the night-time variant of port life and what Joni Mitchell might have described as 'the wind is in from Africa'.

In the hustle, bustle and tobacco smoke, young backpackers and long-haired hippies (the distinction is mine) rubbed shoulders with Moroccans in hooded djellabas and backless leather Babouche slippers. The djellabas, like the cowls of monks in all but their variety of colours, lent the street a cloak and dagger touch as shadowy figures dragged massive trunks and stitched bales of luggage to their night's accommodation. Money changers called from shop doorways, advertising Moroccan dirhams. Hustlers touted ferry tickets. Truckers wheeled massive vehicles through the port gates, leaving them parked for the morning voyage to Africa. They then went off to do whatever truckers did when they waited for sailings to Africa.

In the cafés and tapas bars Spanish men and foreigners mingled in a cauldron of languages: Arabic, Spanish, French, Dutch and English. A couple of hairy-heads in paisley-patterned shirts sipped coffee at a pavement table. A black-skinned man patrolled the avenue, slugging brandy from a bottle. He said he was Senegalese, a seaman down on his luck. He wanted some pesetas. An Algerian family was bedding down for the night in a ramshackle car with French number plates: migrants going home. A horse and cart went down the street, laden with oranges. An oil lamp swung from one of the shafts.

And a great surprise was sprung. Four Americans - a man, two women and a four-year-old boy - were travelling around the world. An Australian had come overland from India. A pin was stuck in our balloon.

It was, I must admit, a yank between relief and dismay: at last we had solid proof that our journey was possible; but the unofficial first Irish overland expedition to India was no longer the only horse on the road.

Nevertheless, as we gathered our wits for the great adventure of the morrow, I was overcome by a feeling that I'd last experienced when empathising with Jim Hawkins as he set foot on the gangway of the Hispaniola in search of the buried treasures of Captain Flint.

At eleven o'clock Tony and I went back to the railway station, creeping in through a side gate with a view to finding us a bed for the night in an idle carriage. But a guard with a flashlight and rifle held a different view. We put in train a tactical retreat and booked into a cheap pension. So cheap that we sprinkled the floor with *Dettol*, dumped the blankets and mattresses, and slept on the box-springs in our sleeping bags.

# Chapter 7
'The Only Hope...'

---

When the Romans came in the first century BC, Tangier was an old town. The legions of Augustus would have heard that it had been founded by Sufax, the son of the Berber goddess Tingis and her husband Änti. The Greeks, on the other hand, would claim that Sufax was the son of Hercules who slept in the Grotte d'Hercule out Cap Spartel way, before going off on one of his labours. Looking out on the Atlantic through the Africa-shaped sea window of that cave, it's easy to feel for the Greek case. But not so, according to the man who sold me a crystal geode from the High Atlas in the city's Petit Socco, thirty-eight years after Tony and I had drunk mint tea in that very spot.

'That,' he assured me, 'is *beacoup de* bullshit.' We became instant friends.

I was on my way home after a ten-week journey in the Mauritanian Sahara when I stopped a few days in Tangier. For years, I'd planned to look up a man called Omar who'd run the Pension Monaco where we'd stayed in 1970. But every time I arrived in Tangier, the address would be back in Ireland. Now, I had it with me. But I was too late. The pension - in Rue Bouselham at the edge of the Medina - was long gone, as was Omar. Nevertheless, by sheer chance, the crystal man had known him. Thin and grey with a clipped moustache, he was in the small square, touting his geodes to passing tourists. When I mentioned Omar's pension in 1970 his eyes rolled back into his shrivelled head.

'A-a-a-ah,' he said, craning his face towards the sky. 'In 1970 the hippies came to Tangier.'

In that instant we were catapulted back to a space we'd shared without ever having met.

The square filled with garrulous ghosts, lingering in the leaning walls, wrought iron overhangs and snaking alleys from a time when Moroccans and young westerners in dark cafés shared hashish pipes and their take on life. There were flashes of pastel walls in cheap rooms where people scrawled psychedelic drawings beside the words of Jack Kerouac, William Burroughs, Allen Ginsberg, Hermann Hesse and Doctor Timothy Leary a.k.a. 'the man who turned on America' who famously said between pops of LSD, 'Drugs are the religion of the people - the only hope is dope.'

Tony and I were there again, eighteen years old, shoulder to shoulder in jeans, combat jackets and boots. We were loping through the ancient Medina alleys with their awnings, mules and spices. We were in the tiny stores and the alcove-workshops where machines were turned by foot. We were among the shuffling djellabas in the listless coffee shops of the hashish men. We were aboard the rusting tub that had long ago brought us from Algeciras to the 18.5 square-kilometre Spanish exclave of Ceuta, a journey of one and a half hours escorted by a school of bottlenosed dolphins.

It's funny how little else I remembered of that first journey across. On a clear day, as you pass Gibraltar, you can already see the African coast and the northern bulwark of the Rif Mountains tumbling seawards, sheer and green, from the heights of Jbel Musa. On the final approach, the white colonial seafront buildings and the high-rise of Ceuta gradually take shape behind a line of date palms and a quay wall that extends eastwards towards the town centre. Yet, on my next visit in 1984 all I could recall of 1970 was the dizziness of boarding a boat with so many veiled women, and men in djellabas, fezzes and turbans, and a bunch of hairy hippies who looked even scruffier than us. And the jolt of arriving in Ceuta to find a bristly-faced Berber who was waiting at the bottom of the gangway with an offer. In a voice that rasped from the hood of his djellaba he spoke the single sentence that would mark the day we departed the familiar world.

'Hey man,' he said, 'you like buy some kif, marijuana, black hash? I make you good price.'

\* \* \*

My first romantic kiss came from Patricia Rafferty when we were both nearly ten. There never was another like it but it didn't stop me going back to look. If there's a place on the planet that is a travel equivalent, then it's Morocco. Which explains why a man called Ahmed who runs a small hotel in the Rif Mountains thinks I'm his Irish cousin. However, that first afternoon it was touch and go.

'You can stick yer black hash up yer arse,' Tony informed the gangway drug lord. Tony had a way with words. This greatly rattled the drug lord.

'Fuck you, dirty fucking tourist. You tell me *arse* in *my* country? Maybe somebody fuck your mother. Maybe somebody fuck your sister.' The drug lord too had a way with words.

## Chapter 7

'Watch yer back,' I advised as we scurried around him, me first. 'And by the way,' I shouted back for the record, 'we're not tourists. We're *travellers!*'

Outside the terminal we regrouped. Down along the quay we could see four other backpackers who'd been on the boat being accosted by two guys without djellabas who looked to me like Bill Sikes and the demon from *The Exorcist*.

'In-juns,' Tony said, alerting me to the possibility of an ambush.

'We need a plan,' I said. 'This is a dangerous place.'

'They could have knives or guns or anything up them djellaba sleeves,' Tony said.

'These guys have no djellabas,' I pointed out.

We waited until five Canadians who'd also been on the boat caught up. Like sardines under attack, the bunching might confuse.

'And if someone's gonna get stabbed,' I flagged up, 'the odds would be on Canada.'

'Good point, boy,' Tony said.

In town we took to walking in the middle of the street, away from any spot from which a knifeman might leap. We took to oscillating back and forth so each could watch the other's back. I know. It was ridiculous. But you couldn't have sold me that on January 26th 1970.

In the bus station, paranoia was further topped up. The five who were ahead had been sold tickets for a bus to Tangier that had already gone. When they complained they were told to get lost.

'Clearly,' Tony said, 'there's no law here.'

Next time around, all eleven of us travellers from the boat set our packs on the ground in front of the Tangiers bus and formed a wagon circle. Tony and the biggest of the Canadians, who looked like a sumo wrestler with a ponytail, went off to buy more tickets, refusing to hand over the money until the man behind the desk - who spoke a few words of English - swore that the bus matched the tickets.

'Swear to Allah,' the big Canadian said.

'No,' the man said.

'Why not?' Tony reasoned. 'If this is the right bus?'

'I am Christian,' the man said. 'This is Spain.' Right enough, when you looked around, there weren't that many djellabas.

Two hours after arriving in Ceuta, we were away again, the eleven of us squashed into four narrow bench-like seats on a bus packed with Moroccan men and women.

'In Tetouan,' the driver told me, 'you change bus. Many seat on bus to Tangier.'

'Many seat on this bus too,' I pointed out. 'Problem is, they all too full.'

'Not too full my friend,' the driver said. 'Only you too big.'

It was a hard one to argue.

* * *

Beyond the town's old fort, we swung along the coast towards the frontier. Behind us, the sea ramparts stretched back towards the cape of Monte Hacho which, along with Gibraltar, formed the ancient Pillars of Hercules. To our left, tin-roofed shacks fronted the beach. Racks of flyblown fish dried in the sun. Multi-coloured fishing boats lay tethered to wooden stakes.

After lengthy Moroccan formalities conducted by friendly cops in dark blue uniforms and white peaked hats, we crossed the frontier under a hill dotted with sentry boxes and took on two more passengers and three goats. We stayed five minutes while a man at the top of the bus begged for alms and another tried to sell some magic potion that would regrow your teeth. Down on the beach the cops fought cat and mouse with would-be migrants trying to dart across to Ceuta. Shortly afterwards the bus was stopped at a police roadblock in a search for contraband.

The man in command was a fat cop in a low-slung peaked hat, grey uniform and thick black moustache who ordered another similarly dressed fat cop of unhappy visage and no moustache to climb up on the roof. Only problem was that when the ladder, which had broken from the back of the bus, was placed on the ground it only reached half way to the roof. This meant that the junior fat cop had to climb as far as he could while the bus driver and conductor held the ladder firm. He would then have to hoist himself the rest of the way. When this wasn't working, two passengers were ordered from the bus and told to push at the climbing cop's legs until he managed to drag himself on to the roof whereupon he ransacked the baggage in a humiliated rage. The cop in charge paraded up and down like Charlie Chaplin in *The Great Dictator*.

'See you later alligator,' he said to us foreigners as the bus moved off again. It was sunny and warm with drifting puffs of cloud in a firmament of eagles, and we'd landed on the moon.

I remember being bombarded by a crackling radio and the vocals

## Chapter 7

of a woman who would've made a great can opener and it sounded fine, fully in harmony with what floated by beyond the windows of the bus.

We were on a potholed tarmac road, on each side of which parallel mule tracks carried the dominant traffic of mules, donkeys and camels. The owners who walked or rode, depending on how heavily they'd loaded their animals, were dressed in a bewildering array of dress. As well as the djellabas and veils we'd seen on the boat, the coastal Berber women wore bright kaftans, or skirts and shawls. The women from the Rif Mountains wore distinctive, red-striped overskirts, shawls, and brimmed, flat-topped, conical hats of straw draped in bright woollen braids. Two of the camels were led by men in blue robes and turbans that covered all but their eyes. One of the Moroccan passengers, with a beard down to his toes, told the big Canadian that these were nomads - men of the Sahara - headed in the wrong direction.

The odd truck went by but most of the road traffic consisted of crowded flatcarts hauled by skinny, sad-looking horses. Periodically, a village without streets climbed the hills in tiers of yellow, white and ochre, many of the houses with chicken coops on the flat roofs. Scrawny dogs howled from behind fences of canegrass and prickly pear. Two donkeys dragged a wheelless wooden plough through a field of stubborn sod and stone. The light was different. The cooking smells were different: tagines simmering over red coals; skewers of meat on charcoal flames. Shops spilled out onto the road, bursting with oranges, figs, olives, dates and lumps of hanging meat. A ceramics stall ran twenty metres along the road, its owners living in an adjoining lean-to. The onion man sold drapes of onions from a wooden frame. On the tops of telegraph poles, storks had built enormous stick nests. Armies of egrets stood to attention in tilled fields or sat in trees like hunched Buddhas. Christianity was gone. The bell towers and spires of France and Spain had been replaced by the square minarets of mosques.

'We could become missionaries,' Tony said. He was joking, him having dumped religion, but I told him he'd want to watch that kind of talk.

Close to Tetouan, pink mountains rose to the west. To the east, the bays and forested cliffs marked the onset of the Barbary coast from which sailed the pirates who sacked Baltimore in West Cork in 1631 and took 108 of its residents into slavery.

'Look out for blue eyes and foxy hair,' Tony said.

On the edge of the old city, goats and cattle grazed between blocks of jaded flats. A couple of sheep had a head-butting session. Below the white climbing layers of the town, the Martil Valley and its imposing crags sat at the western end of an area of the Rif Mountains that grew more rugged and lawless as you travelled east.

It was here, among the villages that dotted the valley, that we came again on the deeds of Leopoldo O'Donnell.

When the Spanish invaded Morocco in November 1859, O'Donnell led the army of 36,000 men. In February 1860 he took Tetouan in a battle in which the lightly-armed Moroccans were decimated by Spanish artillery. He then assumed the title 'Duke of Tetouan'. Shortly afterwards Morocco was forced to sign a treaty ceding Western Sahara, Ceuta and Tetouan to Spain.

In Tetouan where memories were long we refused to mention that O'Donnell's people hailed from our own County Donegal.

\* \* \*

It was dark when we pulled up outside the railway station on Tangier's Avenue Mohammad VI. I felt like a film star. Outside, the pavement was thronged with an enormous reception party of men and boys, all yelling and waving their arms at the foreigners. Others were running from the direction of the Medina's port gate. I acknowledged with a minor Papal wave. This was a warm welcome indeed. *Céad míle fáilte* and all that. To cap it all, the city's mosques opened up with the evening call to prayer, beginning in the main mosque and rippling in a reverberating harmony of '*Allahu akbar*' on up through the hidden alleys of the Medina. Even the stars were twinkling in that Arabian sky.

'Begod boy,' Tony said. 'It's how I expected to be received by the Mir of Hunza.'

Then the door of the bus opened.

I've never been dropped from a height into civil disorder. But if I was, this was how I would imagine it. The crowd surged forward. I was grabbed off the bus and pulled apart by three big yahoos in djellabas. *You like pension? You like kif? You like woman? You like boy?* A Canadian voice shouted *Let go of my fuckin' rucksack!* I grabbed tightly on the straps of mine. A Moroccan voice shouted *Why you paranoid Jew boy?* I looked around to find he was addressing me. I pretended a clash of cultures but that went nowhere. I considered putting up the mitts and going out in a blaze

## Chapter 7

of glory but I was too young and handsome to die on a Tangier street. My head went into a spin. *Ciarán, it yelled, get the fuck outta the middle of this.* Swivelling around, I could see Tony's face in the melee. *Every man for himself* was plastered all over it. I began to battle my way out.

*Pension Royal!* someone shouted. *Pension Miami!* someone else shouted. Suddenly it was all over. Like the Red Sea, the crowd split in two. Seven of us were swept along the streets in one direction towards the Pension Royal. The other four were whisked off to the Pension Miami or a terrible death. Accommodation solved.

Tony and I wound up sharing a damp and dingy room and a communal squat toilet at the Pension Royal with the big ponytailed sumo wrestler Canadian who introduced himself as Tim, and a skinny long-nosed Welshman called Elfred whose features did him no favours. Tim, friendly and florid of complexion, had the warm nature of a teddy bear. Elfred averted eye contact, spoke in a thin tuneless voice and always gave the impression of being hunted. Landed in the room next door were two of the other Canadians from the bus and an Australian with a head like Jimi Hendrix who'd flown from Sydney to Madrid just three days before. Once inside, we barricaded the doors and called for tea while the pension owner fought off the crowd who'd all become 'guides' and wanted a decent levy of commission.

We then discovered that the light switch for the room was outside in the hall. It was beginning to dawn. This extraordinary land was a place where mad things happened.

When the tea came it was full of sugar and mint.

\* \* \*

We spent two nights in that room and were woken each morning at half five by the call to prayer and the braying of donkeys. By the end of that time big Tim had done a Timothy Leary, Elfred had done himself and we were all old Moroccan hands.

No sooner had the voices outside dissipated into the night than Tim sniffed the air. Without a word, he unbarricaded the door and pushed his colossal frame outside. Twenty minutes later I nearly had a heart attack when he bounced back into the room in a purple djellaba and a pair of yellow Babouche slippers. Like someone who'd jumped from a building and landed in a Berber man.

'Fuck's sake Tim,' I said, 'Don't be doing things like that.' But Tim had only started on the cultural assimilation.

'That there,' he said laying a small plastic bag and a packet of Rizla papers on his bed, 'is twenty-eight grams of kif from the finest fields of the Rif.' He lifted the bag and poured what looked like ground tobacco into his palm. 'Smell that.' As if by magic our next-door neighbours came banging on the door.

'No hope without dope!' the Jimi Hendrix Australian whooped, bouncing into the room like a kangaroo. He pulled out a small block of black stuff. 'That there,' he said, 'is the best of Pakistani black.' Tony and I looked at one another. So this was what was pulling all those hairy hippies to Tangier.

In a transformation worthy of the road to Damascus everyone sank in cross-legged reverence to the floor like misers gloating over a stash of gold. (The challenge was to go down, hands-free, in a single move.) Silent eyes were glued on Tim rolling a mixture of kif and tobacco into a traffic cone of a cigarette. I myself watched the door with pumping heart for the Tangier drug squad. Tim laughed and lit a match.

'In a situation like this,' he said, 'there are no leaders, only the led.'

'You keep an eye on me,' I muttered to Tony. 'I don't want to be jumping out any windows.'

'I will,' Tony promised. 'And you keep an eye on me.'

I don't suppose we'd really worked that one out too well.

As it transpired the only casualty was Elfred. Half an hour after Tim had struck the match we were all on our backs, splayed across beds and the floor in the balm of tetrahydrocannabinol euphoria, howling like donkeys at the funniest jokes ever told, when the turn took Elfred.

'Fucking monkeys!' he roared and began lashing at his back. He jumped from the bed and charged around the room like a dog with an itchy tail.

'Fuck's sake, man,' Tim laughed. 'There's no fuckin' monkeys in here. Only hippopotamuses.'

Elfred grabbed his pack and began swinging at the hippopotamuses. It was what they call functioning at a suboptimal intellectual level.

I never saw the likes of it again.

\* \* \*

The transformation continued in the morning in streets that were now bright and cheerful, full of the thrum of commerce and people doing ordinary, everyday things. No hullabaloo like the night before. No monkeys. No hippopotamuses. Just lots of feral cats.

## Chapter 7

As nobody else had stirred, I went out to explore the Medina, a maze of crowded alleys in the old walled city. In a steely pose straight from the pages of *Our Boys*, I strode along like John Wayne. Into the crowd. Into the din. Into the djellabas, veils, fezzes and turbans. Into total sensory overload.

People milled about small shops, buying bread, milk, olives and sheaves of mint. In a dim space no bigger than under your stairs two lads were producing beds and chairs. In a shop as wide as its door and twice that length, a guy with a sewing machine would stitch you up a pair of trousers in twenty minutes. Next door a seated man banged out mosaics. In another the egg man had a tower of thousands packed to the ceiling. Same with the man who sold spools of thread. The olive man's displays ranged from yellow to green, copper, pink, brown and black. Spices were piled in metre-high cones in three shops that sat cheek by jowl. In a small restaurant a waiter was perched on a windowsill, filling his lungs with hash. Other workshops produced leather bags, djellabas and Babouche slippers. Women at corners sold fruit and vegetables. An old man in a striped djellaba sat on a box and sold individual cigarettes. A man festooned in brass cups and ladles, strung across his salmon-coloured robes, sold water from a goatskin bag. Other men hauled mules and donkeys through the crowds. A young boy wheeled bread in a barrow. A crazy man yelled at everyone. Another man dragged himself along on his hands and knees. Three men in white robes sat around a metal tray while a fourth poured tea from a silver pot into small glasses from a height of at least a metre. The pâtisserie sold a hundred varieties of cake. Piercing Moroccan and Egyptian music blared from windows and doorways. The muezzins added their sudden call to prayer. Food smells formed a pot pourri with those of spices, donkey dung, strong coffee and the kif being openly smoked by men and lads as young as ten. Remembering Tony's words of yesterday I kept as best I could to the middle of each alley, some no wider than would allow two people to pass at a squeeze. But passers-by did nothing more than bid me the time of day. With variations.

'Hello. Iss go-o-od? Welcome in Morocco.'

'Hello. What you like? You like smoke? Make you very hap-py. Give you en-er-gy.'

'Excuse me, you come from what place?'

'See you later alligator,' from a perfectly respectable grown man in a fez who followed with, 'In a while, crocodile.'

An hour passed, then another. Without any sense of where I was, I climbed upwards along crooked lanes and long flights of steps that sometimes became tunnels beneath the houses. There were tiled arches, massive wooden doors with studs and iron knockers, tiny dead ends, mosques with horseshoe arches and minarets covered in bright mosaics. Overhead, the buildings leaned at mad angles, overhanging bays supported by rusting angle iron. I passed through an arch into a dusty walled enclosure.

'Kasbah! Kasbah!' Two young boys came running. 'You give dirham,' they demanded on arrival.

'This is the Kasbah?' I asked.

I was in shock. If this was the Kasbah, what was all the *come-with-me-to-the-Kasbah* fuss about? Where was the castle? Where were the belly dancers? Where was Humphrey Bogart? A few dilapidated villas aside, this was an empty shell. But my ponderings were cut short.

'Ferry! Ferry!' I was dragged through a hole in the wall to a spot of rough ground overlooking the harbour and the wooden scimitar-shaped boats that fished the Atlantic waters. 'Tuna! Tuna!' the tallest of the boys shouted. Bluefin tuna migrated through those waters.

I looked about. There was one other person on the promontory, a bear of a man with one clouded eye and a black beard streaked in grey. He was sitting on a low stone wall in a grey djellaba, shading his face with one hand. I nodded.

'Is good view,' he said in a voice far too soft for the size of him.

'Very good,' I said, not making too much eye contact so as to avoid a repeat of the night before.

'What country you from?'

'Ireland.'

'But it is winter,' he said with a blaze of his good eye. 'Why you wear only shirt with sleeves roll up? Maybe you from *Iceland...*?' He grinned with enormous teeth. 'You name...?'

'Ciarán'

'My name Kadar. Welcome in Morocco.'

He hauled himself upright and began to come my way. I felt for the hunting knife in the jacket slung over my arm, and psyched up on old judo throws from long ago training nights back in Gurranabraher parish hall. *If there be war, I be ready.*

'I see you make friend,' he said. He aimed a mock kick at the two boys who ran off with squeals of delight. 'I am carpet seller from Marrakech. Today not busy. Maybe I can show you something?'

## Chapter 7

'No thanks,' I said. Visions of winding up dead in an alley.

'Yes,' he said, turning towards the hole in the wall. 'I have three place I show you. Come.'

I looked after him. Was he deaf or what? Did he have vicious fiends waiting down an alley? Then, a light blinked in a space behind my eyes: I reined myself in, abandoned caution and followed the bearded bear with the clouded eye back into the labyrinth of alleys and steps.

Not long after leaving the Kasbah, we arrived at the first point on Kadar's itinerary: the wrought iron gates of a palatial white villa screened in Bougainvillia.

'This home of very rich woman,' Kadar told me. 'She name Barbara Hutton from USA. Maybe you know? She from Woolworth. You know Woolworth?' I nodded. 'She crazy woman. Very rich. Very crazy. She have many crazy party. One party, she bring many camel from Sahara. She buy this place in 1946. General Franco from *Espagne*, he want buy same, but she pay two times more. When she have party, many people come. In Tangier, we say she Queen of Medina...'

In 1924, when she was twelve years old, Barbara Hutton's grandmother left her $28 million ($375 million today) which was placed in a trust fund administered by her father. By the time she had access to the money at the age of twenty-one, her father had increased it through shrewd investment to $42 million (over $562 million today), making her one of the richest women in the world. In later years, she would become known as the 'Poor Little Rich Girl' for the tragedy of her life. When she died of a heart attack at the Beverley Wiltshire Hotel in May 1979 at the age of sixty-six, all that remained of her vast fortune was $3,500.

In 1970 I had never heard of Barbara Hutton.

'Now,' Kadar said, 'we go Grand Socco.'

\* \* \*

The Grand Socco separated Tangier's old city from the new, but belonged fully to the old. Between the small shops and restaurants that lined the square's eastern side, and the mules and donkeys tethered on the western end, a block of markets and merchants' sleeping quarters huddled under awnings of canvas and tin. The chaotic stalls, gauzy in the haze of charcoal fires, dealt in everything from chickens and fish to pottery and old shoes, fruit and vegetables, miracle cures, spices and unadulterated junk: a spectacle of colour, scent and sound dedicated to haggling and the laborious exchange of precious dirhams. Crossing the square, Kadar filled me in on some local history.

When the rest of Morocco became a French 'protectorate' in 1912, Tangier had special status. In 1923 it became an international city, governed by a colonial commission representing Britain, France, Spain, Portugal, Italy, Belgium, the Netherlands, Sweden and later, the United States. The city remained an international zone (except for a period during World War II when Spain took control) until it was integrated in 1956 into the independent Kingdom of Morocco.

Over the years, Tangier acquired the reputation of a spying and smuggling haven and a base of dodgy foreign capital, masked by the city's political neutrality and commercial liberty. It was from a Tangier bank in 1943 that the Bank of England first got hold of the high-quality counterfeit British currency produced by the Nazis in Operation Bernhard. The plan had been to wreck the British economy by flooding the country with dud notes. In 1970, as we crossed the Grand Socco, Tangier was still deemed the safe house of international spying, with a reputation that was legendary.

During its bohemian heyday of the early 20th century, the city had become home to an eclectic community of poets, writers, artists and European refugees, many still to be found hanging about the Medina.

'After independence,' Kadar said, 'Tangier have big change. Police finish house for woman, house for boy. Now Tangier more quiet. Many foreign person, they leave.'

The beatniks left and the hippies arrived.

On the far side of the Grand Socco, Kadar led the way through a busy Berber pavement market to the entrance of St Andrew's Anglican Church, an Anglo-Moorish slice of old Tangier and our second port of call.

'In this place many famous people dead,' he said. 'You looking.'

Immediately beyond the gateposts, we were in a thick entanglement of eucalyptus, cypress, palms, jacaranda, banana plants, false pepper trees and an undergrowth of shrubs and creepers where lay the graves of some 200 expatriates who never made it home. Among them such colourful characters as Hooker Doolittle, former US Consul to Tangier, and the legendary founder of Dean's Bar whose simple tombstone read: 'Died February 1963. Missed by all and sundry.'

## Chapter 7

The church itself was closed but its hybrid nature was visible from the outside: the crenellated bell tower from which the blue cross of St. Andrew fluttered looked very much a minaret faced in intricately carved latticework while the church porch was a decidedly Islamic horseshoe arch.

'Inside,' Kadar said, 'you have Christian prayer written in Arabic. Very good.'

We now criss-crossed the Medina to a spot called the Café Hafa. This hole in the wall, founded in 1921, looked out over the Strait of Gibraltar like something from an overdose. The restaurant proper, a three-sided affair with white walls and a slanting tin roof, sat on the uppermost level of a series of narrow terraces laid out like the galleries of a mini theatre. Tiled tables on legs of concrete, set among shrubs and cacti served as the longtime haunts of stubble-faced men and men with no stubble who sat hunched over mint teas and café au laits, barely visible in a haze of kif. As we passed to the lowest level, with an unobstructed view of the sea, they looked up in a slow motion Mexican wave, like a single organism with a grin.

'You like buy?' some guy said. 'Sixty dollar, one kilo.'

The writer, Paul Bowles, a regular at the cafés of Tangier, saw them as a revered social institution:

*'Here the men sit with their legs tucked under them and, more often than not, in spite of the official prohibition, pull out their kif pipes and smoke them as they always have done. The cafés are like men's clubs. A man frequents the same one, year in and year out. Often he brings his food and eats there; sometimes he stretches out on the matting and sleeps there. His café is his mail address, and rather than use his home, where there are always womenfolk about, he will use the café for keeping his social appointments. In the smaller cafés, the entrance of anyone from outside the familiar circle of daily habitués has always been regarded with a wary eye and a certain degree of suspicion...*[3]*'*

I was getting the wary eye and certain degree of suspicion.

'This way,' Kadar said, leading me down several flights of steps to our terrace perched on the side of a sloping cliff. To our left, four smokers sat at a table playing a delayed-action version of dominoes. To our right a man of about thirty with leaded eyelids, blackened teeth, scraggy hair and surprising English leaned across.

---

[3] *The Worlds of Tangier* by Paul Bowles – travel article written in 1958.

'Ah my friend,' he mumbled, '*marhaba, marhaba*. You know what *marhaba* means?'

'Welcome?' I guessed.

'Yes my friend. Welcome, welcome. You from...?'

'Ireland.'

'Yes my friend. Welcome you from Ireland. You know this my friend? One man, he say welcome all people. *Marhaba* Ireland. *Marhaba* America. *Marhaba* Deutchland. *Marhaba* Espagne. *Marhaba* Australia. Now my friend, this man, he is dead.'

While I worked on a response to that informative gem he mumbled some advice on what I should drink.

'Coffee is good for you. One coffee every morning. But no milk. The stomach cannot separate the caffeine from the milk. This creates many gases. Very bad for the stomach. These gases, they rise to your neck. They give you like this - gaarh, gaarh! Your neck, it becomes stuck. Mint tea is also very good for you. Gives you energy. Makes you strong. But better without the mint...'

He then leaned over and pulled a wad of kif from his pocket.

'The kif in the village,' he said. 'Tap-tap. Tap-tap. In the village... My mother...' and there it ended. The leaded eyelids widened marginally and fixed on some point in ancient Pangaea.

Beyond the balcony, a colony of rats fought over the spoils of the café rubbish dump. They paid no heed to two men with fishing poles who arrived on a narrow path that climbed from the sea.

'*Bonjour*,' one of the men said.

'*Bonjour*,' I said. The men scrambled over the café balustrade and went on up. Kadar ordered two mint teas. Below, the waves licked at a shoreline dotted with trees and palms. I began to develop a theory.

Morocco was a place where mad things happened all the time. And every now and then they sucked you in and coughed you out again further down the line. Sit long enough in any spot and the madness congealed around you. I imagined walking up to some perfect stranger in Ireland.

'Hello,' I'd say. 'Iss go-o-od? What you like? You like smoke? Make you very hap-py. Give you en-er-gy. See you later alligator.'

'In this place, many famous people come,' Kadar said, interrupting my reverie. 'Mick Jagger from Rolling Stones, he come here 1967.' He then dug into the folds of his djellaba. 'Maybe you like smoke kif?'

## Chapter 7

I don't know what they put in those pipes but a later brand of hashish, developed exclusively in the Rif Mountains, became justifiably known as *Sputnik*.

Kadar produced some cake from the depths of his djellaba and we ate it. 'For munchies,' he explained. He followed with a piece of advice.

'You must not eat with left hand. Left hand is for toilet. If you share food with other persons, you must only touch food with right hand.' Ever afterwards, when dining in the company of right-hand eaters, I developed the rule of sitting on the left one.

For an hour Kadar and I stared out to sea and talked about the possibilities of me taking up carpet making in Marrakech. It seemed plausible. I would learn from him and in no time at all, I'd be dominating the as yet undiscovered Irish carpet market. In later years, I often wondered if perchance Mick Jagger and I had shared similar thoughts on that very same spot.

When we'd finalised the carpet plan we left our perch at the Café Hafa and went back outside.

'OK,' Kadar said. 'Now I go. You have good travels. You know, you start from home of Abu Abdullah Muhammad Ibn Battuta. He 14th century Muslim traveller. He leave Tangier and travel whole world for thirty year. More than Marco Polo. He travel in all North and West Africa, Horn of Africa, south of Europe, east of Europe, Middle East, India, centre of Asia, south east of Asia, and China. And only donkey, camel and boat. More than 120,000 kilometre.'

Kadar shook my hand. 'See you later alligator.'

That put me in my lowly place.

\* \* \*

At noon that day Tony and I hit the Medina as Irish merchants. On my journey with Kadar I'd been asked several times if I had things to sell. 'Anything from Europe,' Kadar had assured me, 'you get good price.' As it turned out Tony had nothing to spare but I had a right little bundle.

A short distance from the port gate of the Medina, we were spotted. A curly-headed man in a brown djellaba bounced from a doorway.

'You have something for sell?' he asked. 'Come! Come! We will drink tea.'

We followed him into a dark cave, feebly lit by an oil lamp and smelling strongly of tanned cowhide. Inside, there was barely room to move with the landslide of leather, pottery, fabrics, jewellery and wood carvings that spilled from ceiling to floor.

'You will have mint tea and biscuits,' he said and sat myself and Tony down on tiny cork stools.

'OK my friend,' he said. 'My name Mohammad. What you have? I make you good price.'

I pulled out my treasures: a sleeveless tunic, a hunting catapult, a rough home-made wallet that I'd fashioned from the back of an old leather jacket, a butcher's knife whittled away to nothing, and a cheap plastic mackintosh.

'I want that blue embroidered shirt,' I said, pointing above his head, 'And a leather bag.'

'You crazy!' he shrieked.

'You crazy!' I shrieked when he wanted my complete haul for the shirt.

I got up and walked away. He came running after me. We bargained again. He jumped up and ran around the shop, praying to Allah. If the bargaining faltered more tea was tossed in as a lubricant.

'Ah you Irish,' he said in the end, agreeing the deal, 'You hard, very hard. You make Moroccan people poor. But maybe some day your son come back in Morocco; then we see...' He then asked us to wait, called *Mohammad* to a passing boy and sent for three more teas.

'If you shouted *Mohammad* out there,' Tony said, 'you'd cause a shaggin' stampede.'

'How many language you speak?' Mohammad of the shop asked when the teas came.

'Irish, English and a little French,' I said, making the best of it.

'Me too,' Tony said, gilding the lily a bit. His only French was *Parlez-vous Francais?*'

'Me?' Mohammad said. 'I learn in my business English, French, German and Spanish. I speak Arabic too. Also I know two Irish: I know *Tá mé go maith.*' [I am well]. 'And I know *Póg mo thóin*. It mean *Kiss my ass.*'

He was delighted.

\* \* \*

In the Medina's conspiratorial Petit Socco, where I'd buy my crystal geode thirty-eight years later, we were hunched over café au laits in the Gran Café Central when the madness began again.

'Ah! Remember me?'

## Chapter 7

We looked up to find one of the more persistent 'guides' from the night we'd arrived heading our way. In grubby leather jacket, jeans minus the knees, long tatty hair and broken nose, he looked like one of those Rockers who'd been battered by the Mods on Brighton beach during the two-day Whitsun free-for-all of 1964.

'Iss go-o-od? You like some smoke? Small piece? I make you good price.'

'No thanks,' I said and looked straight ahead.

'Why you paranoid?' he asked. We ignored him. He became aggressive.

'Why you come Morocco and not talk to Moroccan man? You give me some small money for my mother.' Still we ignored him.

'Fuck you!' he said. 'I am most dangerous man in Tangier.'

Just then, for reasons unknown to this day, he turned and fled into an alley opposite the café.

'De Baróid!' Tony said. 'You're so ugly you scared the hell outta him.'

No sooner had the most dangerous man in Tangier fled, than Benjy of Vancouver dropped into our afternoon. In an establishment patronized by Western hippies and kif-smoking Moroccans, he looked quite out of place. I put him at about forty, thin, tanned, dressed in creased white trousers and shirt and stained Panama hat. No sooner had we sat down than he moved from a nearby table.

'Now you two don't look like your average hippies,' he said. 'Are you over from Gibraltar?'

'No,' I assured him. 'On our way from Ireland to India.'

'Are you not somewhat off track?'

'All part of the plan,' Tony said.

Benjy wanted to know all about the journey down through France and Spain and how we slept rough and ate from a camping stove, and planned to get to India on the pittance in our pockets.

'My maternal grandmother was Irish,' he confided. 'I plan to visit in a month's time, but right now I'm here in Tangier to write a story on Paul Bowles. You know Paul Bowles, the writer? *The Sheltering Sky* and all that? Still comes here to the Petit Socco.'

As with Barbara Hutton, neither Tony nor I had heard of Paul Bowles.

'My goodness,' Benjy said, 'Bowles is probably the reason you guys are here. He led the way. He's been living in Morocco for many moons, studying the deeper realms of consciousness under the accommodating effects of the very hashish that these guys here are smoking. He's been friends with all the great names: Tennessee Williams, Truman Capote, William Borroughs, Brion Gysin, Jack Kerouac. You name 'em, he knows 'em.' He pulled a ragged book from his jacket pocket and flicked it open at a marked page. 'Let me read for you what Norman Mailer said back in 1959: "*Paul Bowles opened the world of Hip. He let in the murder, the drugs, the incest, the death of the Square, the call of the orgy, the end of civilization.*" He also led the way in relationships. He and his wife have been married since 1938, but each has had other relationships with friends of their own gender.'

'This town is full of nutcases,' Tony said.

'Indeed,' Benjy said. 'And now, can I treat you both to dinner? I'd consider it an honour. It's not every day I have the opportunity to buy two of those very nutcases a meal.'

It was dark when we ambled up to one of the restaurants in the Grand Socco where half a dozen stoned hippies were wolfing down plates of fish and chips. Behind them, a great vat of Morocco's famous harira soup filled the air with the scent of tomatoes, lentils, chickpeas, herbs and spices. The owner rushed out, ushered us to a metal table and planted a square of paper and knife and fork before each of us.

'I haf every what you like,' he said, pointing back to a glass-fronted counter beside a raised charcoal fire. 'I haf soup, cheeken, brochettes, feesh, cheeps, omelette. You can choose.' We chose brochettes.

'Begod,' Tony said. 'I never thought I'd see the day when the bould Jesus would walk right by.' A tall pale north European with long black hair, glazed eyes and a tousled beard was stumbling past in a white, flowing Arab chamira.

'White guys going native never works,' Benjy said. 'They look like a bad pantomime.'

The food arrived: charcoal-grilled skewers of mutton (or goat), fresh baguettes and sweet mint tea. We tucked in, cupping a hand around the glasses of tea to ward off some of the night chill. The call to prayer startled when it broke from the Grand Mosque and, in its usual reverberating echo, fanned out from mosque to mosque across the Medina. The hippie in the chamira passed a second time.

'Hi there,' he said, turning our way. 'Isn't this a freaky place?'

*Dutch*, I thought.

# Chapter 7

'A glass of tea,' he called to the restaurant owner and pulled a chair to our table. In full view of the square he leaned back, pulled a kif joint from the folds of the chamira and lit up, staring at his shoes.

'Do you know,' he said, 'that the Grand Mosque of Tangier was built on the site of an old Portuguese cathedral that was built on the site of a Roman temple that was dedicated to Hercules?' He laughed out loud. Ha-ha-ha! 'It is from the time of Sultan Moulay Ismail who ruled Morocco from 1672 to 1727.' He stopped, sucked on the joint for thirty seconds, held his breath until he was set to burst, and exhaled in a choking fit.

'Moulay Ismail, now there was a special man. Do you know he had more than 500 wives and more than one thousand children? By 1703, it was already true that he had 525 sons and 342 daughters. In 1721, when he was seventy-six years old, son number 700 was born. You know he also built the palaces of Meknes - with 25,000 slaves. Many of the slaves, they came from Europe - they were captured by Barbary pirates - and sometimes the Sultan sold them back again...'

'Any from Baltimore in West Cork?' Tony asked but the Dutchmnan wasn't interested. He'd moved on.

'Moulay Ismail was also Moulay the Bloodthirsty. When he would like to frighten his rivals he made the order that the walls of Meknes would be covered with the heads of dead enemies. He was a cruel man...' Another big suck on the joint. 'But maybe you do not care...?'

With that the Dutchman rose to his feet, threw back his glass of tea, said *See you later alligator* and strode off, leaving the tea on our bill.

In the tailspin of what I considered a possible hallucination, Benjy looked at his watch.

'Oh shit,' he said. 'I'm late. Just one word of warning for when you're leaving here. Be careful on the way back to Spain. People like that guy may try and slip drugs into your bags so they can have them collected by accomplices on the far side. But, if *you* get caught, *you* get done. Lots of innocent people are rotting in Spanish jails.'

As quickly as we'd met, Benjy was gone, wishing us luck and speeding off into the Medina for his interview with Paul Bowles. Tony and I went back through the dim night markets and feral cats of the Medina to bravely join the hippies in the Petit Socco, but they too were gone. Later, down by the seafront, under the palms of the central reservation that divided Avenue Mohammad VI, a dark-skinned Algerian with a pockmarked face tried to sell us LSD and heroin.

'Hold it there,' I said and snapped a picture with my Kodak Instamatic.

'Fuck you!' the Algerian said.

* * *

We parted company with Tim and Efred the following morning and moved to the Pension Monaco in the upper end of the Medina. This was the pension run by the Omar I went looking for in 2008.

By comparison, the new accommodation was luxurious: no dampness, an airy room with a rug on the floor and shuttered windows overlooking the quiet arches of Rue Bouselham. Ginny Farrell and Nancy Jordan - Californians studying in Valencia whom we'd met down at Tangier port - were in the adjoining room. Moustachioed Omar and two of his friends, Abdeslam and Ahmed who were visiting from the kif kernel of Ketama, completed the platoon. For those two days we were one big happy family, a convivial atmosphere undoubtedly fuelled by the Ketama kif, the endless mint tea provided by Omar, and the very good natures - and even better looks - of Ginny and Nancy.

Finally, on January 30th Tony and I said our goodbyes, pocketed Ginny and Nancy's address in Valencia, and left Rue Bouselham for the Algeciras ferry and a final exchange with Morocco.

Down at the harbour a school of sardines had surfaced around the anchored fishing boats.

'If we had a line,' Tony pointed out, 'we'd have fish for supper.'

'They Moroccan fish,' a voice answered.

We turned to find before us that most dangerous man in Tangier.

'Oh no,' I said. 'Not you again.'

Having advised us of the sardine lineage, he decided that our packs were full of kif. The conversation goes like this:

'You give me money or I tell police.'

'Get lost.'

'Bloody bastard! You pay me money now.'

'No.'

'You are snake. Moroccan people, they kill snake. Kill everything with the poison - snake, spider. The God, he tell them to do this. If you don't kill them, they come everywhere, like in America. In the house. In the bed. On the neck. Also in our culture, we kill rat. Maybe you are rat?'

## Chapter 7

'Fuck off!' (A calculated eye-balling happens.)

'What? You tell me fuck off in my country? You son-of-a-bitch. I kill you!'

Fists are raised. The dangerous man pulls at Tony's pack.

'That's it,' Tony says. 'He's after planting drugs.'

'Now Tony,' I say, 'In fairness, unless the guy is Houdini this makes no sense.'

None the less Tony begins to empty his pack all over the pavement as the dangerous man becomes more aggressive.

'You call me drug man in my country?' he shouts. 'I kill you!'

Tony would later claim that I lost the head with some suddenness at this point. I only recall that the dangerous man was nowhere to be seen when we reached the ferry terminal.

Two and a half hours later, we were back in Spain being virtually strip-searched by the Servicio Especial de Vigilancia Fiscal at Algeciras terminal. Our nemesis was none other than Gilberto with whom I'd spent the two hours at Algeciras railway station less than a week ago.

'Hippies,' he said, herding us into a small room where a realisation dawned: a hippie was a space in another guy's head.

An hour later, as a reluctant hippie, I realised that a bridge had been crossed in Morocco. By the time we'd booked into a cheap pension everything on the European side of the Strait of Gibraltar existed only in contrast to what lay on the far side. I couldn't wait to get to Asia. I hoped it was a crazy place.

Close to the port, our new personas ran into the Jimi Hendrix Australian who'd been at the Pension Royal. He was trying to console a 19-year-old woman from London called Susan whose sister had been busted coming off an earlier ferry and was now in Algeciras prison.

'She's pretty upset, man,' he told us. 'Her sister was coming from Tangier this afternoon and was caught with some kif in her bag... says it was planted on her.'

Susan, a fragile woman with her hair in two plaits, who looked like she could do with a bag of chips and a sleep, wailed at the thought. There was nothing we could do but buy her a glass of plonk.

The following night, fourteen kilometres east of Málaga, we slept in a boat-club hut and were chased in the morning by two men and a big Alsation.

'The Only Hope...'

*The water-seller, Tangier*

# Chapter 8
Long Way to Rome

On the first of the eighteen days it took to travel from Málaga to Rome, we walked to Cala de Moral, spent a sunny afternoon on an empty beach and slept under a tree to the east of the village.

At first light we woke up to screeching gulls and the shouts of fishermen. They were hauling in nets of whitebait which were being sold by the bucketful to waiting buyers. Wrapped in our sleeping bags, we watched until the rising sun had washed the foreshore in liquid gold and burned the bite off the morning. Time to put on the boots and get on the road. But not before a terrible assault on the natural world of Cala de Moral.

Tony always dreaded bugs of menace - spiders, earwigs, centipedes and the like - and always would. It was a dread hardened back in that earlier-mentioned summer of 1968 as we made our way from Scotland and slept on the grass verge of the A1, ten miles south of Belfast, in the days before it was a dual carriageway.

I had woken at six that morning with crawling skin. Unzipping the sleeping bag and jumping clear, I discovered that we'd slept on the earwig capital of Ireland. They were everywhere - in my clothes, in the folds of the sleeping bag, in my boots, in the cooking pots, even in the packet of tea. And, I had to assume, all over Tony. As I shook the hordes onto the grass, the thought that came wasn't cheerful. How was I going to break this to the peacefully slumbering lad?

'Tony...,' I eventually hesitated. 'Earwigs...'

That was all it took. His eyes shot open and he lay there rigid. Like Christopher Lee in *Dracula* when he's disturbed in the crypt.

*Oh God!* I thought. *It's rigour mortis.*

Then he left the sleeping bag as if propelled by dynamite, and took to the air.

'Jaysus Christ! The bastards!' he screamed, leaping like Rudolf Nureyev all over the A1 and and tearing off his clothes. 'Jaysus Christ! There's millions of 'em!'

In the end he was down to his underpants while his clothes and the contents of his pack adorned a huge swathe of the A1, and the spectacular leaps were still in swing. It took the arrival of a carload of astonished French tourists to subdue him. And that from a lad who, if need be, would have faced a grizzly bear.

Now it was happening again on the beach of Cala de Moral.

He pulled on his left boot and did the lace. He pulled on his right boot and froze, eyes rigid, rigour mortis again. There followed a loud *Jaysus!* The boot flew off and a lizard fell out. Before thinking could happen, the unfortunate creature was a smear in the sand. Tony held his heart with the hyperventilating shock of it.

'Sorry lizard,' he said when he finally caught his breath. 'Tony thought you were a bug and Tony hates bugs.' It was an awesome sight to have beheld.

\* \* \*

We set off separately for Ginny and Nancy's place in Valencia.

Two short lifts and a long walk brought me to Maro. From Maro to Almuñécar the road wound around tortuous mountain bends with sheer vertiginous drops to the sea and large chunks torn from the protective rails. The van driver who gave me a lift along this stretch told of a guy who'd recently gone 150 metres down through one of those gaps and walked out without a broken bone. It was the work, he said, of the Virgin Mary, God bless her.

Olive trees now studded the lower slopes north of the road. Citrus groves and vegetable gardens filled the flats. Massive razor-backed mountains were spattered by the shade of small white clouds. At Almuñécar Tony arrived in a car going to Motril. 'There's my buddy,' he said and I went too. In Motril we cooked a meal on the beach and walked on through the falling night to Torrenueva where we spotted a building site that offered bed space. Just then the village drunk erupted from a small bar. '*Amigos!*' he roared and staggered to our side, all set to join us like Jack Nicholson in *Easy Rider*. Two other drinkers had to manhandle him up the street, still bawling his head off, so we could claim our beds. In the morning we opened our eyes to find surprised workers clambering over us.

Breakfast in the village and we were off along the coast, me some 500 metres ahead of Tony. After three hours, Tony was picked up and *There's my buddy* worked again. We were dropped off in a little town by the sea where we decided it was too hot for further walking. We retreated to the beach, cooled our feet in the surf and lay in the sun. At five o'clock we set off again and from a high point on the road watched the sun go down behind a string of coastal castles. Blazing orange sky. Tiny bands of purple cloud. The closing calls of the birds. The sea silver and motionless as glass. When the glow of

## Chapter 8

the dying sun had faded we agreed that if you were given a pencil and paper you couldn't invent a place more beautiful than the Earth.

'Maybe what people call God was the Big Bang,' Tony theorised. 'But then I don't get that Big Bang at all. How could the universe spring from a dot? And would that make God a dot? Imagine the bother St. Patrick would have trying to explain that on a shamrock: God the Father, God the Son, God the Holy Ghost and God the Dot...'

'Not alone that,' I pointed out, 'but it's supposed to be like a rubber band - all going to reverse back again into the same dot.'

'I can see it now,' Tony said sadly. 'All that work by Noah gone in a flash.'

The deliberations descended in that mode until we found a place in which to lay our philosophical heads.

Next day, on the eastern outskirts of Almería, there happened a serious slip on my part.

It began with the local Chief of Tourism and two of his friends: one an orange-plantation owner; the other an orange-plantation inspector who was driving the car. To help me appreciate the vagaries of oranges, the three men drove me in a two-hour loop. The Tourism Chief explained that Almería province was primarily desert and cactus. This made it popular with the makers of Westerns. Indeed, Sergio Leone's *Fistful of Dollars* had been partly filmed here. The plantation owner insisted we visit his home where I was given a tour of the hacienda and the orange groves that had been coaxed from the parched earth by clever irrigation. The inspector then drove to a restaurant in the grey hills north of the main road where I was treated to a five-course meal on massive plates that we all shared. Finally I was dropped back on the main road, a mere ten kilometres from where I'd started, only to watch the Tourism Chief and his mates bounce off down a potholed track with my jacket still in their car. Passport. Traveller's cheques. Money. The lot.

I plunged into instant panic. *Trip over. How will I even get home? I'll probably end up in one of Franco's jails. Maybe even charged with being British.* I sweated. I swore. I chain-smoked. I kicked a tree. I flagged down a passing cop car; but far from getting out the dusting kit, the cop simply drove off again. 'I'll report you!' I shouted. Finally, I decided to calm down, get out the map, see where the road went. Then a glimmer of hope. According to the map, the road ran only to the sea. If I waited long enough the car might come back again.

Half an hour crawled by. I stared down the empty road, battling the devils of despondency and despair. No car. Another fifteen minutes. Still nothing. The old prayer to St. Jude, Patron Saint of Lost Causes, reared up opportunisticly from the past: *'Pray for me, for I am so helpless and alone. Please help to bring me visible and speedy assistance. Come to my assistance in this great need that I may receive the consolation and help of Heaven in all my necessities, tribulations, and sufferings, particularly in getting back my shaggin' jacket...'*

Then lo and behold, a sight to gladden any eyes, lift any heart: St. Jude - away in the distance towing in his wake a billowing furrow of dust. I grabbed my pack and ran towards it. A car came weaving from the dust, dodging the potholes. St. Jude was hanging out the window, frantically waving my jacket in the air. To this day I can feel the overwhelming joy of being reunited with everything that separated me from destitution. I hugged my saviours. All future failures were excused in advance.

'Here's my parents' address,' I told them, 'in case you ever need a holiday.'

'Thank you,' the Chief of Tourism said. ' Maybe you will be the chief of tourism of Ireland.' We shook hands again and they got back in the car and drove off.

Life having assumed a newly glowing aspect, I went looking for Tony. Just before losing the jacket, I'd seen him on the road.

A few hundred metres back I found him at a roadside shop. He'd teamed up with a shabby, long-haired, bearded Dutchman named Jaep who had massive bags under his eyes. Jaep was a failed geology student from Amsterdam who'd come to Spain to get off the drugs and chase the demons from his head. It hadn't worked. He was on his way to Sorbas with no sense, no money and no sleeping bag.

'I have suffers in my head,' he told us.

'Now,' Tony said, 'you couldn't leave a man like that on the side of the road.'

'Today I make a good friend,' Jaep said (Tony who had bought him a packet of fags). 'Yesterday, only bad police.'

The three of us walked north along a minor road to Rioja, a dreary dusty town on the left hand bank of the Rio Andarax. This was a river so free of water that its bed had converted to citrus groves bordered by prickly pear. We helped ourselves. North of town, in the grey, gulch-riven, desert country of the Sierra de Alhamilla, we

## Chapter 8

stopped for the night in a river basin that was cracked dry. We had a dinner of bread, sardines and oranges.

'Sardines are good for the brain,' Jaep said. 'The oil loosens the connections between the left and the right side.' He thought about this for a minute. 'You know gypsum?'

'In sardines?' Tony said. Jaep ignored him.

'I go to Sorbas for the special gypsum karst landscape which has many potholes and caves with many crystal formations and many bats. Gypsum is a mineral that dissolves soon in water. Because of this, you can find only a small number of gypsum karsts in the world. Sorbas is very special. Because there is little rain, the gypsum does not degrade so fast.'

'Jaep, boy,' Tony said, 'that's an amazing shaggin' story.'

'Gypsum is very toxic for most plants, but you can find some very special plants that live there, like the yellow rock rose that has flowers in the early spring. Also there are some special birds. You can look for bee-eaters and rock martins. Also on the cliffs, some eagles. At the Aguas River in Sorbas you can hear nightingales and reed warblers in the summer and if you are lucky, you can find terrapins or maybe a tortoise.'

'He's harmless,' Tony said when Jaep went to the bushes as they say. 'But I wouldn't mind a nodule of whatever he's on.'

Once darkness had settled, Tony spread his sleeping bag on the ground. The three of us put on every stitch we had. We pulled my sleeping bag up to our noses. And in the spirit of fraternity that governed the times, we froze rigid under a cobalt roof speckled with diamonds.

'Hey Jaep,' Tony asked after about an hour. 'Any spiders?'

'Many,' Jaep said. 'Even the black widow. And there is one dangerous snake: Lataste's viper. And many scorpions. Sometimes they will go in your shoes.'

'Fuck it,' Tony said. 'I knew it.'

In the morning Jaep hailed us saviours and took his suffering head off to Sorbas. In that desert town, where white houses teetered precariously over the ash-grey gorge of the Aguas, he hoped to find himself a terrapin.

'I will bring it back to Amsterdam. It will be my souvenir from the gypsum karsts of Spain.'

* * *

Over the next two days it was mostly bus and train.

The hitchhiking had been hopeless and we were anxious to get to Valencia for the weekend when Ginny and Nancy were free. On the Friday night, as the pubs we couldn't afford were filling up with warmth and chatter, we arrived at Gobernador Viejo. The street, in the city's old quarter, was where our friends shared a top-floor flat with two other gorgeous Californian students named Kay and Mary-Ann. Kay, to our delight, played the guitar.

Tony and I, in preparation for such a moment, had spent years memorising all the Irish folk songs ever written. That night, helped by lots of vino tinto, we knocked those Californian women for six.

'We would undoubtedly have forever been remembered in Gobernador Viejo for that outstanding performance,' Tony said in the morning, 'had the shaggin' *tunas* not turned up.'

They arrived at one in the morning when the women had gone to bed. Imbued with Latin romance, they rang the doorbell, struck up with mandolin and guitar, and began to yahoodle in powerful voices that would've had a bucket of water thrown over them on St. Stephen's morning if they'd been touring Cork's South Parish with the Evergreen Road Wren Boys.[4]

The singing brought Nancy running into the living room where Tony and I were working our way through our last hundred songs. She went to the balcony and looked down as the other three women came tripping behind. Tony and I followed.

'Shit,' Nancy said, turning to myself and Tony. 'You two better lie very low. That's Ginny's boyfriend and mine. They would *not* understand you guys sleeping in here. The boys are 'tunas' and it's a great honour in Spain if the tunas come to serenade a woman but it would be a great problem if they spotted you.' We were only allowed one eye each over the balcony.

Nancy and Ginny got dressed and went downstairs. The music stopped. The night folded in on itself again. Kay and Mary-Ann went back to bed and Tony and I spread our sleeping bags on the tiles of the living room floor.

---

[4] Because the wren had 'betrayed Our Lord' in some way that nobody knew, it was custom to hunt one at Christmas, tie it to a holly branch, dress up, and tour your area, banging doors at five in the morning of St. Stephen's (Boxing) Day, demanding money with squawking menaces such as, 'The wran (sic), the wran, the king of all birds, St. Stephen's Day got caught in the furze, I upped with me stick and I gave him a fall, and I brought him here to visit you all. Knock at the knocker, ring at the bell, please give us a copper for singin' so well....' Great for hangovers. (In Cork, we skipped killing the wren.)

## Chapter 8

'Ciarán boy,' Tony said, 'after all that effort, we got trampled. Tunas are a pain in the arse.'

We stayed three days but justice we did not do to Valencia. This was the third largest city in Spain, with a magnificent old quarter of cobbled streets, verdant squares, ancient bridges, baroque and gothic churches, domed bell towers, lofty palms, crowded markets, and a cathedral that claimed to hold the chalice used at the Last Supper. It was also a gastronomic Elysian Fields, and the birthplace of paella. And it was steeped in history, not least that of the 11th century when Rodrigo Diaz de Vivar, the legendary El Cid, left his indelible mark on Spain's chivalrous age.

'Legend has it,' Kay explained during a break in the nights of song, 'that, having taken the city from the Moors in 1094, El Cid was mortally wounded five years later during a skirmish outside the walls. Realising that the Moors would attack in force once the news leaked out, his wife dressed him in armour the next morning and strapped him to his horse. They then opened the gates and dead El Cid charged out at the head of the army, a crimson cross on his chest and his famous sword, *Tizona*, raised above his head. You couldn't see the Moors for the dust they raised on the way to their boats.'

In actual fact, El Cid died in Valencia on July 10th 1099 of natural causes. Not a Moor was seen to run.

Tony and I did visit the old city on the Saturday, where we climbed the Tower of San Miguelette for the view. But, despite Valencia's many attractions, our trip to town was mostly sparked off by the fact that our singing partners had dates and we'd run out of food and booze at Gobernador Viejo. But the singing was back on track by ten o'clock when the boyfriends had to be home for dinner and it was no longer decent for a young woman to be on the street.

On our final night, Nancy made a point that stirred Tony to delve briefly into history as he put away the guts of a bottle of brandy that he'd bought for thirty-five pence.

'Irish songs are full of narrative,' she said. 'They all tell a story. Some of them quite sad.'

I was about to explain Ireland's 800 years of misery but Tony got there first.

'That's right,' he said. 'As Gilbert Chesterton put it:

*'For the great Gaels of Ireland*
*Are the men that God made mad,*

*For all their wars are merry,*
*And all their songs are sad.'*[5]

'Although, you know what?' he added. 'We never had a merry war in our lives, except maybe when Owen Roe O'Neill beat the crap out of General Monro at the Battle of Benburb.' He lilted into the appropriate line from *Will You Come to The Bower*:

'You can visit Benburb and the storied Blackwater
Where Owen Roe met Monro and his chieftains did slaughter...'

The four women looked at one another, not sure whether Chesterton was a good guy or a bad guy.

'Ciarán,' Tony said in Irish. 'Would you know that I was dr-unk?'

Before I could reply in the negative, he lurched from his chair, veered off towards the bathroom, missed the door and was ill.

The next day, we said sad goodbyes to Ginny, Nancy, Kay and Mary-Anne and agreed to meet again in Ireland or California. We walked to the outskirts of Valencia, and in no time at all were travelling north in the car of a young Spanish hippie with hair to the middle of his back and a joint in his mouth. After a hundred kilometres he dropped us off and we split up, agreeing to meet in Barcelona at the home of Don Emilio Román Sala, the second name on our list of contacts. By seven in the evening I was still thirty kilometres south of Tarragona in pouring rain when a burly guy in his mid twenties with a head like a Catalonian Groucho Marx, picked me up in an old black banger. He told me he was Miguel who sold paintings for a living.

'Barthelona,' he confirmed and raced off into the potholes at 160 kilometres an hour. In Tarragona, the birthplace of Pontius Pilate, he went looking for some girlfriends who lived in the old part of town. There were apparently many but they proved elusive. After an hour of clunking in the dark through a maze of steep alleys full of Roman remains he gave up on finding any of their homes and we left again for Barcelona.

'Sad,' he grimaced, genuinely perturbed. 'If we find, maybe you haf senorita too.'

I thanked him for his kind thoughts. And there had been me,

---

[5] The Ballad of the White Horse.

# Chapter 8

imagining myself abandoned in the car while the bold Miguel lavished himself across the beds of Tarragona.

Outside the city we picked up a couple and their two daughters, aged six and three, who were draped in blankets. The man, with several days' growth on his face, was dressed in a crumpled suit and beret and the woman was wrapped in a long skirt, sweater and shawl. It was still pelting down and the four of them were soaked and shivering. As they got in you could see the bags under the parents' eyes. They explained to Miguel that they were landless peasants attempting to escape the poverty of Galicia on the far side of Spain. They were on their way to Villafranca on the Costa Dorada where the man hoped to find work. They had no money, had only eaten twice in three days and had slept out both nights. We stopped in the next town and bought them some milk, bread, ham, cheese, chocolate for the kids, and cigarettes for the man. We then dropped them off at Villafranca. As we drove off, they looked like refugees, standing in the street, looking one way and the other, wondering where to turn.

'Franco is a fucking, fucking, FUCKING!' Miguel roared at the nonplussed night as he gunned on up for 'Barthelona'. I hold that thought forever.

Later, in Barcelona, there was no room at the inn. Our contact, Don Emilio, dropped us in a dosshouse where we were cooped up for the night with a madman who ran up and down between the dorm beds, banging the door and walls.

\* \* \*

Five weeks after leaving home, Tony and I picked up our mail at the Poste Restante in Barcelona. We then walked to the Plaza de Catalunya, cooked breakfast on a bench beside one of the fountains, and luxuriated in the first news from home. After our night in the dosshouse it was great to hear from Cora that our celebrity status was finally being recognised.

'*Everyone I meet is asking about you. I met Bernard Cronin* [the old school friend who'd considered us delusional] *in town on Saturday and he asked me did I get any news from you and whereabouts were you. I told him I had a card from France and you were going on to Spain from there. He just laughed and walked on as if he didn't believe it...*'

'One day,' Tony said, 'they'll all have to eat their hats.'

We swigged our coffee to that, then wandered down La Rambla to the port to be feng shuied by the lapping of water.

After two more days, another night in a building site and much walking through freezing mountain forests of pine and snow, I crossed the Pyrenees at Bourg-Madame with four French Marxist-Leninists in their early twenties. They introduced themselves as Jean, Paul, Claude and Christine. They were in the mountains making some kind of propaganda film. As all four had been involved in the Paris Uprising of May 1968, they dropped me on the Spanish side of the border. An Irish connection might raise eyebrows on the French side. They needn't have worried. My arrival was a cause of celebration. Another Irishman, one of the French cops told me, had passed through two hours before. *Two* in a single day!

Tony was ahead, on his way to our next meeting in Pisa.

Having picked me up again, the film-makers offered me dinner and the extra bed in Jean's hotel room in the village of Dorres.

'You can maybe be our Irish advisor,' Christine said.

I liked that, and didn't let them down. Jean and I spent the small hours of that very night plotting the finer details of the post-capitalism world that was coming.

Jean's credentials were no joke. He'd travelled to China (virtually closed at the time) and to many of the countries of communist Eastern Europe. He'd trucked with left-wing revolutionaries in India and Brazil. He'd camped with Palestinian commandos in the mountains of Palestine. And he was now on his way back to finish the aborted Paris Uprising. None the less, he was visibly encapsulated by my own recent revolutionary past.

Outraged by an invitation to the British Ambassador to attend the previous May's Choral Festival at Cork City Hall, myself and some twenty stalwarts of Irish republican leaning also turned up. We first burned a Union Jack on the steps of the City Hall to attract any cop who might previously have missed our presence. Four tickets to the festival were then dished out - one each to myself and my 17-year-old brother, Niall, one to a member of the university's Republican Club and one to tall, charismatic, 'Quiff' McAdoo whose flamboyant blond hairdo was a homing beacon to the Special Branch. The plan was that one or both of the latter two would take the stage. Niall and I, strategically spread about the auditorium, would spring up and rouse the masses.

The first part of the plan went like clockwork. Niall and I occupied our seats. We then watched, a little perturbed, as 23-year-old Quiff and the university man sidled in and tried to work their way

# Chapter 8

unnoticed to the stage, followed at a distance of about six feet by fourteen members of the Garda Siochána. The university man got there first, went for the stage, and was immediately grabbed and kicked up the arse out a side door. This did not bode well for the remaining seventy-five per cent of the assault team. However, Quiff bade his time until the first choir came on stage.

'Doooooh...' the conductor went, tapping his tuning fork against the stand of the mike.

'Doooooh...' the choir followed. Then Quiff was on stage, scuttling across crab-like and grabbing at the mike - which fell from his hand. The faces of conductor and choir froze in the Dooooh position.

'Fascist pig...!' Quiff yelled at the British Ambassador. A second later the blond head and all belonging to it vanished in a dense blob of Garda blue that booted him out the same side door. But we weren't done yet. Niall and I jumped to our feet, cheering and clapping wildly, willing the masses to rise. But the only people to rise were the Gardaí who'd been spread about the hall and were now beelining towards our positions. We took stock, abandoned the plan and made for the door. A big Garda who was hot on my heels invited me in a thick Macroom accent to: 'Come back here and fight, ye Nancy-boy.' But I was spurred on by that great maxim that he who fights and runs away will live to fight another day. Ireland might call again.

'That is a great story,' Jean said, looking like he didn't quite know what to say. 'The Irish revolution is lucky to have men like you.'

One could only concur.

In the morning Paul and Claude drove me twenty kilometres of twisting mountain road to Mont-Louis as promising sunlight crept from the peaks. From there a series of short lifts curved down through the Valley of the Tet, chasing the river between the snowfields of the Pyrenees Orientales. At Olette, hot springs steamed from the earth in a saffron haze. To the south, Mount Canigou rose 2,784 metres to its white and splendid peak, first conquered it was claimed locally by the King of Aragon in 1285. (On his return the king reported that he had thrown a stone from the summit into a lake. In response a huge dragon had emerged from the water, flying into the sky and blotting out the sun.) At the 11th century medieval town of Villafranche de Conflent, dwellings were tightly packed behind ancient walls surrounded by forest and vertical slopes. Within the fortifications, narrow lanes were home to craftsmen and their picturesque shops. I stopped to buy some bread and jam. In the fruit-growing district of French Catalonia, vineyards and plantations of apple, pear, peach, orange and apricot stretched as far as the eye could see. From Perpignan I got a lift to Arles where I slept under an old bridge, mindful of the architecture. In Nice, I sat on a stony beach beneath the Promenade des Anglais in the shadow of the Alps, listened to the crunch of stones rolling in the waves, and thought of Isadora Duncan. On a September evening in 1927 on that very promenade, the famed American dancer was a passenger in the Amilcar automobile of a French-Italian mechanic when her long silk scarf caught around the wheel spokes and hurled her to her death.

I walked from Nice to the Principality of Monaco, playground of the rich and one of those European microstates that defy logic. Backed by some of the most expensive real estate on the planet, I sat by the harbour and looked out at the moored boats that starred the Mediterranean with their lights, and had more bread and cheese. I would have graced the place with an overnight stay were it not for the dearth of derelict buildings and a tailing cop who was clearly of the conviction that I belonged to some dark event from his, or Monaco's, past.

Continuing on to Menton, I arrived to a town full of revellers, music, citrus fruits and coloured lights. It was February 13th and they were celebrating La Fete de Citrons (The Festival of Lemons). It was strange to walk anonymously through such a jolly crowd to the other end of town and back into the night, but I had no roots there and no money to spend. Later that night I crossed the French-Italian border and bedded down in an empty car shelter in Ventimiglia.

Some time during the night, I was shaken out of my sleep by a violent electrical storm. Thunder crackled. Lightning lit up the trees and houses. A driving deluge rattled down on my shelter. I went back to sleep and woke in the morning in a lake. Drenched, I took a train to the coastal village of Andora and spent the next four hours drying my clothes and sleeping bag over the radiators of the railway station waiting room.

In Genova, it was the now familiar refrain: the youth hostel was closed for the winter. However, the warden - a humorous man with a good heart - let me in, along with an English couple who turned up later.

# Chapter 8

The road from Genova wound up into the Appenines, briefly leaving the coast before veering down again to the port of Carrara where they were loading ships with precious white Carrara marble, favoured by Michelangelo and mined in the mountains north east of town. Further along the coast, I arrived in Viareggio. Pressed between the Tyrrhenian Sea and the dramatic Apuane Alps, the capital of the northern Tuscan Riviera shared a chromatic history with the former city-state of Lucca, having provided medieval Lucca's only corridor to the sea.

Following the death in 1115 of Matilda of Tuscany who'd controlled all the western passages over the Apennines, Lucca began to constitute itself as a republic. Going on to declare its own charter in 1160, it would - despite its size - remain independent within a feudal Europe for the next 500 years, ruled by men whose names would break your teeth. But independence in feudal Italy had its quirks.

In 1273 and again in 1277 the republic was governed by statesman, poet and Capitano del Popolo (Captain of the People), Luchetto Gattilusion who belonged to a political faction known as the Guelphs.[6] In 1314, internal discord allowed Uguccione della Faggiuola of Pisa, a man of opposing Ghibelline association, to replace Gattilusion as Lord of Lucca. Uguccione was supported by local noble warlord, Castruccio Castracani degli Antelminelli who later provided the critical force in the defeat of the Guelph League at the 1315 Battle of Montecatini. This partnership might have prevailed had Uguccione not grown wary of Castracani's growing popularity and had him jailed and condemned to death. A popular insurrection in 1316 led to the overthrow of Uguccione and the handing over of the republic to Castracani under whose rule it became a leading state in central Italy, rivalling Florence, until Castracani's death in 1328.

There then followed a period of what can only be described as bad luck. Occupied by troops of Louis of Bavaria, the city-state was first offered to Florence, then sold for 30,000 florins to a wealthy Genoese, Gherardino Spinola. In rapid order it was then taken by King John of Bohemia, pawned to the Rossi of Parma, ceded to

---

[6] During the 12th and 13th centuries, a power struggle between the Papacy and the Holy Roman Empire brought turmoil to the internal politics of the Italian city-states. In central and northern Italy the opposing Guelph and Ghibelline factions supported the Pope and the Emperor respectively. Although the central struggle for power drew to a close with the Concordat of Worms in 1122, the conflict between the Guelphs and Ghibellines lasted well into the 15th century.

Martino della Scala of Verona, sold to the Florentines, surrendered to the Pisans, and nominally liberated by Emperor Charles IV to be governed by his vicar. Nevertheless Lucca managed to maintain its 'independence' and paint the word *Libertas* on its flag until the French Revolution of the late 18th century.

From this icon of stability it was a short run to Pisa where - surprise - the city's hostel was open with eight others in residence. There was, however, no sign of Tony. Tired from mountain walking, I wrote some letters and turned in early.

By morning Tony still hadn't arrived. I checked the date, confirming that this was our 'there or dead' day. Outside it was snowing big silent flakes. Six days had passed since we'd parted outside La Garriga, north of Barcelona, where we'd been turned away for the third time by one of our contacts who threatened from behind a locked door to call the cops. (We'd later that night consigned the list to flames so that it served some purpose at last, briefly warming our hands as we bedded down on the concrete floor of a building site.)

As you had to vacate youth hostels in those days between the hours of 10.00am and 5.00pm, regardless of weather, I wrapped up and took myself off to the sights of the old town, principal of which was the city's Cathedral and its free-standing, greatly leaning bell tower.

Although obviously intended to rise vertically, this medieval marvel had been lopsided since reaching its third floor in 1178. At this juncture, most people would've packed up. But in Pisa construction was merely halted for over ninety years as the Pisans fought with the city-states of Genoa, Lucca and Florence. The break, which allowed the underlying soil to settle, saved the tower from collapse and work was resumed in 1272. In an attempt to right the tilt new floors were built with one side taller than the other, giving the tower its peculiar curve. Construction stopped again in 1284 when Pisa was defeated by Genoa at the Battle of Meloria. The seventh floor was finally added in 1319, the bell tower in 1372.

What you might call perseverence.

The visit to the tower was followed by a call at the Cathedral itself, a place either overwhelmingly beautiful or overwhelmingly gaudy. Although much of its original art was destroyed in the great fire of 1595, it still looked like a museum of clutter: gilded ceilings, frescoed dome, apse of mosaics, carved marble pulpit and a litter

## Chapter 8

of sculptures and paintings by Italian masters. I believe I stood on the very spot where a bored Gallileo spawned his theories on the oscillations of pendulums by watching an incense burner swinging in the Cathedral nave.

In the afternoon, I walked the banks of the Arno where rows of tall classical buildings and the snow-dusted hills of Tuscany were lightly reflected in the still water. Young couples were out in force, kissing and knoodling in the flurries of snow. Along the riverside streets - the 'lungarnos' of Pisa - I committed to diary that 'Nancy-boys were carrying bunches of flowers'. You'd never have got that in Cork.

At six o'clock that night, just as I was about to give up on him, Tony walked in out of a blinding blizzard.

# Chapter 9
Petruccia's Folly

We landed on the outskirts of Rome in dark and drizzling misery. After two days of hitchhiking, a night in someone's shed, and a final illegal 14-kilometre amble along the hard shoulder of the autostrada, we were greatly relieved to find a truck waiting for us. It was parked on rough ground, its canvas box open at the back.

When nobody was looking, we heaved our packs over the backboard and climbed in. It was perfect. Plenty of space and a clean, dry wooden floor. I spread my sleeping bag and put boots, jacket and pack in a row, ready to be grabbed should the need arise.

'Here Biggles,' Tony said, 'doesn't God work in strange ways?' He was looking down at a neat stack of blankets on the floor of the truck.

'Tony,' I said, 'is that wise?'

He wouldn't be swayed. He stretched out on his sleeping bag, swaddled himself in blankets like King Tut and drew the zipper to his nose. 'Night-night,' he said and left me with a bad feeling.

An hour later I shot bolt upright. A truck door had slammed. Seconds later the worst was confirmed: it was ours. The engine bucked to life and we jerked backwards towards the street. Our bed was taking to the road.

'Tony!' I shouted, shaking him like a rag-doll. 'It's Mayday!'

'What the hell!' came the reply. 'Is there an earthquake?'

At this point the Biggles preparations paid off. I pulled on my boots, grabbed jacket, pack and sleeping bag and vaulted over the backboard and away from the reversing truck. Tony, however, was stuck in his cocoon. By the time he'd extracted himself, tossed me his jacket and climbed over the backboard, the truck was on its way. The last I saw before losing him to the mizzling night was him bouncing sock-footed along the wet deserted street, one hand hanging onto the truck, the other trying desperately to haul his recalcitrant pack from the far side of the backboard.

*Oopsy-daisy*, I thought. *No plan B.*

Was this the end? As neither of us knew where we were, the chances of him finding his way back seemed remote. Ten long minutes passed. No Tony. I lit a cigarette. Ten more minutes passed. Still no Tony. I was about to abandon my post when, defiant of reason, a forlorn figure appeared in the distance. Glum and wet, he was jumping puddles, boots in hand.

'I lost my jacket,' he said when he got close.

'No, you didn't,' I said. 'It's here.'

'Well, I lost something. Oh shit, it's my sleeping bag.'

'Well, we can't have that!'

A kind of crime had been committed. Like a reverse truck-jacking.

Although Tony doubted my interpretation, he followed as I stormed off to lodge a complaint at the nearest police station. The lads on duty spoke no English and put us through by phone to the central station. But communication was still difficult so central sent a car. As the police forces of Rome rallied to our plight, a skinny, middle-aged, English-speaking plainclothes cop at central station adopted a minority position.

'What colour was the truck?' he asked, like Sherlock Holmes with a long nose and elephant ears. Tony and I looked at one another.

'Make?' he asked. We looked at one another again.

'Number,' he sighed. This we put down to Latin temperament and kept looking at him now. He closed his notebook and drew himself up to his full height.

'It is like this,' he said, bad attitude all over his puss. 'There are many thousands of trucks in Rome. As you do not know the colour, make or number of this truck, you cannot find your sleeping bag. Also, you are lucky that you are not arrested for vagrancy. If I go to your country, I have money. I sleep in a hotel. I do not sleep in somebody else's truck. If you come to my country, you should also have money. I will bring you now to a pensione.'

Buck eejit.

But it was a stroke of luck of sorts. We found a tin of peas in the kitchen and heated them on our stove. Our only food since morning.

The following day I also lost my sleeping bag, leaving it behind at the Colosseum. This was the result of not being able to book into the hostel until evening and having to lug our gear around countless acres of Roman ruins while we learned how Rome was built by two guys who'd been reared by a wolf, how the Vestal Virgins of the Forum Romanum took a thirty-year vow of chastity and were buried alive if they broke it, and how Julius Caesar was stabbed to death by a bunch of hooligans in the Theatre of Pompey on the Ides of March (15th) in 44 BC.

The traumatic loss of sleeping bag was recorded in my travel notes: '*a blow from a hammer... the unbelievable had happened, the absurd became fact - in the space of 14 hours we'd both been parted from our most important possession...*'

In defence of hyperbole, the poor French-made replacements stung us for a mighty £8 each. They were also of such poor quality that, in retaliation, we had to take a long-term loan of a blanket from the city's youth hostel so we could make ponchos to stop us freezing to death on outdoor nights.

I also, by the way, noted the courtesy of Rome's drivers. '*We'd step from the kerb and the whole city would come to a standstill and politely wave us across. On the widest of streets it was perfectly safe to dawdle at ease.*'

I believe things have changed.

\* \* \*

Our visit to the Vatican, with its tombs of popes, paintings by Michelangelo and embalmed bodies of saints, roused Tony's social conscience.

'Remember Eileen Fox!' he whooped at three perambulating priests in long black soutanes. We were on our way back across St. Peter's Square when his mind bounced back to a day, four years earlier, in County Galway.

On a Sunday morning in February 1966, Dr. Thomas Ryan, Bishop of Clonfert, had risen before his fold in St. Brendan's Cathedral, Loughrea, to denounce the 'debasing and disgraceful entertainment' broadcast the previous night on The Late Late Show. Railing against RTE (the national TV network), and the show's compere, Gay Byrne, the bishop told the congregation that he had personally telegrammed Byrne as the programme went out live, telling him that he was 'disgusted with the disgraceful performance'. He called the faithful to arms, a call splashed across the pages of all the newspapers. They were 'entitled to something more in keeping with the traditions of Catholic Ireland,' he told them, and urged them to protest in every way 'short of physical violence' to show RTE that '... we as good Catholic citizens will not stand for this...'

What so exercised the bishop was a game that Byrne had played with a married couple, separately asking them questions and seeing if they both gave the same answer. When he asked the woman, Eileen Fox, what nightwear she wore on her honeymoon, she answered 'None'.

## Chapter 9

Holy horror! Get the fire brigade!

When Dr. Ryan's clarion call hit the streets of Cork and was taken up by the ultra-Catholic Legion of Mary I was a few weeks off fifteen, but distinctly remember having to remind myself that it was the second half of the 20th century.

\* \* \*

As is the form of travellers worth their salt, we were keen to dissemble mysteries. This caused us to take a train up into the mountains east of Rome to check on a story I'd been told at school.

Story was that a mysterious fresco from Albania turned up in a church in a place called Genazzano on the festival of St. Mark in April 1467. The event was witnessed by the whole population as the bells of the village chimed unaided. At the time the church was badly in need of renovation but the only one interested was the widow Petruccia de Geneo who decided to start the renovation herself. She quickly ran out of funds, however, and became the laughing stock of the area, the unfinished church becoming known as 'Petruccia's Folly'. But at four o'clock on the afternoon in question a cloud descended on a low unfinished wall of the church and left behind a portrait of the Madonna and Child. The ensuing dumbstruckness of the people, and a few dozen miracles that followed, clinched Petruccia's case and the cash flowed in. When Petruccia died she was buried out the back.

But the story had another twist. In August 1467, as the Catholic Church conducted an investigation into the goings-on up at Genazzano, two chaps turned up from Albania, attracted by the reports. 'That,' says one, 'is the Madonna of Good Counsel from our little church in old Shkodra.' They had seen it detach itself from the wall, they said, as Ottoman troops laid siege to Shkodra at the foot of the Rozafat citadel, a rocky outcrop of limestone perched 135 metres above the confluence of the rivers Buna and Kir. The fresco had then floated off across the Adriatic to Genazzano. Further investigations in Shkodra were said to have confirmed the absence from the church wall of an image of the same precise dimensions.

The painting, on a layer of plaster as thick as an eggshell, was uncracked and said to be standing upright in the church with no support of any kind except at the base. For well over 500 years, this extraordinary situation had defied the laws of gravity. A church Commission was said to have passed a thread up the front of the icon, over its top, and down the back, demonstrating that it stood alone. During World War II a bomb hit the church, demolishing the high altar and causing widespread damage; but the fresco, a few metres away, was unscathed.

'The bit I find hard to believe,' I said as we climbed into the mountains, 'is the bit about the rocky outcrop being 135 metres high.'

Tony said I'd be hit by lightning.

At Cave, reached in a ripping snowstorm, the railway line came to an abrupt end and we had to slug the muddy streets to the far end of the village before it appeared again. We then continued on through rolling hills of chestnut and olive trees until we whistled to a stop in small medieval Genazzano. We liked the place, nothing more pushed than the trot of a donkey or mule. Here on the wooded southern slopes of the Prenestini Mountains, overlooking the Valle del Sacco, we went in search of the Church of Our Lady of Good Counsel. We had come with a roll of thread to confirm or debunk the mystery.

We were thwarted. The fresco was locked behind glass.

'Ciarán, boy,' Tony said, 'there's no shaggin' justice.'

Disappointed, we left the church in gathering darkness and trudged through a second snowstorm back to the railway station. In the last of the day, village life closed around us. Smiling women passed with groceries and washing balanced on their heads. Men came back from the fields, their donkeys and horse-carts laden with firewood and hay. We watched them. They watched us.

The stationmaster wanted to know what had brought foreigners like us to Genazzano. The fresco, we explained. Delighted by the presence of two Irish 'pilgrims' he offered us the use of the station locker room for the night: TV, heater, table and chairs. The heap.

To this day I would be a bit of a sceptic around Petruccia's fresco. On the other hand, we at home had the later march of the Madonnas.

Although independent motion is not one of the more readily acknowledged properties of concrete, we witnessed in Ireland in the mid 1980s a phenomenon of some twenty moving statues. As the bishops ran for cover - afraid to pronounce for or against - huge pilgrimages got under way. People saw the sun spin through the sky and images of Christ appeared in fireplaces and tea towels. The situation caused such pandemonium on the roads that the Gardaí issued a statue-related traffic warning. In Galway, at an unfinished statueless grotto, a sign appeared saying 'Back in 10 minutes'. Down

## Chapter 9

in Wexford, another said 'Gone fishin'. A Madonna in Sligo had an 'Out of order' sign strung from her neck. Sadly for the people of the North, they never crossed the border.

On the day we left Genazzano, the sun rose on thick fresh snow that glistened brilliantly in the morning light. As the bright sunshine melted the snow, we walked ten kilometres to the village of Colleferro, passing on the way some working girls doing business with motorists up a dirt track. After a relaxed day we reached Collefferro to find it was Saturday evening and we couldn't change a traveller's cheque. But, as Tony came out of a small restaurant where a final vain attempt left us resigned to a food-free weekend, we were saved by a tall dapper man who was on his way in.

'Good evening,' he said. 'My name is George. Can I help you?' Tony explained the situation. 'No problem,' George said. 'Come with me.'

George collected his car, drove Tony to his bank manager's home, drew out some money of his own and cashed us a £5 cheque.

Flush again, we made for the nearest shop, then headed for the railway station in the hope of repeating the night before. But the crotchety old grump of a stationmaster said no. In retaliation we boiled our billy on *his* bench on *his* platform, and scattered our crumbs all over *his* station tiles before going back to the village where we found ourselves a covered alley for the night.

Strange are the things that happen in the night.

Some hours later I was nudged from a sound sleep. An agitated cop, crouching in the beams of a patrol car, had a flashlamp in my face. It took several seconds to realise where I was and who he was. Not understanding a word he was saying, I pointed to myself and said '*Irlanda*'.

'Ah,' he sighed, '*Irlanda...*' He pushed my head back on my jacket, pulled the sleeping bag over my face and said something about '*dormir*' (sleep) and the car drove off.

Tony, that lad of principle, lost not a wink through the whole commotion.

## Chapter 10

No Dough, No Show.

On the morning of February 27th we sailed south along the mountainous coast of closed Maoist Albania on a ferry belonging to the Hellenic Mediterranean Lines. I had a glass of orange juice to celebrate my 19th birthday.

We'd left Italy the night before and were on our way to the Greek island of Kerkyra, nowadays better known as Corfu. It was a mixed morning. Dolphins in a deep black sea. Screeching gulls following the ship. A coastline of craggy snowcapped beauty beyond which sat the dictator Enver Hoxha who'd ruled Albania with a brutal fist since the end of World War II, turning a semi-feudal relic of the Ottoman Empire into the most tightly controlled and isolated country in Europe.

More than twenty young travellers who'd spent the previous night socialising among the communal bunks and hot showers in the belly of the ship were now on deck. Not since Tangier had there been such a coming together. Everyone was everyone's friend. Everyone was looking forward to landing in Greece. Everyone was fixed on the hulking coastline. Everyone was going on to someplace else. Everyone was sorry for the people of Albania.

Although the distance was relatively short and we'd travelled separately, it had taken four days to cross the spine of Italy from the alley in Collefferro to the port of Brindisi, much of it a labour of foot. Long days of intermittent rain. Steep hauls up switchback tracks to villages built on the tops of mountains. Downhill shortcuts through muddy fields. Forests, valleys and snowy peaks. Birds in the morning and evening. Lifts from donkey carts on roads yet to meet the internal combustion engine.

In the town of Cassino, rebuilt after one of the bloodiest battles of World War II, my bed was two storeys up in a building site, down on which gazed the lights of the massive restored Monte Cassino Abbey, showing no signs of the 1,400 tons of bombs pointlessly dropped on it by American planes in February 1944.

In the hilltop village of Gambateza, I found another building site set back in an alley, where dinner was carved from a loaf of bread so heavy and large that you could've fitted it to a bicycle. It was a

## Chapter 10

cold night. Even with my new poncho, the shivers drove me out at 6.30am.

That evening I'd probably have made it to Brindisi and a civilised bed had it not been for a group of students who ambushed me in Foggia, holding me for two hours of English practice. As a result I closed the day on the outskirts of Bari where the bedroom was a culvert under the main road.

The fourth morning was memorable for its vineyards, olive groves, blossoming apple trees and a 40-kilometre run down the shimmering Adriatic coast. En route I noted that the whitewashed coastal houses, tiny compared to those of the mountains, were all daubed in red paint with the letters 'C.V.'

In Brindisi I was told that they were under the 'protection' of the shadowy Comitato Vigilanza - the Citizens Vigilance Committee. True or false, I don't know. Nor do I know if it was shadowy.

\* \* \*

The plan was to catch the ferry from Brindisi and meet again with Tony in Kerkyra. But I learned at the port that there was no boat until the following night. When I checked about for possible signs of Tony, I ran instead into a square-headed American body builder with a crew cut, who was planning to sail that night to Athens. Ron, who'd come straight from Muscle Beach on the west side of Los Angeles, gave the impression of a man who'd been pummelled flat by a pile driver. This was on account of him being very broad but not very tall. You could imagine that he was once the famous small guy who got the sand kicked in his eyes on some other beach.

'Are you OK?' he asked. I explained the Tony thing. 'Ah,' he said. 'I have a few hours to spare. I'll help you look for him.'

The good thing about walking the streets with Ron was that nobody was going to mess with us. The bad thing was that he made odd connections.

'Man,' he said, 'I lost a friend too. Two years ago I woke up to find that my old buddy from high school who'd been conscripted into the army had been blown away in the Tet Offensive [Vietnam]. Two days later I started to save money so I could get away from the country that forced the guy to die for something he didn't believe in.'

'But my friend is alive,' I pointed out.

'Yes,' he said. 'And Brindisi is alive. In its time it was a Roman naval station, a sailing point for the Crusades and a gateway to the East for the silk trade... Now it's crawling with white slavers.'

'What?' I said. This signalled I was sceptical.

'Yep. This is a big base for it. White women kidnapped all over Europe and shipped out to the Middle East. Some GIs in the local base told me that their captain's 16-year-old daughter was drugged and taken on board a ship here. The ship was ready to sail when it was raided and she was freed.'

I tried to imagine western women running around unnoticed in the harems of sheikhs and pirates.

'It's true,' he insisted. 'Maybe your friend has been kidnapped too?'

'He's a guy,' I said.

'Fancy a pizza?' Ron pointed towards a small workers' tavern. At first I didn't let on that I'd never heard of such a thing.

Once inside, I looked at the bilingual menu. Along with stewed horse chops with celery and pecorino (a cheese made from sheep's milk), and roulade of tripe in a spicy broth, it offered a long selection under 'Pizza'. But no clue as to what might constitute a pizza.

'What's a pizza?' I asked in the end.

'I don't *believe* it,' Ron bawled. 'You don't know *pizza*? My gawd! It's a kind of bread, with cheese and tomato sauce and pepperoni and things. It's all over Italy.'

'Never heard of it,' I told him. 'I've been living on bread and salami.'

'You don't have pizza in Ireland?'

'No,' I said. 'Do you have pig's head and cabbage in California?'

That shut him up.

'Check this,' Ron said, nodding towards two young men, strolling along, linking arms as the nightly passeggiata got under way. This was when the locals strolled the streets to meet friends and family for coffee or ice cream in the bars and gelaterie before heading home for dinner. 'At home you'd never get away with that. But here all the guys do it.'

We agreed: men linking arms were ridiculous.

After we'd eaten, Ron came up good: he fixed my accommodation.

'I stayed last night in a campervan down by the waterfront,' he explained. 'The owners have gone to Greece and it's being looked after by a Canadian couple who are stopped nearby in a van of their own. I'm sure they'd let you have it.'

He brought me around and I had a bed for the night. Free, comfortable and up off the ground. After the night in the railway station and four nights sleeping rough, it felt like I'd inherited the

# Chapter 10

Marriott. I could sit to a meal and savour in comfort the grubbiness of five days' travel.

Accompanying Ron back to the ferry terminal, I bumped into a Canadian who'd been in the hostel at Pisa. He told me that Tony was in town and looking for me. Although a later scouring of old Brindisi failed to locate him, we'd be on the one boat to Kerkyra.

* * *

In the morning I opened the van door to find standing before me a bespectacled long-haired Japanese lad of about twenty.

'Hello,' he said, sticking out his hand. 'I am Keiichi Kochi. I am Japon man.'

Keiichi was a student taking what would later be known as a gap year. Same as myself, he was planning to sail from Brindisi to Kerkyra. I invited him to join me for breakfast.

'Can you watch out for my friend?' I asked him. 'He is tall, like this, [I gave the measure of about six feet]. He has black hair, and a jacket and rucksack like mine.' I showed him both. He looked at me sideways.

'You fliend?' he asked. 'Why he not take his lucksack?'

'No. This is *my* lucksack - damn it - rucksack. My friend is somewhere in Brindisi with the same rucksack.'

'Ah, you fliend live Blindisi.'

'No. My friend lives in Ireland. But we are travelling together and he is somewhere here in Brindisi.'

'A-a-aah! You fliend, he live Ileland. Why you look for you fliend in Blindisi?'

'Keiichi,' I said, losing it a little now. 'My friend is in fuckin' Brindisi but I can't *find* him.'

'A-a-aah,' Keiichi said. 'You lose fliend? Unbeliebable!'

This, I concluded, was how nations went to war.

Two hours later, Tony arrived by chance at the van, trailing behind him a saucer-eyed, 22-year-old Italian, half hidden behind a mass of straw curls that looked like an oversized mop.

'This is Urk,' Tony said. 'We met yesterday and he kindly arranged to have me put up for the night with some friends of his from the local Communist Party. Then this morning I met that Canadian from Pisa and he told me you were in town. We've been on the lookout ever since.'

'I am a poet and a philosopher,' Urk said, clearly smashed out of his head. 'I believe in nothing except God and the total liberty of man. My ambition is to be free and to travel in every corner of the world before I die. Soon I will go to India to write poetry and philosophy, but first I must find a companion. Maybe an Indian yogi. Only crazy people travel alone in Orient.'

Tony drilled an index finger into his temple. '*Níl sé ar fónamh,*' [He's not well] he mouthed.

'One time I had to slit a guy's throat,' Urk continued. 'He was bothering me.'

He pulled out a few pages of scribbled English rantings and began to read from them as Keiichi Kochi turned up a second time. I introduced Tony to a very puzzled Japon man.

'I will go to India,' Urk concluded. 'On the way I will stay some time in Afghanistan.'

'Ah,' Keiichi said. 'India, many people.'

Urk pulled out some more poetry, this time in Italian, and began to translate, much to the consternation of Keiichi who could neither understand the Italian nor the English.

'Me Japon man,' he reminded Urk.

Poetry session concluded, Urk insisted that Tony, Keiichi and I follow him back into the old historic quarter to visit a tall column that marked the end of the ancient Appian Way. On the broad steps leading to the column we were joined by Antonio Frongillo, a jolly, long-haired, 36-year-old, self-proclaimed hippie from Rome who loped his eagle nose through the streets like a panther and insisted that we all accompany him for wine and hard-boiled eggs in a small tavern lined with oak.

'Good vino,' Antonio said.

'Yes,' I agreed. 'Very good. There is a simple relationship with wine. The higher the alcohol and the lower the price, the better the wine. What we are drinking fits the bill.'

'You are funny man,' Antonio said. He then downed a bottle of red by the neck in the time it took the rest of us to get through our first glass. Urk got drink-on-dope drunk and slumped over a table. Keiichi wanted to know if he was going to India any time soon.

'On the way to India,' Urk mumbled, face pressed to the wood, 'you will pass through Afghanistan. There you can buy much hashish in every place. You smoke plenty and you will understand the life. You will understand the love. The road to India is the road of love.' With that he pulled himself upright and staggered off to collect Tony's gear.

## Chapter 10

'Where the hell is Afghanistan,' I asked Tony.
'Haven't a bulls,' he said.

\* \* \*

Disembarking in Kerkyra town on the east coast of Kerkyra island, we squeezed our way through a labyrinth of rough cobblestones searching for the baker's and the morning's bread. We were suddenly in Greece, a country under the dictatorship of the Regime of the Colonels since April 1967 when democracy was overthrown in a coup d'état, supported by the United States. On every side, giant billboards proclaimed the virtues of the new rulers. Matchboxes in the shops sported an image of a yellow Phoenix rising from the flames, fronted by the black silhouette of a soldier with upright rifle and fixed bayonet - the omnipresent emblem of the junta. In every sense we were now a long way from home: dark-skinned moustachioed men fingered worry beads; black-cossacked Greek Orthodox priests stroked long beards; horse-drawn carriages rattled the cobbles of the wider streets; old matriarchs in long black dresses rode saddlebagged donkeys to market, swishing at flies with long sheaves of grass. Flowerpots spilled over from wrought iron balconies. Watches went forward another hour. We bought our bread, supplemented it with a slab of 'old' cheese and two tomatoes and sat down to take stock.

In a mirror we didn't look that good. Our jackets and jeans had grown shabby, the boots were irrevocably scuffed, we'd lost significant weight, and our faces were lined and burned from sun and wind. But, with 4,800 kilometres behind us, we were closing in on Istanbul which had now become the place where the road to India really began. Ever since Tangiers, the pull had been Asia. Morocco had turned the world on its head and decades would pass before Europe would beckon again as a goal that was worth the candle.

'Gee golly,' Tony said, imitating an American accent. 'If the folks back home could see us now, they'd say *There go men of shteel, hewn out of the sholid rock.*'

The musings, however, were cut short by a sudden deluge that caused a bolt for a cheap hotel at the eastern end of town close to an old Byzantine fort. On the plus side, we broke all records with nothing short of a miracle - a second shower in twenty-four hours.

'If this keeps up,' Tony said, 'we'll end up like the guy in *The Third Policeman* who spent so long on his bike that the transfer of molecules made him half man, half bicycle. We'll have shower-heads spoutin' out of our shaggin' ears.' Tony had been hugely influenced by Myles na gCopaleen's atomic theory of the bicycle.[7]

When the rain stopped, we went outside to find young people in fancy dress dancing through the streets, singing, shouting and playing music. It was the beginning of Apokries, they told us, a two-week festival dating back to the worship of Dionysus, god of wine and ritual madness. In the olden days, revellers ran through the streets brandishing giant phalluses and singing bawdy songs. Nowadays, coming before lent, celebrations were more decorous. However it was still a festival of wine. In a small bar we made the acquaintance of Retsina, a wine flavoured with the pine resin that Garnoc Pumphrey had mentioned back in the Málaga Mountains. Soon we too were singing, shouting and demonstrating to a bemused cop the intricacies of the Irish céilí swing.

Next day we left Kerkyra by ferry and docked two hours later on the Greek mainland amid the wooden fishing boats of Igoumenitsa. It was a glorious afternoon. From behind the town, snow-covered mountains and forests swept down from a blue sky to a sea that was calm as a Hindu cow. Despite losing the last of the afternoon to cooking, we enjoyed a great sunset and set off into the forested hills after dark, bent on putting good distance between ourselves and the Adriatic. But Apokries wouldn't let go. Six kilometres out of town strange music drifted up from somewhere down in the woods.

We followed the sound along a dirt track to a packed, smoke-filled bar where festivities had reached a pitch akin to the tail end of a wet summer's night in Kruger Kavanagh's pub in the west Kerry village of Ballyferriter. Greek folk music was being hammered out on bouzoukis and fiddles; dancers were swirling around the floor, whooping, stomping and hanging on to one another with handkerchiefs; and everyone was tossing back Retsina, beer and various suspicious liquids, to beat the band. We felt entirely at home. However, when we walked in, everything stopped.

'*Irlandia*,' I said, pointing to ourselves. There were gasps of amazement. Then events moved at speed.

We were grabbed and hauled to a table. A woman in a black dress shoved a bottle of clear liquid in our faces. She was about forty

---

[7] Myles na gCopaleen was the pen name of Brian O'Nolan, Irish novelist, playwright and satirist who wrote *The Third Policeman*.

## Chapter 10

and had a mug that shone like buffed leather, with eyes circled in something black that probably passed as make-up.

'*Ouzo! Ouzo!*' she barked, thumb jabbing to mouth, indicating that we should drink as a matter of urgency. Everyone cheered. We poured a shot each and sipped. An unholy Poitín-and-liquorice type mix burned holes in our gullets. We screwed up our faces. The woman grabbed both our hands and tipped the rest of the poison down our throats. The place erupted. The music and madness resumed. We had joined the gang. An old boy advised us to add water to the Ouzo. Amazing, we said, how it changed to milky white. *Ha-ha-ha!* everyone went. A circle gathered. Old women kissed us. Nikos, a thick-set guy with long black curls who spoke passable English and specialised in making foreigners welcome, poured two more Ouzos down our necks.

'*Tsamiko* is best dance,' he said. 'You must try.'

'Do you see any green in my eye?' Tony asked.

He tried to drag us into the middle of the floor where a group of his mates were pursuing a death tryst. Those who were upright were spinning others around the floor at terrifying speed. The others were horizontally dangling from the ends of handkerchiefs. Hair was swiping the stone floor.

'Lock your legs around the leg of the table,' I advised Tony.

'No have afraid,' Nikos laughed.

'Pull the other one,' Tony said.

We were rescued by a Canadian who'd lived in Greece for years, a balding man in his late thirties with the belly of a whale and a nose as red as a plum. Although he was so drunk that he couldn't remember his name or where in Canada he hailed from, he managed to pull Nikos off and joined us at the table.

'Where...you...from...?' he asked. We told him. He stared into his glass for a few minutes. 'Where... you... from...?' he asked again. Gradually his words dissolved into nothing more than a load of letters, then a kind of 'zhaaah' sound until he fell forward into the table. At the end of the night, however, he resurrected himself. He stumbled out the front door, mounted a motorbike and took off into the darkness on all sides of the road - with a drunken uniformed cop riding pillion. Tony and I went back to Igoumenitza to a building site we'd spotted earlier.

'You know what?' Tony said, sitting on his sleeping bag like Buddha O'Connor with a slur to his words. 'You couldn't buy this if you won the Pools. Here we are, living on buttons, walking till we drop, sleeping in ditches and building sites, but would you swap it for the world?'

'Tony,' I said, also with a little slur, 'this is how the world was meant to be.'

'If my oul' man could see us now,' Tony concluded, 'he'd either be very proud or he'd have us committed.'

Next day was Sunday. As no workers were likely to appear, we slept until hunger drove us again to the baker's. But when we arrived we had to join a queue stretching the length of the street. Carrying pots and pans, the citizens were lining up to have their dinners cooked in the ovens.

\* \* \*

At noon we left Igoumenitza for a second day running, this time managing a good pace into the forests of the Pindus Mountains. At about five o'clock we stopped in a village to eat. When we were about to leave again we were called to one side by a thin, stubbled old man who was standing at one of the stone huts. Wrapped in an overcoat tied with cord, he'd been talking to a group of shepherds in cloaks of coarse black wool who, with their hoods drawn up against the cold, looked like the celebrants of a black mass.

'American?' he asked.

'*Irlandia*,' I said.

'Ah,' he said. '*Ollandia*. You stop my house dis night.'

We didn't need to be asked twice. At this height the evenings closed with a petrifying vengeance.

'Thank you. Thank you.' I spluttered. '*Ir-landia*,' I said again when we reached the hut.

'*Ol-landia* very good,' he said.

'*IR-LANDIA*,' I persisted.

The shepherds eyed me suspiciously.

'My name Owua,' our host said when we'd crossed his threshold. 'From Albania. I eighty year old. I have family here before. Ten children. All gone.'

He didn't mention a wife but she was also all gone.

'All people this village. All refugee Albania. All leave when communists come in Albania.'

This took some digesting: that displaced people could find enough space in another country to establish their own village and have their own lands to farm. Owua must have seen the confusion so he added to it.

'Albania people in Greeken many year. From 13th century. Some long time Christian. Other - Cham Albania people - long time Muslim. Many dem Muslim help German in World War. Kill many, many Greeken people. No good.' He shook his head and pursed his lips into what looked like a sink-plunger. 'After war, bad Albania people run fast. Go back Albania.'

It seemed that when Owua crossed over, Albanians were fleeing in both directions.

One of these days I'll go back and try and make sense of all of this. It's been doing my head in for forty-odd years. Only problem is that I don't remember the name of the village. When Owua wrote his address for me the next day, he did so in a script that - as they say - might as well have been Greek. I know. I know.

Owua's single-roomed hut was spotless. Heated by a wood fire, its furnishings consisted of a small table, two chairs and a long communal bed where the entire family of twelve once slept. A basin provided the washing facilities.

'You eat apple?' he asked and cut up the only piece of fruit in the house.

As our eyes accustomed to the dim interior, Owua told us that he'd learned his English when living in the U.S. for a time. He'd also got rightly browned off with the war in Vietnam.

'No good,' he said. 'Vietnam. All dem young boys. All dead.'

Later, the three of us went to the local bar, a scrubbed friendly place with a log fire, rough wooden beams and a stone floor where Tony and I again delved into the chemical wonders of Ouzo and held a conversation of monosylables with Owua, doing our best to explain the difference between *Irlandia* and *Ollandia*. But *Irlandia* was the dark side of the moon.

'No good,' Owua would say if conversation dried up. 'Vietnam. All dem young boys. All dead.'

As the night wore on and the fire threw long shadows across the floor, songs were sung by myself and Tony to raise village hearts. When it was time to go and we rose somewhat unsteadily to face out into the twinkling frost, Owua put his arms around both of us.

'Remember me,' he said. Then after a little pause: 'No good. Vietnam. All dem young boys. All dead.'

\* \* \*

From Owua's village, we walked twenty-five kilometres across the mountains. It was a bright crisp day of dense forests, cliffs and towering snow peaks that swept a chill down the winding road. We walked briskly, soaking in the glorious sense of isolation and freedom that lived in that place. For much of the journey we followed the line of a river, crossing numerous streams of gurgling meltwater that tumbled down into the silver flow. Far below, smoke rose from the chimneys of half hidden villages basking in wintry sunshine and surrounded by patchworks of small fields. On the slopes above and below, shepherds and goatherds in their black cloaks watched over their flocks. They waved as we passed. An old woman in long black skirts and leading a donkey, gave a furtive nod from the far side of the road. In her left hand she had a ball of sheep's wool, kneading it out between thumb and forefinger and collecting the rough yarn on a wooden spool held in her right hand. At the top of a pass a young shepherdess sang to herself as she turned out a beautiful piece of embroidery. She'd been there for a thousand years. Shortly after sunset, as temperatures dipped precipitously, a car rolled down from the top of the pass and we stuck out our thumbs. The driver brought us to Ioannina. As we got in, he loaded a shotgun and placed it between himself and the driver's door.

'In case we see rabbit,' he said.

Afterwards we heard that two German hitchhikers had murdered six Greeks some time before. This may or may not have been true or relevant.

\* \* \*

Sitting 500 metres above sea level on the shores of Lake Pambotis, Ioannina was a town of cobbled streets, tiled houses, balconies and flower baskets. To the east and south east it was fringed by the highest of the Pindus peaks. Torrents from Mount Mitsikeli fed the lake where 10-kilometre-long Nissi Island was home to several monasteries. They included that of Panteleimon where Ali Pasha met a bad end in February 1822. The bullet marks were still on the floor.

In the centre of town we found ourselves a building site for the night but had to retreat to the park at half seven in the morning when the workers turned up. After three freezing hours we bought some cheap gloves and moved to the uncostly Hotel Metrepole, having decided to stay a couple of days so we could visit the cave wonders of the adjacent Grottos of Perama. We also got to meet a chunk of the townspeople. Everywhere we went, people wanted to talk to us, wanted to know who we were and where we were going. In return they shared with us the tale of Ali Pasha.

## Chapter 10

After helping the Turks in their war of 1787 against Austria, Ali was made Pasha of Trikkala in 1788. Immediately, he seized Ioannina, then a town of 35,000 inhabitants, and made it his headquarters. The new ruler, formerly leader of a bunch of brigands in the Albanian mountains, soon earned a reputation as a ruthless and clever tactician. Gradually he extended his power and territory, forging foreign relationships with the major western powers of the time who supplied his army with advisors and artillery. In 1809, when Lord Byron visited his court, Ali Pasha had a harem of over 600 women, and wealth and power to burn. In 1812 he plumbed for immortality and ordered an alchemical laboratory from Venice. Five years later, when his scientists had failed to find the cure for death, he had them hanged. And rightly so.

Eventually Ali Pasha overstepped himself and his enemies appealed to the Ottoman Sultan to have him removed. In 1822 Ioannina was besieged by 20,000 Turkish troops whereupon Ali's allies and his own sons ditched him. However, when promised a pardon, he ordered the town to surrender and retreated to Nissi in anticipation. He was killed there by a Turkish agent and his head sent to Istanbul for public display.

That was the end of Ali Pasha.

*   *   *

On our third morning in Ioannina Tony and I left the Metropole and were cooking breakfast in hypothermic conditions in a nearby park when we attracted a young woman hoping to do business. Aged about eighteen, she had the loveliest of smiles but the lousiest nose for opportunity. Still living on bread and whatever came cheapest, and wrapped in fading combat jackets and jeans, we were a bad target. Half an hour later we were about to leave town when we were collared by some friendly students. Leandros, the keg-chested leader, advised that we take a bus over the Katara Pass to Larisa.

'If you hitchhike,' he said, 'very dangeroose. Crazy dangeroose. Katara is 1,705 metre high. Very cold. Much big snow. No automobile. But no bus now to Larisa. Only one bus every day. Bus tomorrow. Seven o'clock in morning.'

We went back into town and called in at the old castle of Ali Pasha and the Alsan Pasa mosque before booking in at the youth hostel. Being the only guests, the warden made us a huge charcoal fire in a one-legged bronze brazier and gave us charge of the building for the night. And as the white-hot coals made strange patterns against the blackened bronze, the one issue we'd avoided when taking stock in Kerkyra mushroomed out of the flickering flames.

'You know what?' Tony said in slow motion. 'I was counting my money. I'm not going to make it to India. I'm down to thirty-five quid and whatever drachmas I have in my pocket. I'm probably going to have to turn back from Istanbul...'

I can't say I was knocked off my feet although I'd been hoping that, somehow, Tony's money was more elastic than mine.

'How about you?' he asked.

'I have sixty quid.'

'Do you think you'll make it on that?'

'Dunno. But I'd like to try. Maybe we could both keep going? Pool the lot and make a run for it together?'

We thought about that for a long minute before Tony shook his head.

'Ciarán boy,' he said, 'nice thought, but there's no point. Whatever chance one mad bastard might have of making it from here to India on sixty quid. Two mad bastards would never make it on ninety-five. Then we'd have to get back again.'

'If we could make it to Delhi,' I said, 'we could sell our passports on the black market. Then when the money runs out, we'll just front up to the Irish embassy for repatriation.'

'Wouldn't doubt ya boy!' Tony howled. 'You're outta yer head. But if you think you can make it, do it for both of us, for the first Irish overland expedition to India. I'll head back to England and look up the relatives. If I can pick up a job I'll wait for you there. Just make sure you come back in one piece.'

He tore a page from his travel diary and wrote me the addresses of his grandmother and aunt Ann who lived in Maidenhead in Berkshire.

'That's the way it goes,' he sighed. 'No dough, no show.'

After that it was a funny kind of lonely night that led to a day that almost led to no other nights when the Larisa bus lost its purchase on a hairpin bend in the high forests and blizzards of the Katara Pass and plunged backwards towards the abyss. Another metre on the fresh crust that had fallen since the morning efforts of the snowploughs, and money wouldn't have mattered any more. Our thoughts would've been on the snapping, silvered branches of spruce and pine, and the leisurely cascade of grinding metal and collapsing snow.

## Chapter 10

\* \* \*

Six hours after leaving Ioannina, we arrived in Larisa. We spent the next six hours trying to hitchhike out again but abandoned the effort at nightfall and booked ourselves into yet another building site to look down from five stories up on the second weekend of Apokries.

A train brought us to Alexandroupolis, passing under the shadow of the 2,917-metre massif of Mount Olympus, crossing the flats of Central Macedonia, and following the foothills of the Falakron Mountains to the coastal plains of Thrace. The following afternoon we took a bus to the Greek border post. The bus would, we understood, bring us to Ipsala. However, when we reached the Greek post our gear was dumped on the road and we were gruffly ordered off along with an English couple bound for Thailand. Border formalities, however, were swift and the four of us were soon on our way again, walking across a bridge that divided Greece from Turkey. On the Greek side two soldiers in red hats, blue coats, white tights (my gawd!) and shoes with woolly tossles, marched up and down with rifles and fixed bayonets on their shoulders. How could you take them seriously? On the Turkish side the corresponding two soldiers looked on from their sentry boxes with big grins.

We now faced an eight-kilometre hike to Ipsala. Briefly, it looked like our luck was in when a Swiss campervan stopped; but they could only take two. We tossed a coin. Tony and I lost and walked to Ipsala. But, luck is a strange fellow. Had we not walked, we would've missed the Turkish folk group that played their hearts out on the late bus from Ipsala to Keysan. At Keysan we changed vehicles for the final four-hour run to Istanbul.

# Chapter 11
## The Pudding Shop
_____

Cities have primary focal points. Like beating hearts, they pump the lifeblood of the metropolis. Istanbul's is undoubtedly the Blue Mosque, a bijou of splendour sitting triumphantly for the past 400 years on the site of the old Imperial Palace of Christian Byzantium[8]. Overlooking the Hippodrome, a massive square where crowds roared and chariots raced in Roman times, this colossal structure with its cascade of domes and its six slender minarets is one of the wonders of the Islamic world. The early 17th century masterwork of Ottoman architect Sedefkâr Mehmet Aga is also credited with having caused a considerable scandal in its day. Its six minarets (normally Turkish mosques have from one to four) put the Blue Mosque on a collision course with the great Haram Mosque of Mecca - the holiest of holies - which also had six. Ultimately, a seventh had to be added in Mecca to resolve the row. No visitor to Istanbul fails to gape before the towering minarets of monumental Sultanahmet Camii, to give it its Turkish name.

However cities have fringe places too.

For the young travellers for whom all the roads of Europe converged on Istanbul, the alternative wasn't to be found at The Tomb of The Sultans where Sultan Ahmet I, patron of the Blue Mosque, lay alongside his wife, Kösem, (strangled to death in the harem of Topkapi Palace) and sons, Sultan Osman II and Sultan Murat IV.

It wasn't to be found in the alleys of the Grand Bazaar where small tea shops with hubble-bubble pipes sat among 4,000 other shops selling everything from shoes and carpets to gold and ceramics, specific trades packed under the painted vaulted ceilings of specific streets and the lot feeding a frenzy of barter and selling.

Nor yet under the physics-defying dome of Ayasofya where Mehmet the Conqueror had symbolically ended the Byzantine Empire when he took the city for the Ottomans in 1453.

No. It was in a rundown café beside the broken kerbs of Divan Yolu - diagonally across the Hippodrome square from the Blue

_____
[8] The old Greek name for Istanbul.

## Chapter 11

Mosque - where the ancient road from Constantinople[9] to Rome once began. The attraction was that, here at the Pudding Shop, the road to Asia also began.

On the night we'd arrived a businessman on the bus paid a taxi to take us to a cheap hotel. After a drive through dense suburbs stilled by night, the taxi landed us in a dive where we paid about twenty-five pence each to share a room with two doped-out Frenchmen and a doped-out Malaysian. In the morning we moved out and landed in Divan Yolu as if led by a divining rod. No sooner had we done so than we spotted the young travellers pooling about the door of the Pudding Shop, among them the Canadian we'd met in Pisa and Brindisi. He was turning north for the Balkans in a few days. 'By the way,' he said, 'my name is Paul.'

He was surprised that I was attempting India on my now remaining £50.

'Every step you take is one you'll have to take back again. Every cent you spend is one that's gone. What happens if you can't sell your passport in India? I mean, an Irish passport in the hands of someone called Abdul or Sanjay might raise an eyebrow or two...'

'You're wasting your time,' Tony said. 'He fell off a lorry when he was young.'

'While this may be true,' I assured Paul, 'it's also irrelevant.'

'Maybe we could travel together?' Paul suggested to Tony when he heard that he too was turning north.

'Not on my money,' Tony said. 'I'll be hitchhiking the day long and sleeping rough, and experience has told me that one guy travels faster than two.'

'Actually,' Paul said, 'neither hitchhiking nor sleeping rough had really been on my mind...' He turned back to me. 'But you there, you'll need to get yourself in here and gather as much information as you can. You might find some guy coming through from India who can tell you how to stretch that £50 over 5,000 kms.' He led the way into the crowded café.

The collision of images between the café interior and the pavements of Divan Yolu could not have been more profound. Consequently, much approbrium fell on the brothers Çolpan who ran the Pudding Shop.

On one side of the door, moustachioed men in baggy pinstriped

---

[9] The Christian name for Istanbul, so called after the Roman Emperor, Constantine I.

trousers, open shirts and skull caps staggered up and down the pavement, bent double under large saddle-like 'pads' on which they lugged loads as big as cars. Others pushed long, two-wheeled handcarts piled three metres high with merchandise. Muslim women in tesettür (headscarf and light coverall topcoat) or colourful blouses, shawls and great ballooning trousers, shopped for bread and breakfast groceries. Shoeshine boys on brass thrones wanted to polish our battered boots. Muezzins called from the minarets of the Blue Mosque and a dozen others within hearing distance. Single decker trolley buses, four-wheeled horse-drawn flatcarts, bicycles and relics of cars trundled down the street. Men stood idly at corners, fingering circular strings of worry beads. And every direction led off into an Islamic city of some 2.5 million souls, tightly crammed around the Bosphorous Strait that separated Europe from Asia, and along the seven-kilometre natural harbour of the Golden Horn.

On the other side of the door, enveloped in the ragged romance of adventure, a diametrically opposed lifestyle played out.

In a haze of smoke and contemporary rock, young sandal-shod and barefooted travellers sat cross-legged on couches and metal stools. Decoration was minimal: plain white walls hung with occasional prints and photographs with no running theme, and a bunch of postcards from various corners of the world stuck behind the counter. But the lack of decor didn't make for meek or glum. All the life and ambience that you could ever want was brought to the tables by those of long hair, Indian trousers and glassy eyes who walked through the door. In a further division, they too were given to a kind of caste structure. There were those who had closed in on Istanbul from the trails of Europe and for whom the city was the grand finale. There were others like myself who'd been on the road for a while and now faced the run to India. And there were those coming back from the east. The peace and love ones who'd found an inner light. These made in India people, unless they were strung out on junk, were the Brahmins of the Pudding Shop.

Surrounded by piles of books, the three castes, united in opposition to the rest of the world, swapped travel yarns and doom-mongering horror tales not heard since Ibn Battuta of Tangier had passed this way. In the café booths, they laughed at one another's close shaves, and sang and played instruments. And everywhere they scribbled notes on journals and scraps of paper. Everyone was soaking up what people coming the other way had to offer. The

## Chapter 11

best places to stay in Tehran. The cost of the bus from Istanbul to Izmir. The times of the Orient Express up through the Balkans. The cheapest way to get to Baghdad. How much you should pay for an ounce of Lebanese Red in Beirut. Where to stay in Belgrade. How to get work in Germany. The price of an Afghan jacket or goatskin bag in places nobody ever heard of. With no such thing as guide books, your compass was the guy at the next table.

Tony and I didn't have a lot to offer: not too many people were that keen on the last building site in Alexandroupolis, or that alley back in Colleferro.

The three of us sat to a table and ordered coffees and rice pudding. In the middle of the floor a young woman of carrot-juice figure in a long dress, sandals and headband, clearly out of her head, was singing some song of The Who and dancing in slow motion. Shiny blonde curls covered her face. She didn't give a flying fiddler's about who thought what.

'Now here's a thought,' Paul said. 'When you folks left Ireland, how did you expect to get even this far on the money you had?'

Tony explained it in simple terms.

'Back in Ireland, whenever a few of us went away for the weekend, we'd have £1 each. Fifty pence would be for drink, twenty-five for fags, and the rest - unless there was some other call on it - would be for food. We multiplied that last twenty-five pence by 180 days and reckoned that we'd need about £43 for food over six months if we stuck mainly to bread and cheese. That would leave us heaps for accommodation and travel, and we planned to keep both of those costs to a minimum.'

'What about scurvy?' Paul asked. 'Or anorexia?'

'We had the odd orange too,' I countered. 'And we cooked a meal whenever we got the chance.' (It wasn't as if we were dumbos.) 'And we had a few cheap feeds in restaurants. I had a pizza in Brindisi.'

Paul stared from one of us to the other.

'So what the hell are you worried about?' he said. 'With the survival kits you have in those bags and *all* the money you have left, you two should be able to make it to China!'

I didn't think he was right about that and told him so.

'China is closed.'

After leaving Paul, we booked in at the cheap Sultan Ahmet Hotel, also on Divan Yolu. It was clean, friendly and a stone's throw from the Pudding Shop, which meant that we were able to drop in several times a day. Every time we did, I asked if anyone was going east. But those going east had all either gone or hadn't arrived yet. We scoured the notice board on the wall, ignoring anything yellow with age.

Rosie from Manchester wanted Denis to know that she'd be back from India in May 1969 [she was running late]. Hans and Gabi, parked behind the Blue Mosque in a 'clapped-out ambulance', were offering two seats to Stuttgart for $7.50 each. 'Jules' could fix you up with a bum student card or passport, or buy your unsigned travellers' cheques for half face value. You could sleep free in Sikh temples in Punjab. You could sponge off a Buddhist if you were down on your luck. They did a good buffalo steak in the Star Restaurant in Kathmandu: all you had to do was get there. Watch out for Dodgy Ali who sold opium from Afghanistan and hash from Pakistan on the corner of Tahvukhane Sok. Be careful at night in the cobbled alleys behind the Spice Bazaar. Don't wear a ring or someone might chop your finger off. Belly dancing was good on the far side of the Golden Horn. John Lennon might show up at the next full moon party in Goa. It wasn't worth hitchhiking in Asia: public transport was dirt cheap; it was safer and often saved a night's accommodation.

Down at the bottom of the board, Hanna from Copenhagen wanted to know 'how the fuck am I going to get home after losing my passport and money'. (Some heartless bastard had scribbled below: 'Swap your arse for a camel.') But nobody was going to India. Eventually I stuck my own note on the board: 'Going east anybody? Hoping to leave on Friday 13th March 1970.'

Maybe I should've picked a more auspicious day.

Between visits to the Pudding Shop,[10] the first Irish overland expedition to India spent its final days scaling the hills and lanes of the old quarter of Istanbul. It called twice at the Blue Mosque: the first time to see it; the second to verify the relative lack of blueness in the 16th century Iznik tiles that coated the interior

'You know what?' the Tony side said. 'We'll just have to write a complaint to the Mufti of Istanbul.'

At Ayasofya, we stood under the dome of what was, for a thousand

---

[10] In later years the Pudding Shop would undergo the scourge of gentrification. Today it still stands on a greatly regenerated Divan Yolu, proclaiming itself 'the world famous'. Inside, polished wooden tables are served by waiters in waistcoats and ties, behind whom are to be found a few old black and white blown-up photos of the café's heyday when it served as the Istanbul base of the hippie trail. It's a sad soulless place for old wanderers.

years, the largest cathedral in the world and the religious centre of the Eastern Orthodox Church until Mehmet II took the city on behalf of the Ottoman Turks. In an incredible military operation, the Turks dragged seventy ships overland on a road of greased logs from the Bosphorus to the Golden Horn to circumvent the Byzantine harbour defences, and deployed the biggest cannon ever seen against the city's walls. After a siege of fifty-four days, they breached the walls on May 29th 1453 and the Ottoman army entered in an orgy of plunder, rape and massacre. The last Byzantine Emperor, Constantine XI, died fighting in the streets. Mehmet the Conqueror then rode to the great Byzantine cathedral, cleared it of relics, said a prayer and declared it a mosque.

A short walk from Ayasofya, and we were at Yerebatan Saray Sarnıçi, the Sunken Palace Cistern. Built in the 6th century, the underground chamber was capable of holding 80,000 cubic metres of water. Its arched brick ceilings were supported by 336 columns, nine metres high and arranged in twelve rows. One column was engraved with a symbolic hen's eye and tears, remembering the hundreds of slaves who died during construction. Carved and engraved out of various types of marble and granite, the majority of the columns were believed to have been recycled from the ruins of older buildings and brought to Constantinople from various parts of the Byzantine empire.

In some of the older streets we found remnants of Ottoman-era wooden houses, two and three storeys tall, with magnificent protruding bays and clear views to the moored ships that dotted the Sea of Marmara. A woman in one of those houses changed a $12 money draft I'd received from home as a birthday present after the banks of Istanbul told me that, in order to change it, they'd have to send it to America!

We spent a day at the Grand Bazaar, eating kebabs and drinking sweet black tea from dainty tulip-shaped glasses held by the rim. After each tea we were offered the hubble-bubble. Some guy who had a brother in Germany wanted to sell me the carpet on his back. Someone else had onyx eggs for sale. A man shot past with a tray of tea balanced at forty-five degrees. We were dragged into shops to view chaotic congestions of treasure and bling. In one I was tempted by a ceramic plaque with a quote from a 1934 speech by Mustafa Kemal Atatürk. Atatürk (Father of the Turks), commanded the Turkish forces who defeated the Allies at Gallipoli, and later led the secular revolution that created modern Turkey from the shattered remains of the Ottaman Empire. As the most revered man in the land, he stared down from public spaces all over Istanbul, including the Pudding Shop. What Atatürk had to say related to the senseless slaughter at Gallipoli:

*'Those heroes that shed their blood and lost their lives... You are now lying in the soil of a friendly country. Therefore rest in peace. There is no difference between the Johnnies and the Mehmets to us where they lie side by side now here in this country of ours... you, the mothers, who sent their sons from faraway countries, wipe away your tears; your sons are now lying in our bosom and are in peace. After having lost their lives on this land, they have become our sons as well.'*

Even at nineteen I thought it a remarkable sentiment from a commander who'd lost more than 80,000 men to Allied guns at Gallipoli.

At night, between electricity blackouts, we'd peramble up and down Divan Yolu and its surrounding streets to sniff the breeze and eat from smoky stalls that sold kebabs, chestnuts, roasted corn, pickled vegetables, soft drinks, hot tea and full meals produced on three-wheeled handcarts complete with cooking fires. We'd skite around the man who was selling the hash. Tony was for asking if he was Dodgy Ali but he looked like a lad who'd give you a smack in the teeth.

Alternatively we'd meander down Alemdar Avenue, along the outer walls of Topkapi Palace, and continue to the waters of the Golden Horn. Immediately east of the Galata Bridge we'd stop for fish sandwiches, prepared on small curved boats bobbing against the quay wall, by fishermen who spat in the face of fortune. Throwing down the gauntlet, they first lit fires in shallow steel boxes on the floors of their boats. As if that wasn't enough, they added pans of sizzling oil on which the fish were fried. Every now and again the pans would burst into flame, threatening to engulf the wooden boats, but not a bother was raised in men like that. After sandwiches, we'd stroll across the Galata Bridge, a floating wonder (long since replaced) that caused the moored ferries and white ships, and the skyline of domes and minarets, to heave and sway; and we'd shoot the dizzy breeze with the anglers who hauled on huge bending rods along the entire length of the bridge.

Then the times ran out and it was our last night in the city.

## Chapter 11

On our way home we had given a hand to two men who were trying to force a massive roll of paper onto the kerb and through a doorway. In gratitude, they'd invited us in to the brightly lit printing works of *Sabah*, where the presses were hammering out the morning's edition. We were given thick black coffee and everybody thanked everybody else. Afterwards, we sat in our room at the Sultan Ahmet and made a pact: in a few years time we'd come back again, this time with Cora and Tony's girlfriend - whoever she was - and we'd all go east together.

'Ciarán boy,' Tony said, 'life is long. There's always another day.'

But he was wrong on both counts. Life is short and that other day would never come. Neither of us could've guessed that, although we'd remain the closest of friends, we'd never travel together again.

In the morning I had some visa photographs taken by a local photographer. We both then went to the Iranian Consulate where I presented them along with my application for a visa. I wanted multiple-entry but was informed that this wasn't available to Irish nationals. However, the Consul had a soft spot for Ireland.

'Perhaps we can bend the rules,' he said. 'Come again tomorrow.'

Back at the Sultan Ahmet I took a room for one. We sat and had a Coke and made small talk as the distance of leaving ate all the space in the room.

An hour later we walked to the bus stop for Edirne and didn't say a lot. From a café wall, Atatürk smiled down on us. An old man in an overcoat and wool hat wanted to take our picture. His camera was a wooden box on a wooden tripod, with a lens poking from the front.

'No thanks,' I said. 'No money.'

'Tell him you're on your way to India too,' Tony said. 'See what he makes of that.'

There wasn't much time for goodbyes. There wasn't much mood for goodbyes. We just shook hands and wished one another a safe journey.

'See you in Maidenhead,' I said. 'Good luck with the hitchhiking.'

'Ciarán boy,' Tony said, 'I'll be waiting. And if you see that Mir of Hunza on your way through Pakistan say hello for me. Tell him O'Connor will call in person next time.'

He boarded the bus, the doors closed and he was gone. And I was suddenly left standing at a very empty bus stop in a city full of strangers.

# The Pudding Shop

 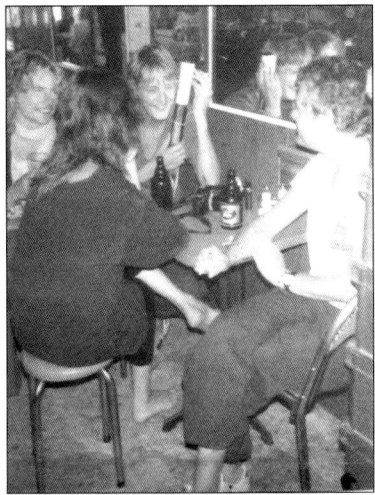

*Young travellers in the Pudding Shop, Istanbul*

# THE ONLY IRISHMAN IN KABUL

*'Twenty years from now you will be more disappointed by the things you didn't do than by the ones you did...'*

Mark Twain (1835-1910)

*The author, village stop in Afghanistan, March 1970*

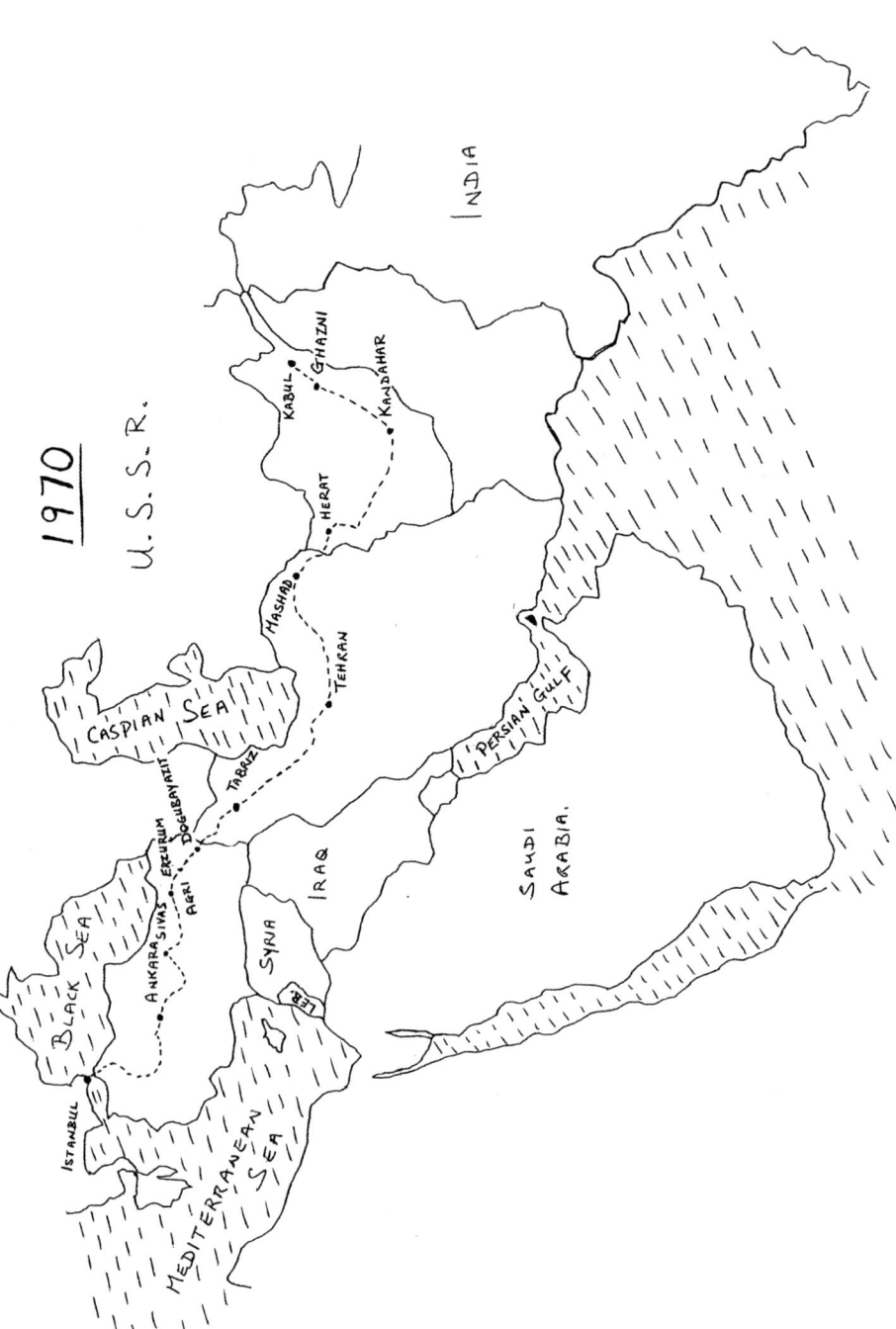

# Chapter 12

## The Erzurum Express

More than half a mile wide, the Bosphorus connects the Sea of Marmara and the Black Sea, separating Europe from Asia.

Its name (the cow-crossing) comes from the story of Io, daughter of the river god Inachus. When Zeus, god of the sky, began to get loose with Io, his wife Hera became suspicious and followed him to Earth. With the wind up him, Zeus panicked and turned Io into a heifer. Hera, however, was wise to that. She took the heifer to Olympus and placed it under the guard of the monster, Argus, who had a hundred eyes and never closed them all at once.

Perplexed by this, Zeus asked his son, Hermes, to go and free Io. Hermes, god of eloquence and commerce and patron of travellers and thieves, grabbed his winged sandals and magic wand and set off for Olympus. There he spun Argus a long-winded tale that sent half the monster's eyes to sleep. He then shook opium poppies over the other half, lopped off Argus's head, and rescued Io. When Hera found out she flew into a rage, flung Argus's eyes into the tail of the peacock and sent a vicious gadfly to torment Io. Chased by the gadfly, Io charged madly from country to country until Zeus caught up with her in Egypt and turned her back into a woman again[11]. She was spotted crossing the Bosphorus on her way to Anatolia.

Further west at the Hellespont, the strait between the Aegean Sea and the Sea of Marmara, Alexander the Great crossed into Anatolia in 334 BC. At the age of twenty-one he'd arrived with his boyfriend, Hephaestion, and an army of 35,000 Macedonians and Greeks with the goal of liberating the Greek cities of Anatolia and conquering the Persian Empire. A hundred kilometres west of Ankara, he came upon the mysterious Gordion Knot, tied by the Phrygian king to fix a yoke to his ox-cart. An oracle had foretold that whoever undid this knot would be lord of Asia. Alexander sliced through it with a single blow of his sword. Within three years he had conquered the Persian Empire.

Yours truly crossed the Bosphorus to Üsküdar on the afternoon of Friday March 13th 1970, and was thinking neither of Io nor

---

[11] An alternative Irish view has her going to Ireland and settling in Mullingar.

## Chapter 12

Alexander. Very aware of being the only non-Turkish person on the ferry, I was thinking of what Urk had said back in Brindisi: 'Only crazy people travel alone in Orient.'

From the days spent in Istanbul, I knew that there were real threats. Disease. Bandits. Wild terrain. Scorpions. Snakes. Crazy roads. Mad accidents. The horror stories that do for travellers what ghost stories do for children were up a notch at the Pudding Shop. *But if you worried about stuff like that*, my hero-self reasoned, *you'd stay under the bed*. None the less, people knew people who had died in Asia. I was also very conscious that I didn't have enough money, although the consequences of running out were mitigated a little by the irrational belief that, no matter what, I could make my way home again. With hindsight, it was like walking out onto a frozen lake with no idea of the strength of the ice. For everything to work, luck would need to hold on many fronts.

Streaming out from the old city for the 15-minute ride to Asia, I was looking down at shoals of pulsing jellyfish and already regretting an earlier impetuosity. When I went to collect the Iranian visa, I met two English guys who were also planning to leave for Asia in the afternoon. But they first wanted to buy student cards on the black market. Back at the Pudding Shop they were told they'd have to wait until the morrow. It was too much for me: the mind was set on leaving.

At one o'clock, as the vehicles[12] and passengers streamed off on the Asian side under the minarets of the Mihrimah Sultan Mosque, my regrets were compounded by the gaping stares of passers-by. And children who ran away. When I began to ask for directions to the railway station I realised that pretty much nobody spoke a word of English. Beyond *teşekkür ederim* (thank you), I didn't speak a word of Turkish.

'Train station?' I asked a passer-by. He looked shocked

'Estacion,' I tried on the next. 'La gare des trains.'

It was a waste of time. Of those who didn't flee, none understood my efforts. I tried every variation of 'train' and 'station' that I could conjure up, but to no avail. Eventually, in desperation, I confronted a kebab man, blocking his way with a shrill 'Choo-choo!' and two arms pumping like pistons. At first he backed off as if assailed by an imbecile. Then he saw that I was actually a communication wizard.

---

[12] There were no bridges across the Bosphorus in 1970.

'Haydarpasa,' he said and pointed south.

I complimented myself and set off along the seashore for the one-hour walk to the first railway station in Asia. Coots smiled from the water. A cormorant with outstretched wings said *how ya doin'* from the end of a rickety wooden wharf. Starlings sang the Beatles' *Michelle*, my favourite tune. A crow winked. The sun danced in the sky. Ferries glided by, gleefully tossing their wash at the fishing boats bobbing on the silver sheen of the Bosphorus.

I stopped to view what I assumed to be a palace. I learned later that it was the old Barrack Hospital of Scutari where Florence Nightingale was based during the Crimean War. Her lamp was said to still reside there.

\* \* \*

Jutting out into the the Bosphorus on reclaimed land, Haydarpasa Station stood as a reminder of the grandiose Berlin-Baghdad railway scheme, part of the German Empire's strategic Drang nach Osten - 'Drive to the East' - of the late 19th and early 20th centuries. Designed by architects Otto Ritter and Helmuth Conu, the station was completed in 1909 and presented to Sultan Mehmed V as a gift from Kaiser Bill. Standing on eleven hundred wooden piles, each twenty-one metres long and driven into the mushy shore by steam hammer, Haydarpasa was staggering in size and décor.

From an adjacent quay, flights of marble steps led up to great polished wooden doors set among stained-glass windows and a massive facade of yellow sandstone flanked by turrets with conical roofs. This was further augmented by balconies, moulded cornices and a crest-like central clock tower. The interior walls, pillars, arches and huge vaulted ceilings were painted in trailing foliage garlands. Beyond the station building the railyard was 200 metres wide and packed with trains and shunting carriages. The platforms ran forever.

On the afternoon of March 13th 1970 it was a noisy and crowded place where I had to battle to the ticket desk to buy my third-class ticket for the 41-hour journey to Erzurum in eastern Turkey. Ticket in pocket, I then took myself off into a corner. With seven hours to wait for the night train, I sat down on the marble floor against one of the massive columns that supported the station arches to watch the passing parade. I was particularly fascinated by a group of women in black veils that covered all but their eyes, who'd been in the Erzurum queue. However, biter bitten. No sooner had I

## Chapter 12

settled than a crowd began to muster, a deep semicircle of jostling faces that gradually pressed in to stare at *me* until I began to fear being pancaked in a catastrophic humanslide. I tried smiling. I tried nonchalance. I feigned boredom. I tried shooing them away. But the crowd simply got bigger. Seven hours of this was going to be tough.

'*Effendi! Effendi!* You come.' a gruff voice called. I turned to my left to find a big man with a square chin and cropped hair on his toes on the outer edge of the crowd. When I couldn't extract myself from the wall, he pulled a pistol from inside his coat, waved it in the air and scattered my admirers with a roar. My saviour was a plainclothes cop who led me to the station waiting room.

'You careful,' he said as he cleared a space for me on one of the benches. 'Turkish man is bad man.' This was either a load of baloney or true. Either way it was unnerving.

'But, on the train?' I asked. 'Is it OK on the train?'

'You careful,' he said. 'You one person. Maybe you sleep and you have danger.'

It was a long day of skirmishing thoughts on that bench. Looking out at the ferries and the smoke they belched into the sky, I mulled over my retreat options; but eventually at ten to nine the Erzurum Express was ready for boarding and I decided to take a chance. I left the waiting room and pushed my way out to what had become an arena of chaos. Throngs of people were hauling cases, boxes and massive stitched bales along the platforms. Others, half shrouded in the drifting smoke of a steam engine, were dragging similar loads across the tracks. Trains were being stoked and topped up with water. Passengers were forcing their way onto carriages while others were simultaneously forcing their way off. Porters were bulldozing overloaded handcarts through the crush. It didn't look like any place in which I could ever hope to board a train. But I was wrong. By allowing myself to be swept along, I was carried down a platform, through the door of my train and down the corridor a short distance before two powerful arms yanked me sideways into a compartment.

As soon as I was through the sliding door, it was slammed shut.

*Shit*, I thought, *I've been kidnapped!* I could see the headlines: *The Gentleman Vanishes* or *Murder On The Erzurum Express*. However, when I regained composure I recognised three fellow sufferers from the hours in the waiting room - two men in their late twenties and a women of about fifty. We'd been exchanging foolish smiles all day. Now we were all nodding and doing it again. The woman was sitting by one of the windows. The man with the powerful arms had his boots firmly against the handle of the door. I was privileged. Nobody else was getting in. The woman indicated that I should take the second window seat.

'*Teşekkür ederim*,' said I. I plonked myself down on the wooden bench with my pack beside me. *Now what?*

'Erzurum?' the man with the powerful arms asked. I nodded. He smiled and pointed at himself and the others. 'Erzurum,' he said. Fierce nodding by all three.

'*Deutschland?*'

I shook my head. The conversation dried up while the big lad dredged for the next topic. It was going to be a long ride.

Over the course of the coming hour I managed to learn that my companions were mother and sons. They lived in a village to the south of Erzurum and the one who had grabbed me - Ismet - had just come back from Germany where he'd been working for a year. The other brother, Suleyman, and their mother, Fareeda, had come from the east to give Ismet a hand in offloading some of those German marks in the alleys of the Grand Bazaar. The spoils were straining the luggage racks.

Ismet and Suleyman were two versions of the same pea: harsh black strokes of moustaches, bushy black eyebrows, sharp noses, tobacco-stained teeth, shabby grey suits with floppy lapels, and cloth caps. But, whereas Ismet was built like Tarzan, Suleyman could have done with a feed. I couldn't help wonder if there was some connection between that state of affairs and the mighty frame of Fareeda.

Some people would say they'd eat a horse. Fareeda had clearly done so just before arriving in Haydarpasa. Dressed in baggy pantaloons, sweater, jacket and yashmak, with a strand of greying hair hanging down over one eye, she could easily have passed for herself and her twin sister. My thought on this was that I wouldn't fancy stretching my hand in any competiton for dinner; and that Ismet, away for a year with no Fareeda grabbing at the grub, had managed to get his hands on bigger fare.

Clearly in charge, the big woman fired exhausting questions at me through her offspring and was in no way discouraged by my not understanding a word. Ismet would smile encouragingly. Suleyman would shrug his shoulders. Finally, at ten o'clock on

## Chapter 12

the nail, the train lurched forward and in a rip of whistle, we slid out of magnificent Haydarpasa. Fareeda spoke and Ismet's boots were removed from the door. We were safe. Staring out at the dark receding city as the train rocked gently into outer Asia, my heart did a conga drum. *This is it boy*, it said. Then Fareeda exploded from her seat and I thought I was dead.

One minute she was sitting there. The next she was on her feet, teetering my way like a disaster zone. She hadn't planned it that way. Her initial move was towards the bag of food that lay on the rack above Suleyman's head. But the train had lurched again and she was propelled my way by an acceleration that I later learned was due to the vector sum of non-gravitational forces acting on an object free to move. In other words she was an out-of-control inverted pyramid heading my way with a g-force of 5.3. You have no idea how terrifying such a sight can be. Nor the damage of such an impact.

I threw up both hands but to no avail. When Fareeda struck it was like being hit by a juggernaut. I went down in a suffocating heap. Then *she* panicked - that was a joke! - and started jabbing her fingers in my ears and eyes. Beyond the darkness I could hear the commotion as Ismet and Suleyman dealt with the shock and tried to haul their mother off the unlucky visitor to their country. It took some time and to be quite honest, I didn't expect to surface with all the bits attached. Eventually, however, light reappeared and I was able to readjust my squashed head and check to see if I could still wriggle my toes. There followed great expressions of sorrow and many more smiles. Suleyman calmed the mother. The mother smoothed her hair into place beneath the yashmak. Ismet pulled down the bag of food and I was showered for the next hour with boiled eggs, goat's cheese, bread, bananas, black coffee and Turkish cigarettes. Fareeda then pulled out a blanket and rolled herself along most of the far seat, leaving barely enough room for Suleyman who'd now been posted on the door. Soon reduced to a whistling nasal symphony, the big woman spread a relative peace over the compartment and the two boys began to doze.

For another hour I stared out the window through a space I'd cleared in the fogged glass. In the creaking and swaying of the carriage, I mostly saw only the reflections of my three pals; but every now and then, the darkness would be starred by the distant lights of homes and villages. Or we'd suddenly plough into cities, or small towns with obscure stations, and the train would jar to an unsteady halt, a signal for the boots of Fareeda's sons. No matter how many people banged on our door as they thumped cases, boxes and sacks along the corridor the defences never faltered. Even the yelling station vendors who beat their way onto the train with sandwiches, eggs, tea, sweets and soft drinks had no mission at our door.

Eventually I put my pack between my knees and drifted off into a semi-sleep, my head buried in the canvas and the seat of my jeans on fire from the heating pipes that ran under the wooden benches. Even with the sleeping bag as a buffer I was cooked ham.

\* \* \*

I woke at six to the clicking wheels of the train and the awful sight of Fareeda on her feet again. Outside, yellow light danced along a row of treeless hills, casting long shadows in the folds that shunned the rising sun. Across a dry watercourse, a flock of small birds rose in a heart formation. A horseman rode by in the distance. Fareeda got out the food. I pulled out a bag of fruit. We all had breakfast.

Four hours later the train pulled into Ankara and stopped for a breather. Twenty minutes into its stay, the corridor filled with commotion. Suleyman opened our door, then beckoned. A tall guy with blond Medusa locks and a square pack from which hung a portable typewriter was pushing his way up the train. Thin and bony, he was muffed up in boots, jeans and a once-white sheepskin jacket. Behind him came a dark-haired woman in a long black wrinkled coat, red shirt and denims, carrying a bedroll. They were being followed through the train by a group of jostling jeering men, the result of an encounter that began on the platform where the woman's good looks had attracted the wrong attention.

'In here!' I shouted. I was the man at the gates of the Alamo.

'Shit!' the guy said. 'It's Doctor Livingstone!' That was an exaggeration. However, they swept forward and in through the door, promptly slammed shut by Suleyman. I was delighted. Two Americans in their early twenties. Kindred spirits. People who spoke English. A small familiar on the Erzurum Express. I helped them squeeze their bags into the few spaces not occupied by Fareeda's swag.

'Are you from *Ireland?*' the woman asked once they'd settled and the mob outside had dispersed.

'I am,' I said and outlined the sad end of the Irish expedition.

'Gee,' she said. 'You guys sound like you took the tough way. You'd probably qualify for the Nobel Prize for effort.'

## Chapter 12

I have to admit, I hadn't thought about it like that.

'Where are you going?' I asked.

'Kabul,' the guy said.

'Me too - well, India actually - but Kabul will do for a start. Maybe we could travel together.'

'That would be cool,' the woman said. 'But is India not a long way on your sort-of reduced budget?'

'I'm going to sell my passport in Delhi...' I explained.

'That's a nifty plan,' the guy said. 'Put it there.' he reached out to shake the hand of the man with the nifty plan. 'I'm Max,' he said. 'Benjamin C. Witting the third to be precise, but call me Max. And this is Sharon.'

'Would that be Max the third?' I asked.

'Yeah,' Max said. 'Ha-ha! That's a good one.'

Max the third came from Adelphi in Maryland, named after a mill established in 1796 along the northwest branch of the Anacostia River. He spoke loud and funny but to a Turk he might've just sounded loud.

'Where in Ireland are you from?' he wanted to know.

'Cork,' I said. 'In the south.'

'Cork? You ever heard of Mother Jones?'

'No,' I had to admit.

'She was from Cork.'

'Was she?'

'Yeah man, she sure was. She used to be a schoolteacher in Memphis, Tennessee.'

'Still never heard of her.'

'When her husband and children died of yellow fever she moved to Chicago and set up a dressmaking business. Then she lost the lot in the Great Chicago Fire of 1871. After that she began to work for the Mine Workers Union, helping miners and their families organise against the mine owners. In 1902, when she was sixty-five, she was being tried for ignoring an injunction banning meetings by striking miners, when the district attorney called her "the most dangerous woman in America. She crooks her finger" he said, "and 20,000 contented men lie down."

'In 1903 she organized the Children's March from Philadelphia to the home of Roosevelt in New York to protest against child labour in the Pennsylvania mines and mills. Then she supported the coal miners during the Paint Creek mine war in West Virginia in 1912 and

1913, standing up in public during a shooting war between members of the Mine Workers Union and the private armies of the mines. When they brought in martial law, she was arrested and charged with conspiracy to murder and was jailed by a military court. And she spent the last years of her life with a family in Adelphi. And you never heard of Mother Jones?'

'Have you ever heard of Andy Gaw?' I asked.[13] 'He's from Cork too.' I knew I'd get him with that.

Sharon, surname Von Ostermayer, came from Berwyn, Pennsylvania, an area within the Easttown Township of Philadelphia and part of its Main Line suburbs, built, according to Max, by Philadelphia's elite. He wasn't exactly accusing Sharon of anything but he did mention 'old money' and 'multimillion-dollar stone colonial homes along the banks of the Schuylkill River'.

'Our connection is more with the Welsh,' Sharon said. 'The land that became Easttown Township used to be part of the Welsh Tract. It was promised by William Penn, the founder of the Province of Pennsylvania, to a bunch of Welsh Quakers as a place where they could speak, and conduct business, in Welsh. Although it never really took off, several Welsh place names still exist, such as Berwyn. Our other claim to fame is that our Revolutionary War hero, Mad Anthony Wayne - indeed, whose father was from Ireland - came from the western part of the township. Some of him is buried there.'

I asked the obvious question: '*Some* of him?'

'Yeah,' Sharon said. 'After the War of Independence, he died of gout during a return trip to Pennsylvania from Detroit and was buried en route. But in 1809, his son had the body dug up. Then they boiled it to get rid of any flesh that was left and two saddlebags were stuffed with as many of his bones as would fit. He - part of him anyway - was then reburied in St. David's Episcopal Church near where I live. Legend has it that half the bones got lost along the way and that his ghost can be seen once a year staggering along Route 322 looking for the rest of him.'

'We met in Crete,' Max said as if to distance himself from the ghost of Mad Anthony. 'I was walking the beach asking every chick

---

[13] Andy Gaw, a small man who suffered from the shakes, dribbled, spoke only in mumbles, and never worked a day, was Cork's most loved citizen back in 1970. As he drifted up and down Patrick Street and the Grand Parade people gave him pennies which he then recycled to passing children.

## Chapter 12

I met if she slept with strangers, namely myself. Been living in the caves down in Matala for the past five months.'

'We've hitchhiked from Istanbul,' Sharon added, 'and haven't slept for the past three nights. Hence the sunken bloodshot eyes.'

'Not worth it,' Max said. 'Too much hassle for chicks.'

An hour had passed. Fareeda was stirring ominously. From the scowls directed at Max and Sharon, she seemed to be taking umbrage at the alternative society brewing in her carriage. She raised her voice and the sons took up the cudgel. A bag of Grand Bazaar swag was accidentally dropped on Max's head. Ismet shouted Turkish abuse at Sharons' rucksack. Suleyman opened the door to the crowd that had gathered again outside. The crowd jeered. Suleyman closed the door again. Another bag was dropped on Max's head.

'You know what?' Max said in the end. 'Peace and love, man. But we're outta here.'

He and Sharon gathered up their packs. Ismet curtsied and Suleyman opened the door. I rose to follow but Fareeda blocked my way: I was still the privileged one, the one on whom angels smiled, the one who walked in the light.

'We'll catch up in Erzurum,' Sharon said.

I felt empty. Staring out at the grey and brown mountains, void and arid as a desert, I pondered the tyranny of courtesy. *I should've gone*, I said to myself, *with the yankee-doodles*.

Finally at about five o'clock the Holy Ghost floated in through an open crack in the window, landed on my shoulder, reminded me that I was named after two Irish saints, and a hermit who lived in the 5th century, and said: *Courtesy is a load of oul' rashers. Follow me.*

I lifted my pack, weathered Fareeda's drumbeats of love, said goodbye to herself and her sons, and went in search of Max and Sharon.

I found them holed up in the corridor between the last carriage and the rear engine, still being harassed and suffering the abominable stench of the hole-in-the-floor toilets which had been going downhill since Üsküdar.

'Man,' Max said. 'Are we glad to see you. We need all the reinforcements we can get.'

We chased the harassers back into the last carriage and secured the door. Some time around ten, we reckoned it was safe to spread our sleeping bags in the narrow space. Three hours later I opened my eyes to find the ceiling replaced by an overhang of Turkish men. Rising like a vengeful Cerberus, I spread my arms, glared Cork-fashion-narrow-eyes, and hustled the enemy back behind the carriage door. I then stood, back to the door, while America slept. The only dropping of the guard was a quick nip to the loo, now a toxic danger zone; but in that brief interlude three men breached the defences. By the time I reappeared one was groping the unconscious Sharon.

They'd crossed the wrong man. Cork-fashion-narrow-eyes again, and they were running for their lives.

Shortly after five that morning a sympathetic conductor, armed with a pistol, reached the end of his train and found us in the toilet fumes. He shook Max and Sharon awake and told us to follow him. Two carriages down, he ordered a Kurdish family of five to take their boots from the door and let us in.

\* \* \*

As soon as the dining car opened, we went for coffee and discovered three other travellers on the train. To my great amazement, two were the Englishmen I'd met at the Iranian Consulate in Istanbul. Tom Smith, a low-sized guy with a mop of hair that fell to his eyebrows, and stout, easy-going Bill Oakes of sandy hair and pale tawny moustache were both from Leeds. On their second journey to India, they had left on the same train after all. They would pick up their bum student cards in Kabul. The third guy was a long-haired, happy-go-lucky bearded American - 'just Zigg' - who saw fun in everything on account of him having escaped from his life as an accountant. I remember little more background apart from the fact that they were determined guys who belonged to those times. Regretfully, I didn't take enough notes because - hey - how could I forget those who shared that trail when the fire was in our souls.

'We've been looking out for you for thirty-six hours,' Tom said. 'Where the hell have you been?'

I explained the Fareeda situation. Outside, the sun rose over the yellow steppes of eastern Anatolia as we slowed down into a siding. Five minutes later we were hit broadside by a roaring blast of air as one of the massive, black, billowing steam trains of the Turkish Railways thundered by in a masterpiece of timing that they would never, ever want to get wrong.

Forty-one hours after leaving Üsküdar our little band was still in the dining car when we reached the end of the line at Erzurum. It was three in the afternoon. From here, we'd have to travel on by road.

## Chapter 12

Max, Sharon and I went back to our Kurdish friends to retrieve our bags. But trust - or stupidity - had cost me a rifled pack. A fancy Parker pen, my Instamatic camera and half the photos I'd taken to date were gone. While the family shrugged and gazed in wonder at how a cat burglar must've come up through the floor, I was a boiling cauldron. Pen and camera were parting gifts from Cora. I later wrote a long considered piece in my diary about bastards, tokens of love and things that were priceless. With time, however, it lost its voltage and balance.

In Erzurum station, we were joined by Gunter Effinger, a Swiss medical student also going to Kabul. Thin and jaunty with a dark-blue jaw and collar-length hair, Gunter was the original silent partner. He hardly ever spoke. Even when his camera was later stolen, he simply shrugged. After scooping Gunter into the gang, we checked our new bearings on this far side of Turkey.

Set in a great bowl at almost 2,000 metres and ringed by snow-covered mountains, Erzurum was a city of contrasts: broad central avenues of six- to eight-storey blocks and grubby back streets with cramped, bleak shacks. Horse carts and bullock carts and the odd fancy car from Germany. There were contrasts too in how we were received by passers-by: some were friendly; others threw looks that would have salted Lot's wife if she hadn't already been done.

'The magnificent seven,' Zigg laughed, leading the way along the pavements of Erzurum looking for somewhere to stay, and a cheap kebab.

'If our president could see me now,' Max said, 'he'd be a proud fuckin' man.'

No harm to Max, but I had my doubts.

# Chapter 13
## Viktor

'Ha!' he bellowed as he boarded the bus and spotted the rest of us. 'This is a FUCKING place! Two days I have been trying to hitchhike to Iran and every time I get picked up by these fucking men. They want money or sex. So every time I get out and have to walk back here. Where is this bus going?'

'Agri,' Tom said.

'Good. Then I will join you. I go to Kabul.'

And so entered Viktor Strommler, 21-year-old psychology student and part-time disc jockey on a break from his studies in Munich, in what was then West Germany. In Erzurum bus station, a place of hustle and appalling toilets, he looked like a guy going to a dance. While the rest of us were in a state of general disrepair, he appeared in a dazzling blue shirt, grey creased trousers, navy reefer jacket with shiny brass buttons, tan suede shoes, and a cherubic face framed in blond shoulder-length hair, coiffed to perfection. As soon as he sat down, he took off his shoes and dabbed some talc between his toes. He then opened his shirt and sprayed his underarms with deodorant.

'Man,' Max said, 'did you just step out of the Erzurum Boutique?'

'For that,' Viktor said, 'you will have to buy me vodka.'

Dandy as Viktor was, he and I became instant friends. This was not unconnected to the two hours it took to reach Agri, during which he shared with me his take on life. It began with the assertion that, one day, governments would be run by dope-smoking hippies with big hearts, that his macrobiotic grandfather would find a cure for death in the meadows of the Bavarian Alps, and that wise women of a certain size, lost deep in the forests of the Amazon, would burst forth to enlighten the regular medical profession with their ability to swing an axe.

'They will chop their fucking heads off,' was the belief here.

'You know something?' he said. 'If you can squeeze under a big cupboard, you can find many good things in your head.[14] You can separate yin from yang.'

---

[14] Some years later mutual friends of ours would come home one night to their London flat to find Viktor in exactly such a position, but unable to extricate himself. The sideboard had to be lifted off.

'What?' I said. 'Yin? Yang?'

'Irish,' he admonished. 'You don't know this?' I felt like someone who'd neglected his homework. 'It is an old Chinese philosophy. Everything in the universe is yin or yang. But nothing is complete yin or yang. For example, when the day becomes the night, it is yang changing to yin. Every part of the body also has some yin and some yang. The liver is mostly yang; the kidneys are yin. Therefore you must find the best foods for each part and keep everything in balance. Sometimes you can feel too yin: maybe you have a cold or you are feeling tired or depressed. Then you must become more yang. You must do exercise, wear bright colours, eat potatoes and fish. If you feel too yang - maybe you are stressed or angry, or your girlfriend has run away - you must meditate, light candles, eat fruit salad, wear light colours, listen to the birds. Then you have yin-yang balance again.'

These views were of interest to me. I was keen to bring back to Ireland something that might update Catholicism.

'Did the Chinese write this down?' I asked. 'Or are you kind-of making it up?'

'A-a-aargh,' he growled. 'You think I am the founder of Taoism?'

As Viktor rattled on, I wrote down as much as I could with a view to looking into it at some later date. Meanwhile the road to Agri, barely wide enough for a single vehicle, carved its way across a wide plateau, hemmed in north and south by snow-topped mountains. It was a landscape that changed like the ebb and flow of a tide.

Where the mountains closed in, we were dwarfed by towering massifs or funneled through narrow gorges with signs that warned of falling rock. In the less inhospitable parts of the steppes, villages of stone and mud brick would occasionally rise from the earth. Surrounding them were patchwork fields where stooped men broke the soil with heavy, ox-drawn wooden ploughs. Women planted crops and drew water from bore wells. Children tended flocks of sheep and goats. Smoke curled up from holes in flat adobe roofs and wafted across the road. Beside each house, a cone-shaped heap of dried dung provided the cooking fuel. Traffic was sparse, mostly flatcarts pulled by horses and bullocks. On a bend on one of the passes, a brown bear stood beside the road in the snow.

'Does somebody own him?' I asked. Zigg looked at me like I was five-eighths stupid.

'I guess you don't have them in Ireland...Huh?'

Indignant, I continued to search for the owner.

When we reached Agri, a town composed largely of stone or mud huts and dirt streets, we discovered that the regular buses to the border were finished for the day. However, we could catch a dolmus (private minibus). While gathering this information, Tom and I had to slap a wave of picking hands from the many pockets of our combat jackets.

'You must keeep a rat in every pocket,' Viktor advised.

Treacherous ice-packed roads and a driver who gave no quarter brought us to Dogubayazit, a shabby border town made up of a few central, tree-lined streets and scattered stone and adobe shacks that spread out on all sides like bunkers. Horse-drawn carts trotted the byways. Large stacks of cut trees sat at corners to provide firewood for the citizens. The women of the town were draped in long Hessian-type dresses and heavy coats, or the black chadors that had crossed the border from Iran.

I later learned that, seven years earlier in this very town, Waterford-born Dervla Murphy - cycling towards India at the time - had fired a .25 bullet through a hotel ceiling when she was accosted in her room in the middle of the night by a scantily dressed Kurd. The gunshot, apparently, caused not a stir.

After dropping most of our fellow passengers, the bus continued into a bleak white land of bare hills and stunted trees, dominated to the north by the 5,165-metre twin peaks of Mount Ararat. Late in the afternoon, we were dumped in packed snow at an isolated frontier post over which fluttered the Turkish flag. Husky-type dogs and armed soldiers watched as we negotiated Customs and Immigration and walked across the border into Iran.

\* \* \*

We were greeted by laughing officials. They stamped our passports, joked about the freezing temperatures, welcomed us to Iran, advised us to put our watches forward by one and a half hours, and paid little heed to our packs. We shared cigarettes and they gave us glasses of hot sugary tea, brewed under a gigantic poster of the Shah of Iran, his wife and their son. Max in his Afghan jacket and Tom in his combat jacket, now augmented by a woollen hat pulled down over his ears, were discussing the Shah.

'He looks like a bit of a ponce,' Max said. 'He's got a diamond tiara on his head.'

'Careful,' Tom warned. 'Or you'll find yourself in front of a firing squad.'

## Chapter 13

'No shit?' Max said.

'No shit,' Tom echoed. 'The secret police are everywhere. They drag people off if they suspect that they're even thinking bad about the Shah. They'd drill holes through your fingernails and pull out your teeth.'

That conversation sorted and formalities taken care of, we asked about buses.

'No bus today,' one of the customs officers said. 'Bus in the morning.'

'Vodka,' Viktor said. 'You have some here?' The officials laughed. Viktor said nothing but took this as a sign. 'They are hiding it,' he confided.

'Peace, man,' Zigg said to all the Customs people.

We left customs and stepped back out into the bitter wind that howled down from Ararat onto the 2,600-metre border post. To the east, the mountain snows were washed in silver light, filling us with a buoyant energy. Joking and laughing, we set off from the top of the pass.

'Everybody STOP!' Viktor shouted from the rear. He took a photograph. I have it still: an image of freedom and devil-may-care, and carefree young ragtags on the cutting cusp of life.

We decided to walk two kilometers down the mountain, out of the snow, towards the first Iranian village. Half a kilometre before the village, we made camp at the base of a large rock. Leaving Max, Sharon and Viktor to guard the packs, the other five of us continued to the village to buy food. We arrived in Bazargan, a strip of concrete, stone and adobe huts set in a flat basin and shaded by trees, in the Muslim year of 1348.

No sooner were we spotted than the children burst from the houses. Dogs barked and snapped at our heels. Sheep and goats skittered about. Men in turbans and woollen hats, and women in long, colourful dresses and shawls, sprang from the houses and tiny shops. Once our needs had been established, an older woman in a black shawl, with blue tattoos on her face, took control. She dragged us to and fro, showing us where we could buy potatoes, bread, cheese, onions and dates. The men shook our hands. The children practiced their few words of English which mostly amounted to, 'Hello mister, what is your name?'

When the crowd finally deemed that we had sufficient food and water, they warned us to be on our guard. There were bandits in the mountains. We thanked them and left the village, with all the children following us back to our rock. On the far side of Bazargan a man on horseback, his grey cloak billowing in the wind, galloped across the flats in spirals of dust, startling a pair of water buffaloes. Zigg claimed it was Lawrence of Arabia.

'Gone to rouse the bandits,' he added.

Back at the rock, Viktor was disgusted that we hadn't found vodka.

'You and me Irish,' he said, 'after eating, we go back to the border. They have vodka. They always have vodka at the border.'

I considered this reasonable and as the last light drained from the hills and our fire snapped at the frigid air spilling down from Ararat, we headed for the mountain post.

'Iran Muslim country,' they told us when we arrived. 'No alcohol.'

'In the cupboards,' Viktor said. 'You have it in the cupboards.' The border guards took it in good humour.

'Get out now,' one of them roared. 'Or we will bury you in the snow.'

Back at camp, the fire was still flickering. The three Americans were asleep, Sharon happily ensconced in Viktor's sleeping bag.

'She left all her gear in Rhodes,' I explained.

'The fucking hell!' Viktor said. Sharon got up.

As it happened, Max and I shared an identical taste in cheap Italian sleeping bags. We zipped the two together and had room for all three of us.

In the early hours I woke up to find Viktor patrolling the rock. He let out a manic chuckle and I realised he was smoking something he'd carried with him from Istanbul. I got up to keep him company.

'I watch for the bandits,' he told me. 'They will come from the mountains after they have finished eating. They will come on elephants.' Another manic chuckle, followed by a voice from the depths of Zigg's sleeping bag directly below.

'They have *nice* bandits in India.'

A few minutes later the big bearded American was also on bandit patrol.

'You know of the dacoits?' he said.

'They are living in the jungle,' Viktor said, staring into the dark. 'They can see in the night. They can levitate when the police come.'

Looking back, I do believe that, at that moment, Viktor may well have had such a being in his line of vision.

'Not quite,' Zigg said. 'When I last checked, they couldn't see in

# Chapter 13

the dark and they couldn't levitate. Mostly, the dacoits are caste-based and don't bother foreigners which is what makes them *nice* bandits. But some have ferocious reputations. And they're not shy when it comes to shooting cops. Having said that, the Indian cops aren't too shy about shooting them either.'

'Dacoits,' Viktor said. 'Dacoits make the things happen.' He then leaned forward into my face.

'Irish,' he said in a grim monotone, 'I think you have escaped from the Foreign Legion.' His eyes were periscopic in the glow of what was cupped in his hands.

I correctly guessed that Viktor and I were going to get along just fine.

In the morning the sun threw a golden sheen across the snows of Ararat and Bill swore he could see Noah's Ark. It was all hands astir as we packed in the shivering cold and made our way into Bazargan where everybody was waiting to see us catch the dawn bus to Maku. The sun crept down the mountainsides. Birds flitted between the village trees. Roosters crowed. Sheep mewled. Smoke curled from the huts. Steam billowed from the nostrils of horses and water buffaloes. Back in Ireland, it was St. Patrick's Day. When the bus drew up in the centre of the village, all the men shook our hands again. We wished them peace and love which was now being doled out at a terrific rate. The women laughed and joked among themselves. Max's Medusa locks were particularly funny.

Nobody in Bazargan had ever heard of St. Patrick.

Twenty kilometers down the mountain road and we were in Maku. Tucked into a narrow gorge, the town had been built on the site of an ancient Armenian civilization, remains of which lay folded into a ledge under a massive overhang in the cliffs that towered above the town.

Sometimes I say stupid things. Sometimes companions mistake them for sound ideas. That morning I said something like, *We could climb up there.*

'It would pass the time,' Tom said.

Several of the others agreed, although none was as exuberant as myself. Such was my haste that, half way up, I hit my head a thundering wallop on an overhanging piece of cast iron pipe and was knocked clean out. When I came to, my hair, face and jacket were covered in blood and Gunter, the *medical student*, was pouring water over my head from a rusty tin!

'Gunter,' I heard myself bleat. 'Have you never heard of fuckin' lockjaw?'

'Irish,' Viktor said, 'you should not have left the Foreign Legion.'

# Chapter 14
## Ashura

The bus to Tabriz meandered through an enormous landscape of mountains, snow and semi-desert, broken occasionally by nomad tents and barely noticeable villages sheltered by clusters of trees. In the open spaces, camels, sheep and goats grazed on sparse vegetation. Gradually, particularly in the towns, the dress of the women changed from bright wide skirts and shawls to full-length, black chadors. The mosque domes of Turkey gave way to enormous high-arched portals set in recessed doorways and flanked by twin mosaic-coated minarets.

Three hundred and ten kilometres from the border, we arrived in Tabriz. Cradled in a valley that sloped westward towards Lake Orumieh, it was flanked to the north by the red 3,750-metre Sahand Mountains, to the south by the foothills of the Eynali ranges. Its idyllic setting, however, was somewhat offset by a natural disadvantage: it was prone to regular and devastating earthquakes.

A city of gardens, carpets, art, music and literature, Tabriz was home to the largest covered bazaar in the world, once among the most important commercial centres of the old Silk Road. But when we went to wander its labyrinths, we were advised that it was closed for Ashura.

We assumed this was some kind of maintenance project.

People gathered around us. They were fascinated to find that we belonged to five separate nationalities. One older man in a skullcap told us he was Armenian and Christian, belonging to a community that had been in Tabriz since the earliest days of Christianity.

'Many Christian church here,' he said. 'Marco Polo, he come in Tabriz. He visit Christian church of Tabriz.'

He then advised that we should call at the Armenian cemetery where we would find the grave of an unlikely Iranian hero.

'American,' he said. 'He die in Constitutional Revolution of Persia.'

The story went like this.

After a popular struggle against the rule of the royal family, Shah Mozafar o-Din, was forced in 1906 to establish a Persian constitution and an elected parliament that would curb the power of the royal family. But when Mohammad Ali Mirza ascended the throne in January 1907, he reneged on the agreement. After several rows with parliament, he used his Russian-led, Persian Cossacks Brigade to bomb the parliament building in June 1908. The assembly was closed and many of the Constitutional Movement's leaders were hanged. Resistance erupted across Persia, with Tabriz as its epicentre.

When the Shah attacked in 1908, the citizens were outnumbered, outgunned and short on supplies, but they held firm. However, in the early months of 1909 the city suffered a sustained bombardment by Russian forces and their domestic allies. In late April, in an attempt to break the stranglehold that was starving the city, the Constitutionalist fighters attacked the royalist blockade. Among their ranks was Howard Baskerville of Nebraska.

Baskerville, a Presbyterian missionary, had come to Tabriz to teach at the American Memorial School. He arrived in 1907 fresh out of Princeton Theological Seminary, and was immediately swept up in the revolutionary mood of the country. When war came to Tabriz, he could have easily sought out the safety of the US Consulate, but chose instead to pick up a rifle. On April 19th 1909, nine days after his 24th birthday, he led 150 nationalist student fighters in an attack on the royalist blockade. He was killed by a single bullet through the heart. In recognition of his courage, a Persian carpet from Tabriz, into which his picture had been woven, was later presented to his mother in Nebraska and his bust was placed in Tabriz's Constitution House, the official bed of the rising.

\* \* \*

On the night bus that covered the 740 kilometres from Tabriz to Tehran we were joined by a small excitable French Canadian named Pierre, and by Andy Fidler, a 23-year-old Englishman from Warwickshire whose blond curls and granny spectacles gave him a professorial air. Andy had been on the road since February and had travelled down through Lebanon and Iraq. Back home he used to be a plasterer. 'Not a good one,' he said. 'I kept getting the shit in my eye and thought, *to hell, I'm outta here.*' Andy explained that Ashura was definitely not a maintenance project.

'We're gonna hit Tehran just in time for it. It's the big Shia festival. The whole place will be closed down for the day.'

'Big party,' Max said.

'Seriously religious, man,' Andy said. 'They have it on the 10th day of the Muharram holy month of the Islamic calendar. It

## Chapter 14

commemorates the beheading of Imam Hosain ibn Ali in the 7th century. He was the grandson of Mohammad and was killed by Caliph Yazid at the Battle of Karbala in Iraq.'

'So what happens?' Max asked.

'Dunno,' Andy said. 'But you can bet yer arse that Keith Richards won't be tuning up his geetar.'

At 4.45am on the morning of March 18th we arrived in Tehran and booked in to the dilapidated Fars Hotel for a few hours sleep. We woke up in our dormitory rooms to find the city closed down as Andy had predicted, and caught in the juxtaposition of two cultures, one spearheaded by the Shah, the other guarded by the country's mullahs.

Shah Mohammad Reza Pahlavi had come to power in 1941, following the removal by British and Soviet troops of his father who was suspected of collaborating with the Germans. The new Shah initially introduced some land redistribution and promoted literacy. He also advocated the emancipation of women and attempted to westernise Iran through his 'White Revolution', setting himself on a collision course with the mullahs.

In 1953 the Shah was ousted by the democratically elected Dr. Mohammad Mussadeq, who intended to use Iran's oil wealth to advance the lot of Iranians rather than that of US and British oil companies. But democracy was quickly overthrown when the CIA and the British MI6 engineered a coup and re-installed Pahlavi as the Shah-an-Shah (King of Kings) on the Peacock Throne. Pahlavi, who had briefly fled Iran after Mussadeq's election, now returned as a western poodle. Gradually, he put in place intense political repression to facilitate the siphoning of Iran's wealth to indigenous and foreign freebooters, and keep the angry mullahs in check. Under CIA guidance, SAVAK, the Shah's brutal secret police, was formed in 1957 and was trained primarily by Israel and the British.

Over the years, SAVAK became a law unto itself, with authority to arrest, jail and torture anyone who fell foul of it. Crimes worthy of torture and imprisonment included reading or possessing the wrong books and, according to Tom, thinking poorly of the Shah.

By 1970, the capital of the oil-rich country sported tall apartment blocks and broad avenues with shops that sold Western clothes and goods, and great cakes. The ski resorts in the Elburz Mountains, north of the city, rivalled those of the Alps. Narrow back streets simultaneously hid the poor and sheltered the old ways. Wealth and poverty sat cheek by jowl in a city of palaces and slums and beautiful mosques and religious madrassas with ornate doors and mosaics, behind which sat the mullahs. Thrumming their tables and wielding a silent power, the turbaned clerics scorned the Americanisation of their country, blatantly symbolised by the advertising billboards and Western fare that flooded the central squares. But, most damning of all were the young women with the rouged lips and flowing uncovered tresses who voted secular and strode the broad boulevards in leather boots, bell-bottoms and Satan's thigh-high skirts.

Order was still maintained, however, by visiting SAVAK terror on anyone looking for radical change (a policy responsible for the forced exile of one Ayatollah Ruhollah Khomeini, Shia mystic and Islamic revolutionary whose star was yet to rise). Yet, anyone in the centre of Tehran on the morning of March 18th 1970 would've needed little imagination to gauge the force of the Islamic hydra lying just below the surface of modernised Tehran.

Ashura, as it manifested itself on the streets, was an unnerving spectacle: thousands of men in black shirts, chanting in unison, marched under a sea of black flags and banners, while vast crowds lined the streets. Each marcher carried a T-shaped stick with several lengths of chain attached. Every so often the procession would grind to a standstill while the marchers chanted and flogged themselves, swinging the T-sticks over their shoulders and drowning all other sound with the swish of chains and the thump of steel on flesh.

An attempt on my part to take a picture with Viktor's camera brought a white-turbaned mullah in flowing brown robes racing from the crowd, a mad look in his eyes and a finger running across his throat in that unmistakeable message of love. Many's the man would've stood his ground; but, pack and all, I legged it. This, I have no doubt, impressed the women onlookers. I could hear them shouting after me and some were very beautiful indeed.

'Irish,' Viktor grinned when my heart was back to normal and I'd located the lads again, 'did you get your photograph?' He then pointed at another mullah over there. 'Hey Mr. Mullah,' he half-called. 'Is it OK if the Irish would ask one of your Iranian girls for a date?'

'Viktor,' I said. 'That is *not* fuckin' funny!' Nor was it.

Although these were the supposedly tolerant days of the Shah, even the beam of the likes of that, aimed at the almond-eyed

## Chapter 14

women lining the streets in their black chadors, would've been terrible mullah bait. And the mullahs seemed wild short of a sense of humour.

'The pity of it,' Tom lamented, 'is that these women are so beautiful.' He then expounded to us his Theory on the Comeliness of Iranian Women. 'Simple,' he said. 'The old Persian kings brought back the most beautiful women of their empires to the harems and the genes have stayed.' Unlikely, but there you go.

Feeling that we should move on, we retreated to muddy back streets of adobe houses, outside which songbirds hung in small cages and people washed their pots and pans in the open drains. In one street, where green parrots and doves rose from the pavement trees, the smell of baking bread sucked us into a deep cavern. Inside, two barefooted, bare-chested men were crouched over a glowing hole that blasted heat from the middle of the floor like the entrance to Hell. Into the hole, the sweating bakers were whacking enormous, elongated flats of unleavened dough which stuck to the domed mud interiors. Minutes later, the finished loaves were hooked out.

We bought some of the hot gritty bread, and picked up a chunk of goat's cheese and a couple of cucumbers from a street vendor who was sucking tea from a saucer through a sugar cube clenched between his teeth. Sitting on our packs close to the baker's we made gritty sandwiches and washed them down with glasses of sweet tea.

'What kind of bread do you have in Ireland?' Max wanted to know.

'We have skulls, ducks and bastable loaves[15],' I said. Max was flummoxed.

\* \* \*

Max and Sharon left us in Tehran. They were hitchhiking onwards to Kabul. The rest of us took a night train to Mashad.

Initially, we had trouble getting tickets: Bill reckoned the officials wanted to keep us out of Mashad, sacred city to the Shia, during Ashura. Finally we spoke to the stationmaster and tickets were produced. We then milled about the railway station, attracting to us a large group of teenage boys and girls from some local grammar-type school, all keen to practice their English.

'Why do you go to India?' a gangly lad in shirt and tie asked Viktor.

'Because everything is possible in India,' Viktor said although he'd never been there. 'India is one big crazy place where I can learn

---

[15] All well-known loaves of bread around Cork.

to float in the air like a balloon. I can learn to play the flute to the cobra. Or maybe walk on the fire. And in India they like the hippies, the freaks.[16] Especially the holy men - the holy men like the freaks very much.'

'In Iran, holy men do not like hippie,' the student said. 'Iranian holy men say hippie is bad person. Say hippie woman is very bad person. But Iranian students, we like hippie very much. We want to go to Europe. Maybe also India.'

'If you come to Germany,' Viktor said, 'you can visit me.' He reached into the inside pocket of his reefer jacket and pulled out, of all things, a business card. *Viktor Strommler, disc jockey.*

'Peace,' he said and gave the V-sign. By now we had spread more peace than the U.N.

This prompted much address swapping and promises of marriage. By the time our train creaked out of the station, we had an army of cheering well wishers waving us off to the empty wastes that separated Tehran from the north eastern city of Mashad.

'In Mashad, you must be careful,' one of the girls shouted. 'It is pilgrim place where Shia go to pray at holy place of Imam Reza. No foreign person can go that place.'

'Last time I was through,' Tom said, 'I heard some people got stoned for going too near the shrine.'

Imam Reza was allegedly assassinated in 817 AD by the Sunni Caliph Mamoun during a journey from the village of Sanabad to Baghdad. The Mashad shrine was built on the site of Sanabad. Foreigners, we were advised, shouldn't go there. True or false, the big bearded Zigg was taking no chances.

'Man,' he said, 'that's heavy. I've already got an Afghan visa. There's no need for hanging about. I'm gonna shoot straight through Mashad. I wanna be in cool Afghanistan.'

At prayer time, the train became a speeding mosque, with every Iranian on board stretched in prayer along the aisles. It happened again in the morning as we crawled across the desert through camel herds and flocks of hardy sheep that managed to graze on sparse nothing, burnt by drought. To the north, the snows of Kuh-e Binalud glistened in the sunshine.

---

[16] 'Freaks' was the term most widely used by those on the hippie trail to describe themselves. The British *Observer* newspaper would later claim that this was to save others the effort of inventing a derogatory term.

## Chapter 14

'That is where the gods live,' Viktor declared. 'Up in that mountain. I go there tomorrow.'

He didn't.

In Mashad, Zigg floated off into the ether with peace signs to everyone. The rest of us made our way to the Afghan Consulate to pick up visas. We then booked into a cheap hotel in the shade of some chenar trees in a falling-down street. In one of the rooms, we found an Englishman, a Canadian, a German and an Austrian - lying on the floor out of their skulls around a battered copy of Herman Hesse's *Journey To The East*. They'd bought some hash in Tehran.

'Maniacs!' Andy from Warwickshire said. 'Do you want to get yourselves shot?' He then thought about it. 'Ah, what the heck,' he added. 'No harm in seeing if it was worth the risk.'

An hour later, Viktor and I slipped down town to grab furtive glimpses of the Holy Shrine with its vast square, giant arches and domes of gold and turquoise. The place being awash with white-turbaned mullahs, we didn't hang about. Returning to base, we headed for a back street restaurant, where we swapped information with the Herman Hesse devotees over a dinner of mutton stew, raw onions and bread.

Out in the street, Mashad's horse-drawn taxis rattled by as they had for centuries.

# Chapter 15
## The Land of the Great Hashish

───────────────────────

'You must relax,' the Immigration official at the Iranian border post said. 'No hurry. Two hours? That is nothing.'

'But we need to get to Herat,' I protested. 'It's almost dark.'

'Tomorrow, Herat is still in Herat,' he assured me.

Despite the lack of traffic between Mashad and the border, the post was the perfection of bedlam. The only way to the Immigration desk was to engage in the equivalent of a rugby scrum with knots of men with long beards, traditional Afghan kurtas (knee-length shirts), loose-fitting baggy trousers, waistcoats and a mix of turbans, astrakhan hats and karakul caps. Older men, with homespun shawls or blankets over their shoulders egged on their teams from the wings, supported in turn by smaller numbers of women in black chadors, bright shalwar-kameezes with skintight leggings or Afghan burkahs with lace visors. Some people had no papers; others didn't seem to know what they were. People yelled and argued and money changed hands. Mounds of baggage littered the floor. On the eastern horizon, the dark, storied mountains of Afghanistan rose jagged into a turquoise sky. Dust devils came through the door. And still we waited for a third hour before we secured a spot at the Immigration desk.

'Stamp. Stamp.' the official said. 'Now you go Customs. Have good times.'

Viktor, Andy and I were through but Gunter, Tom and Bill were still in the queue when the unmistakeable voice of Max the third broke through the din.

'Hey man, what the hell are you guys doin' here?' Sharon was trailing behind. They both looked pretty rough.

'We have a lift from a trucker to Herat,' Sharon said, 'provided we ever get outta here.'

'Behind you!' Viktor roared, screwing up his nose and jabbing a finger. 'People *shitting* in the road.'

Two men had casually dropped their baggy trousers. Further along, another man squatted in an open sewer. A chap downstream rinsed a tin mug and a pot. Another was cleaning his teeth.

## Chapter 15

'Just think,' Viktor said. 'Every time you drink the tea, you will wonder what really makes the colour...'

'Viktor,' I said. 'We don't need that.' I was very calm. Max said I reminded him of Ghandi.

\* \* \*

Night had long fallen by the time we'd rattled the thirty kilometres of corrugated dirt to the Afghan border post. Transport was a wreck of a bus with wooden benches, a door hanging loose, six windows missing, a floor covered in sheep shit, two bouncing, fume-spewing drums of petrol in the back, and a bulky, black-turbaned, bushy-bearded lunatic named Omar at the wheel.

Our fellow passengers were mainly tribal Afghans, not the least bit phased by the three hours it now took to get through Afghan Immigration and Customs. It was therefore a bit of a surprise to learn that, with great precision, someone had decided that, timewise, Afghanistan should be one hour and ten minutes ahead of Iran. (Maybe that was a joke but we couldn't check as none of us had a watch. Carrying a watch, binding peace and love to time, would've been a hanging offence.) While we waited we were beseiged by people wanting to change money and sell hash. Eventually, we entered Afghanistan through a rickety boom supported by an oil drum. A camel, caught in our headlights, bolted in front of the bus.

At two in the morning we arrived in Herat, frozen stiff and covered in dust, to find that the only accomodation available was a table in the kitchen of a building that passed itself as a hotel. Sharing the kitchen were some twenty Afghans spread across other tables and the floor. In one corner, a huddle of men squatted at a guttering candle. They were drinking tea, mumbling, and smoking through an enormous, gurgling clay hookah, the chillum filled with a piece of hash the size of a matchbox and topped with charcoal. When it came his turn, each man would fall to like a flure-sucker[17] until the coals were whipped into maddening flames. This would send columns of smoke rushing down the stem of the pipe, through the cooling water, and straight into the lungs. In the dark the smokers' faces, turbans and hennaed beards would periodically shine like spectres in the ball of flame that erupted from the pipe each time the man on the stem came up for a coughing fit. Those waiting their turn would daintily sip from their little tea-glasses, half filled with

---

[17] Ulster-Scots for a vacuum-cleaner.

sugar, or dunk a cube in the tea, stick it in their mouths and suck the tea through the sugar.

'Hey Irish,' Viktor said, 'we must do the culture.'

A small man with a goatee and skullcap glided across the room. 'I have some thing,' he said to Viktor. He pulled a slab of black hash from the pocket of his waistcoat. 'You buy?' He was the hotel manager.

Purchase made, we hunkered down with the men at the candle who greeted us with courteous nods; and while the people on the tables snored like trains, Viktor fuelled the hookah. '*Tesekkur*,' each man said as he went at the stem like an industrial bellows, then lurched backwards in his own private fit. To their astonishment I outdid them all in the coughing stakes. As a matter of fact I had to rush outside to throw up.

You can't bate the Irish, I always say.

In the morning the manager found us rooms, one of them shared by Viktor, Andy and myself. They were basic, with earthen floors, mice, ants, doors frayed to splinters, and yellow walls carved with meaningful messages. They were also not far from the communal washroom where the Afghan men performed their matinal hawking; but they were a step up from the tables. The three of us thanked the man for blessings, then stepped out into warm sunshine and a small medieval Tajik city with dusty steets of steel-doored shops and tiny kitchen industries. To the north, a line of low dry hills met the sky.

In the sudden sunlight it took a second or two for the street to meet our eyes; but when it did, it was the full knock-me-down, like something pulled from the sleeping hours. Andy was the only one to speak. 'Far out, man,' was what he said.

Men dressed in the clothing we'd seen at the border rode by on bicycles, donkeys, ponies, camels, and decorated two-wheeled gharries (taxis) drawn by horses with heads virtually enclosed in dancing red pom-poms. Others heaved pushcarts along the street. Two men came our way hauling an unimaginable load of eight massive wooden crates stacked ten feet high on a supercart known as a karachy. This looked more like something a horse would pull and was specially adapted to take the weight by being set on the recycled axle and wheels of a truck. Poor consolation to the guys attached to it. There were also those who sat at intervals along the pavement, perfecting the precious art of doing frig-all. The few visible women slid by like ghosts in their burkahs. Many people

## Chapter 15

went barefoot. Others wore studded 'Aladdin' shoes with pointed toes that curled back on themselves.

Directly in front, the morning sky was dominated by the great earthworks of the Pai Hesar, founded by Alexander the Great and sacked, 1,550 years later, by Genghis Khan who was still an incendiary subject around Herat.

In 1221 the city had surrendered to the Khan army. But it later rebelled, killing the Mongol garrison and bringing down the wrath of 80,000 Mongol troops, led by Genghis himself, who slaughtered all but forty of the inhabitants.

'Genghis Khan,' our hotel owner told us. 'He burn Herat.' As if it had happened yesterday.

'We are in the Arabian fantastics,' Viktor said as two tall men strode past, turbans trailing to their waists and flintlock rifles under their arms. They were followed by a family leading five camels and eight donkeys. They in turn were followed by a Kuchi woman from the desert. Instead of a burkah, the nomadic Kuchi woman wore an embroidered black dress and blue shawl, and masses of jewellery forged from white metal and coloured glass. A silver headpiece was draped across her tattooed forehead and a small blue stud glinted from the side of her nose. She stopped and stared open-mouthed. We were the exotics.

Shaded by a verandah, we set off along a broken and buckled pavement lined with caged birds and the agricultural bounty of the surrounding Hari valley. Immediately, a man in an enormous black turban rushed out from one of many identical shops that sold many identical goods.

'Welcome!' he shouted. 'You are guests in my country. I am happy to give you some tea. It is a small gesture of friendship.'

It was the beginning of a pattern. Right across Afghanistan, we'd find proud, fiercely independent people full of charm and hospitality. Every service, no matter how mundane, would be delivered with endless courtesy and dignified bowing; and there was always that cup of sugary tea. Of course we would also encounter rogues, but they were a minority among whom could still be found the enduring national charm.

'Thank you,' Andy said. We followed the man into a tiny space.

'Sit,' he said, pointing to a mat on the floor. A great fuss was made and the tea was brewed on a bulky stove that looked homemade.

'You will do a tour of Herat,' our host said, sweeping away some breadcrumbs from around Viktor's feet. 'You will begin at the Masjid-i-Jami. That is the Friday Mosque. It is dating back to the 13th century.'

Tea over, we followed his advice and made our way to a tree-shaded square to view this blue-tiled architectural triumph that owed much of its grace to pishtaqs, squinch-net vaults, mihrab niches, spandrels, iwans and muqarnas vaulting. And what are they you might ask. Well, to use the undying words of Chief Superintendent Murphy of the Garda Síochána who led the hunt for kidnapped racehorse, Shergar, back in 1983: *a clue, a clue, that's what we haven't got.*

Leaving the mosque, we cut between mud-brick compounds where an occasional open door offered glimpses of everyday life in the domed houses: a woman washing clothes in a bucket; a group of hookah-smoking men on a rug; young boys building a kite. We continued until we arrived at a collection of six crumbling minarets beside a small river on the northern edge of town - all that remained of Queen Gawhar Shad's Musallah Madrassa. The renowned centre of learning was built in the 15th century by the enlightened wife of Tamerlane's youngest son. It was destroyed in 1885 by the unenlightened British so their artillery could have a clear line of fire against a Russian army that never came. The queen's maousoleum stood in remarkably good condition among the ruins.

Returning to the city centre, we stopped at a chai-khana[18] in one of the covered bazaars, a street of tin and canvas awnings crammed with hawkers, barbers, carpet sellers, foodcarts and men snoozing on rope-and-bamboo charpoys. Horses and camels were tethered to posts. Goats, dogs and chickens dug through piles of rubbish. A woman rode out of a small store on a donkey.

The chai-khana, with its charcoal pit, was the local social hub and our means of taking in liquid. The shop next door was the butcher's where slices of meat were hacked from fly-blackened carcasses. Kebabs for the brave.

'*Chai*,' I said, raising three fingers and hoping it wasn't some kind of insult.

'Welcome,' the owner boomed. 'You sit.' He was an older man with a greying beard and a massive striped turban twisted around a shaven crown.

---
[18] Tea shop

# Chapter 15

We planted ourselves on battered cushions beside three men in turbans and shawls. The chai-khana man told them we were mystics on our way to India.

'They say you maybe Sufi,' he told us. I think they were taking the Mickey.

'No,' Andy said, not wanting to become embroiled in the semantics of Islamic theological debate. 'Sadhu. Hindu sadhu.' All three men raised their glasses and took another sip of tea.

'Check out,' Viktor said, pointing up the street where the open sewers were serving the usual range of washing purposes. 'They are splashing the shit-water on the fruit and nuts to make them fresh!' Further along, a man squatted over the sewer that provided the water for the fruit and nut man. 'I will make a book,' Viktor said. 'It will be about all the ways you can use the shit-water.'

'What do the women do?' I asked the chai-khana man, 'They never squat in the street.' This turned out to be a rude question. It remains to this day a complete mystery.

Before we left the chai-khana the three wise men flamed a hookah and offered us a smoke.

'Today,' Viktor said, 'we are in the Land of the Great Hashish.'

As so often happens when wisdom blossoms, one could only agree.

On the way back to the hotel we stumbled on a row of workshops where traditional crafts were followed in traditional ways: a weaver at a wooden loom; a blacksmith at his anvil; the yoghurt man with his cultures and bowls; the knife-sharpener leaning over a shower of sparks. In the recycling departments, men turned old tyres into sandals and buckets, old tins into oil lamps and stash-boxes, car parts into a water pump. In the glassblower's shop, we were offered *Herat Blue* glassware.

'Very fam-oose,' the glass blower said. 'No break-ing.' To demonstrate he threw a glass on the floor. It shattered to sparkling smithereens.

'Maybe this one does not break,' Viktor said, raising the most expensive-looking piece above his head.

'You *bloody* man!' the glass blower shrieked. 'It fall, I *keel* you!' With his yellow, opium-filled eyes, he had morphed into the Beelzebub of Herat.

Down the street we had a great laugh. Ha-ha-ha! Have another smoke.

\* \* \*

The bus to Kandahar was an old Mercedes with a Bedford engine and little to recommend either. Despite its decrepit nature, however, we took off at buck-mad speed once the driver had evicted the beggars who'd flocked aboard at the tumbledown bus station. Whizzing through the narrow streets, we stopped several times to pick up passengers. Our last stop was outside a skin shop draped in massive wolf pelts whose owner climbed aboard with a bundle of animal skins. Then we were out into a belt of rice paddies, vegetables and trees that stayed until we'd cleared the Hari River floodbasin. Beyond Herat's oasis, two lines of pines stretched a little further until they petered out in a rock-strewn moonscape of red, pink, yellow and purple mountains rising stark and slatelike against a translucent sky.

With crackling Afghan music howling in our ears, we careered along in good spirits on the Russian-built road where conditions were fairly good, but there was little regard for the nerves. We overtook trucks and buses on blind bends. We swung around corners on the right and left. We swerved into the desert to avoid annihilation. A bus came towards us with the passengers on the roof and the interior full of sheep. Another drove beside us in an Afghan chariot race. Inside it was full of bearded tribesmen; on the roof a trussed-up camel. Finally they overtook us, horn blaring, faces smiling, on yet another blind bend.

An old man with yellow eyes, rotten teeth, a straggly white beard and a filthy grey turban, flopped onto Viktor's shoulder. Earlier he'd been smoking opium.

'You must sit up, like this!' Viktor demanded, heaving him off. He flopped back again. 'Maybe he would give me some opium and I could be happy too,' Viktor complained, repairing the hairdo.

With the rising sun, we discovered that the windows of the bus were jammed shut. This added nothing to the broken seats, the flies that dropped from the ceiling, or the half-inch ants that scurried about our feet. But mystics all on our way to India, we smiled. Something greatly boosted by plentiful exotic refreshments.

Everywhere there were ailments. People wanted medicine for sick stomachs, runny eyes, broken fingers, scalds and sore heads. One man, missing most of his upper lip and nose tugged at my jacket, but nothing I had would cure leprosy or fill the missing lip or the twin holes that were his nose. Another man's eyes were covered in cataracts: he wanted 'Aspirin'. Gunter gave him one and he crushed

## Chapter 15

it and rinsed his eyes. I don't imagine it did much in the line of good.

Half an hour out of Herat we had our first breakdown. The driver and his helper sorted it with bits of wire, a ball of string and a hammer. Over the next fourteen hours we had five more breakdowns, several prayer stops and a puncture. Each time we stopped, the engine cut out, requiring all passengers to push a jump-start. The puncture, which came in the afternoon at an abandoned camel rest on the flat northern reaches of the Desert of Death, truly tested the bus crew's ingenuity. With the exception of a foot pump, we had no repair kit. Undeterred, the driver instructed us to push the bus off the road. Passengers who'd been through this before began to stick rocks under the axle and dig a hole below the wheel so it could be removed. A piece of rubber was then put over the puncture and fused into place with charcoal, reddened over a small fire. The wheel was re-fitted and inflated, the soil replaced, the stones knocked away, and the bus heaved back on the road for another push-start.

'Just like we do in Germany,' Viktor said. Then off we went, already anticipating our next breakdown

*Push-starting the bus after repair of puncture.*

The desert scenes that unfolded between Herat and Kandahar could not have been better woven by a Yacqui shaman on peyote: painted mountains rising in morning pastels; camel trains slinging down shimmering dunes; circling vultures over an old mud fort or abandoned village; flats of blinding salt; bejewelled Kuchi women with tattooed faces plodding the dunes alongside determined men with flintlock rifles; a cluster of black goat-hair tents flapping gently in the sands; mirages - great lakes and cities - unfurling in the emptiness; termite hills and darting lizards; lonely tombs of stone and broken glass, the more recent topped with small crude flags not yet shredded by desert winds; a family driving camels, goats and sheep into the empty searing south that ran all the way to Pakistan; and the opium man springing to life for a burst of hoarse and terrible song and a yellow grin from childhood's nightmares.

In walled villages of domed houses where an intermittent spring allowed a few rice paddies and trees to flourish, the Afghan men would pray and take a ritual wash while we foreigners were ushered into the tea room by barefoot little girls in shalwar-kameezes and glittering nose studs. In a similar abode, lunch of rice, meat and potatoes was slapped up before we had time to think. Then it was back to the stifling bus with the stuck windows until, finally, the blood of sunset closed the day.

Watching the moon cloak the desert in shadow and silver, and Kuchis and camels darting through the beam of our one flickering headlight, I drew the future for Viktor.

'Some day when I have money, I'm coming back to spend time with the Kuchis.'

'That is a mad thought,' Viktor said. 'They will eat you.'

But the future of Afghanistan put paid to all of that.

\* \* \*

Kandahar was another small, old world city, much of its housing like the mud-brick villages of the desert. Built beside the tamarisk- and poplar-lined Aghandab River, its dirt streets led from all directions to the Char Suq, a central square of squat buildings where a cop on a blue domed rostrum blew his whistle at passing bicycles, gharries, carts, rickshaws, camels and men with pushcarts. As in Herat, the pavements were lined with hawkers who sat under awnings and pines and stunted mulberry trees and measured weights with rocks lobbed onto hand-held scales. Food was cooked on charcoal fires. Tea shops and food stalls smelled of spices and burning hash. Near the northern edge of the city, the Kherqa Sherif Zariat, the most sacred shrine in Afghanistan, was said to contain the cloak of Mohammad, given to the city by the Amir of Bokhara as part of a treaty in 1768.

## Chapter 15

The surrounding region harboured some of the oldest human settlements. The remains of Deh Morasi Ghundai, an early farming village dating back to 5,000 BC, lay twenty-seven kilometres southwest of the city. Another Bronze Age village, with multi-roomed, mud-brick buildings from the same period, was discovered at nearby Said Qala. Seven thousand years of human history passed under our feet.

The six of us booked into one room at the Ariana Hotel, a place of green walls, white ceilings and dark corridors where everything was either broken, dangerously exposed, underpowered, or scuttling across the floor. We were immediately visited by a young pockmarked man who politely knocked on our door before entering.

'My friends,' he smiled with a regal curtsey, 'welcome to Kandahar. My name is Hafizullah. I have here for you very good hashish and opium. You will see we have four qualities of hashish and two qualities of opium. I can sell you as much as you like. We can hide it in sandals, sitars, gas cylinders. Whatever you can think. In Europe you can make many dollars.'

'We are not hippies,' Andy said.

'Very well my friends,' Hafizullah said. 'Maybe tomorrow you are hippies.'

When he left, Andy rolled a smoke. Two tokes and Viktor was chasing flies across the beds.

'The flies,' he said. 'They spread the plague.'

'That was rats,' Tom said.

'Rats do not FLY,' Viktor enlightened him.

'Kandahar is the fly capital of the world,' Bill said, passing around a packet of dry biscuits. 'Flying rats, flying bats and flying flies.' It was the kind of conversation that inspired men like Aristotle.

'It is now in order that we walk through the back streets to mingle with the citizenry,' Tom said. Despite the kite-flying children taking us for fools, we moved into the lanes of Kandahar. 'Look,' Tom said. 'A group of dignified, silver-bearded men in turbans smoking a hookah.'

The dignified men invited us to sit with them on one of many wooden street platforms to engage in the now familiar national pastime of rolling prayer beads, smoking hash, drinking tea, beating off the flies and eating the seasonal pomegranates.

On our second day in Kandahar, Viktor lay on his bed and continued to indulge in the national pastime, but without the prayer-beads, tea or pomegranates. This caused a dose of the jim-jams, a state much induced by an overtaxing of the inner man.

Mid morning, the rest of us went to the post office where it took an hour to buy postcard stamps and watch them being franked as a precaution against having them peeled off and used again as per travellers' lore. We then went back to where Viktor had fused to the bed.

'MUNICH!' the blond head roared when we came through the door. 'There is no place called *MUNICH!*' The hair, no longer coiffed, was sticking out at goblin angles. The breath was ragged. 'There is a German city of *München* where I live.'

'I think you're wrong,' stout Bill from Leeds said. 'I was definitely in Munich at least twice.'

'SHADDUP!' Viktor choked, burying his head under the pillow. Then slowly, like a hermit crab emerging from its shell, the two eyes reappeared, brimming with the light of payback. The lips peeled back in a saccharine grin. 'Piggy from Lo-o-o-oods,' came the run of brute revenge. 'Piggy from fucking *Lo-o-o-oods*.'

Viktor would have made a great diplmat.

Having sorted the München issue he went off to trace the adventures of kings and queens, soldiers, horses and Indians, who were climbing the green walls.

Down in the street, a young Australian was trying to explain the purpose of a surfboard to desert tribesmen: the nearest sea was on the far side of Pakistan.

\* \* \*

A dusty street in Kandahar was where that first trip most likely came unstuck. That's the sad fact of it.

'Did you just drink from that tap?' Bill asked. We were on our way home from the bazaar. It was a hot afternoon and the tap was attached to a wooden post in the street.

'I've been drinking the water all the way from Istanbul,' I told him and let him in on the Theory of Immunity. 'Seeing as I've had a healthy upbringing, I should be OK.'

Bill's jaw dropped. 'Either that,' he said, 'or you're gonna need ten good Guardian Angels.'

Bill's would prove the more sound theory.

Later on, the monosyllabic Gunter rose from the dead. In an incredible transformation, the silent Swiss led us all out of town to a chain of rugged hills east of Kandahar. These, he told us, had once formed part of the old city's defences. He then found a steep rock face where a flight of forty-two carved steps - the Chihil Zina - led to a shrine carved out of the limestone. It commemorated the victories of 16th century Moghul Emperor Babur, and his son Humayun.

'Also, a big battle happened here late in the 19th century. The army of Amir Abdur Rahman beat the army of his cousin, Ayub Khan. This was the beginning of Afghanistan as one nation.' There was a silence.

'Gunter,' Viktor said. 'You have been smoking too much.'

On the heights of the Chihil Zina, we watched the hills west of the city melt to a dusky rose against an orange sky. Gradually, the sky passed through a tumult of blood, torn by shards of purple and pink, until it faded to a soft green. A little longer and a solitary star drained the last light from the sky. Almost immediately the moon rose, huge, bone-yellow and wrapped in a great silver aureole.

In a time before the awful wars of Afghanistan, that was Kandahar.

*The author and Gunter Effinger at desert graves, Afghanistan, March 1970.*

# Chapter 16
## The Fall

There's a point in every journey when you hear about the possibilities: rabies, malaria, cholera, dengue fever, typhoid, elephantiasis, hepatitis. There's no end. But when you're carried along by a belief in your own invincibility, the fall is great indeed.

Qaderi Bus Transport brought us to the capital, eight and a half hours from the Desert of Death through a series of dead riverbeds and spectacular gorges to the southern flanks of the Hindu Kush, pink with snow in the close of the day. This time, the road had been built by the Americans, part of the ongoing tug-of-war for strategic Afghanistan that had been the country's curse for centuries. Eventually, as we now know, both the USSR and US would throw off all pretence and invade in turn. The end result would be the destruction of Afghanistan (for the good of the Afghans) and the slaughter of its innocents by the thousand.

Wedged 1,800 metres up in the folds of the Hindu Kush, and spreading out from both banks of the Kabul River, the centre of the 3,000-year-old city was a collection of bazaars, mosques, flat-roofed peeling buildings, tree-lined streets and dirt alleys. Some led to relatively affluent suburbs. Most led to sprawls of mud brick that fanned out from the centre and climbed the surrounding hills, home to many of the city's half million inhabitants. Outside of the occasional garish bus or truck, traffic was mainly confined to camels, donkeys, pushcarts, bicycles and the familiar horse-drawn gharries.

In the Royal Palace, Muhammad Zahir Shah ruled over a feudal kingdom where his power was almost absolute. While local councils were sometimes called to advise him, these bodies had no real power, nor did they in any way represent the Afghan people. They acted more as cabals of tribal elders. The landowners and patriarchs who controlled the countryside, benefited from the king's patronage and held in check the bearded men with the flintlock rifles who walked the teeming bazaars.

We got off the bus and headed for the Ferh Hotel on Jade Timur Shahi. It was fruit season: along the pavements, turbaned men sat on the ground selling oranges and pomegranates. On the walls that corralled the Kabul River, carpet sellers displayed their pieces.

## Chapter 16

A muezzin called from a small blue-domed mosque with a single slender minaret. Some guy in a corner did a squat business in the street.

'If it's Monday,' Bill said, 'it must be Kabul.'

'Piggy from Lo-o-o-o-ds,' stoned, unrelenting Viktor drooled.

Despite the lack of funds, I concluded at this stage that I couldn't leave Afghanistan without picking up a sheepskin jacket, symbol of many made in India men. Viktor and I went out into the skin bazaar where I bought such a garment and he bumped into everyone in sight. (This garment subsequently skulked in dark corners until I came back from abroad one time to find that a herd of Irish moths had finally killed it.)

That night in the Ferh Hotel the folly of the Theory of Immunity fell upon me. I woke up at half past two with a thumping headache, a ripping pain in my stomach, and a severe dose of the gallops.

'Could be amoebic dysentery,' Tom said in the morning. 'If it is, you're gonna need a doctor.'

'What's amoebic dysentery?' I asked.

'It can kill you in days,' Tom said with a grimace. I assumed he had some kind of warped sense of humour.

After breakfast of tea and bread - about all I could manage - I went out with Viktor to the bazaars of the Shar-e-Nau district, where they sold the flintlock rifles, but I was back in an hour, burning with fever and too weak to walk. In the afternoon I tried to go out again with Gunter but barely made it to the hotel door. By half past five I was passing rivers of blood. By nine o'clock my pulse rate, normally at the lower end of the spectrum, was clocking in at 105 beats a minute, and I was simultaneously sweating and shivering. Gunter gave me two antibiotics and I fell into bed.

'Dehydration,' I heard Tom say. 'It's the biggest killer.'

By morning the fever had eased. But for the first time since leaving home, I felt all reserves of energy and optimism sucked away. The coming days passed in doldrums of sleeping, drinking tea, running to the loo, eating little and venturing out in short shaky sorties. In that state I began to think the unthinkable. Maybe, after all, I wasn't meant to go to India.

Somewhere in the haze Tom, Bill and Gunter upped in the middle of the night and left for Bamiyan in the north - they were going to see the giant Buddhas; Viktor went over to the German Embassy and managed to scrounge $25, part of which he used to buy a white

Afghan coat and a lump of hash; and he and I, on one of my brief sorties, ran smack into Sharon, speed-walking down Jade Timur Shahi, pursued by five amorous Afghan men.

'Jesus Christ, am I glad to see you guys,' she squealed as the crestfallen suitors fell back. 'Man!' she added, looking at me. 'You look *sick*.' She invited us back to her hotel. 'Zigg is there too,' she said. 'We met him shortly after we got here.'

At the Hotel Saadat, Max, Zigg, and a tall, lank, ponytailed, peace-loving Frenchman named Antoine were out of their lids.

'Isn't this just a far-out place,' Max said with ferocious concentration. He was sprawled on the bed like a shot man. 'Imagine, in the next life, we could all come back as little maggots, crawling about, waiting for some bastard to stamp on us. Squish!'

'You can buy much hashish in every place,' Urk had advised in Brindisi. 'You smoke plenty and you will understand the life.' Max was getting there.

As the evening wore on much conversation was devoted to the state of one's bowels. It had been so since Istanbul. The bowels were the thing.

'The safest way to travel,' Viktor said, 'is eat nothing and meditate. Like those people who live in the Himalayas.' Viktor made these things up.

The Kabul cops looked exceedingly funny that night as Viktor and I walked home. How we avoided telling them is a mystery.

Fourteen years on, I was hitchhiking one evening from Dijon to Frankfurt when a strange thing happened. I was close to the German border on the entrance to the autoroute and expecting to be in Frankfurt by nightfall, when some halfwit hijacked me and dropped me off in a godforsaken village in the arse-end of nowhere.

'Bless you!' I roared after him or something to that effect. I surveyed the gathering darkness, the empty road, and the half dozen houses and one pub that made up the village. No chance now of getting to Frankfurt. For fifteen minutes nothing happened. Then a balding, long-haired man with a walrus moustache staggered from the pub, flopped into a battered van, and drove towards me. He stopped and picked me up. He looked like someone I knew, but I couldn't place the face. Given the circumstances, the conversation quickly turned to travelling. He had travelled and I had travelled. He'd been to Afghanistan and I'd been to Afghanistan. And we'd both spent a hazy evening in a Kabul hotel in 1970 with Benjamin C. Witting the third.

## Chapter 16

It was Antoine of Kabul.

Although much of that first visit to Kabul was a haze of fever, I rallied long enough to climb a hill outside the city where the unexpected boom of the noon gun almost blew me from my perch. Looking down on Kabul and the flat-roofed mud shanties that climbed the opposite hill, I checked my funds. I had £15 in travellers' cheques and just under £8 of Afghan currency. That and amoebic dysentery. On that splendid hill, I finally capitulated. I was going home.

Climbing back down I came across a broad open sewer and suddenly wanted to kill people. There they were, with their flat pushcarts and buckled wheels, unloading fruit and vegetables so they could wash them in the pestilential swill and poison poor souls like me.

On our final night in Kabul, Viktor, Andy and I joined Max, Sharon, and Zigg for an evening meal and a few hours back at the Hotel Saadat.

'Who are we all?' Zigg asked from the flat of his back. 'All us freaks on the road? We've got nothing in common: class, culture, language, nationality, nothing. Just that we're the generation that had to watch all those insane fuckers explode all those nuclear bombs through the sixties. Any wonder we're on the road doing dope?'

'Yeah man,' Max said. 'But dope is OK. In fact it's compulsory.'

'You speak like the Buddha,' Viktor said.

In the morning Viktor and I were turning back towards Iran. Andy was leaving for India and Sri Lanka. Max, Sharon and the big bearded Zigg, were planning to follow Tom, Bill and Gunter to Bamiyan to see the giant Buddhas carved into the cliffs.

'Man,' Zigg said. 'They've been there for the last fifteen hundred years and will probably be there until the mountains fall down.'

Zigg of course was confused. In March 2001, the Afghan Taliban would see to that. With the zeal and ignorance of the fundamentalist, they blew the world-treasured Buddhas of Bamiyan, their greatest cultural inheritance, to chippings.

Towards the end of the night we swapped addresses and swore to write and visit and keep in touch; but apart from myself and Viktor, we never did.

'You know what's just come into my head?' Sharon said, 'Some day we can all tell our grandchildren that when we were young we did this.'

'Maybe they'll be doing it too,' Zigg said.

'Naw,' Sharon said and in this she proved the prophet. 'This scene won't last. Too many others will come behind and all sorts will be in that mix. Even the drinkers will come.'

I might add that there were two classes of people who were shunned by all respectable hippie-trail travellers: people who were into hard drugs and people who were into booze.

'Speaking of others...' I said. 'Anyone seen any Irish people about.'

'No man,' Max said. 'You're the only Irishman in Kabul.'

'Hey Irish,' Viktor asked without looking up, 'are you really from the Foreign Legion...?'

# Chapter 17
Carted Off

---

All was well again until it wasn't. I don't know if it was a relapse or a second independent attack but when I woke up in the middle of the night in one of the more rundown quarters of Tehran I suspected that it wasn't going to matter much.

We'd reached the capital at 7.20am the previous morning. Exhausted, the six of us who were now travelling together had booked into a single room in a cheap hotel in Amir Kabir Lane and went for breakfast. I felt weak but put it down to lack of sleep. In the evening I again accompanied the others to eat but barely touched the food and couldn't drag myself to conversation. I went back to the room and crawled into bed.

Just after 3.00am I was woken by a violent headache, ripping cramps and a burning fever. Shaking, sweating, shivering and in need of the loo, I crept from the room to the communal foul-smelling hole in the ground down the hall where I found to my horror that I was splashing the porcelain in blood. Rivers of it. Far worse than Kabul. I was no sooner back in bed than the rush was on again. And again. As the night wore on and I lost more and more fluid, I knew I needed help but hadn't the wit to do anything about it.

Viktor was somewhere in the room - in one of the other beds - but I didn't want to go looking for him in the dark in case I disturbed the others whom I didn't know that well. We'd only joined forces on the bus from Herat to the Afghan border and I was afraid I might already have given them the heebees on the train from Mashad. In the delirium of the earlier sickness, I'd threatened the physical annihilation of a not so nice Dutchman who was tossing my rucksack about. Afterwards I knew I'd gone over the top but the damage was done. *Madboy* was tattooed across my forehead. I would probably, I reckoned, have to now live under another name.

By seven-thirty, when the others woke up, I was dehydrated, bleeding from the nose and too weak to stand unsupported, heading in short for *Tír na n-Óg*.[19] Georgio, the Italian among the four newcomers, didn't do anything to change that notion.

---

[19] The afterlife Land of Everlasting Youth in Irish mythology.

'This is not good,' he said. 'You can die from this.' The worst of that statement was that Georgio was generally a pool of light.

The man from Venice had climbed aboard the battered Afghan bus at Herat wearing a dark green velvet suit and carrying three flintlock rifles that he'd picked up in Kandahar. With long dark hair and a biker's moustache, he looked like he'd stepped from the Sonora Desert of a hundred years before.

'You,' he'd said, taking the measure of me, 'are like a dying man.' I felt reassured. He could've said dead man.

Back at the Iranian border, when I'd been worried about being quarantined for not having a completed set of cholera vaccinations, he'd been the ray of calm.

'What can you do?' he'd advised. 'Only to think positively.'

Later he had come to my rescue in the corridor of the overnight train from Mashad.

At 7.30pm we'd pulled into a station and most of the passengers got off to pray on the platform: hundreds of people facing towards the Kaaba in Mecca and moving together in a great wave under the station lights. As we left again, a young Iranian guy sat down beside me. He smiled in a way that made his oblong face look like a split egg.

'You no pray?'

'No,' I said. 'Christian.' (kind-of.)

'Christian no pray?'

'Not at seven-thirty.'

'What you think about Islam?'

'I only know a little about Islam,' I admitted.

'Islam is from Prophet Mohammad from 7th century,' he explained. 'Allah, he tell Qur'an to Muhammad. Qur'an is word of Allah. Islam mean give yourself to Allah. When you are Muslim, you must obey Allah. You must give to poor person. You must not eat or drink or have woman in daytime in holy month of Ramadan. You know Ramadan?'

'Yes,' I said.

'Maybe you can be Muslim? Muslim people believe many prophet - Abraham, Jesus, Moses - but Mohammad only true prophet.'

'What about the place of the woman in Muslim society?' I asked.

Big mistake.

'In Islam, woman must be *modest*. Not like in Europe. Europe woman have no modest. Europe woman come in Iran. Iran woman see she not wear chador. Only dress like man. Only have small shirt.

## Chapter 17

This no good for Iran. Maybe some young Iran people think this OK. Maybe some Iran woman, maybe she think this OK. But my friend, THIS NO OK!'

'This yes OK,' I said.

Big other mistake, causing savage look.

'Fuck you American!' he said.

For the second time in a single day I was under siege. Until Georgio, who'd been dozing, leaned across

'You go sleep now,' he said. 'My friend sick. Tomorrow Tehran.'

The Iranian took one look at the green velvet suit and three rifles, decided Georgio was an infidel lunatic, and backed off.

Now the same Georgio was telling me I could die.

'Do you think you should go to the hospital?' Viktor said after Georgio's diagnosis. I shook my head. Harry from England sprang from his sleep which doubled up as a yogic trance.

'There's no thinking,' he said. 'We need a taxi, and we need it now.'

This was also disconcerting as Harry was an ascetic practitioner of meditation. Of thinning blond hair and light moustache, and draped in a white Afghan jacket and Indian trousers, he had taken up an entire seat on the bus to the Afghan border so he could sit in the lotus position, an activity that could go on for hours.

'It lost me a wife in Sweden,' he told us.

Having Harry excited, seeing him run outside shouting for a taxi, was indeed frightening. Seeing him run back in after ten minutes was a heart stopper.

'Right!' he ordered. 'Lift!'

Harry, Viktor and Georgio grabbed my arms and legs, carried me from the hotel, bundled me into the front seat of the taxi and hopped in behind. Doubled up in pain, head slumped forward, I saw the blood from my nose trickling down my shirt. *I'm dead alright*, I sadly said to myself.

As we left the hotel, I could see the worried faces of my other two companions. Paul, despite a shaven head and mean looks, was a Frenchman of gentle heart.

'You must not listen to Georgio,' he shouted. 'He has ze problem with ze 'ead.'

Tony Lee from Sydney, the last of the company, shouted something about 'the fightin' Irish'.

Short, stocky - and ancient at twenty-six – Tony had left Sydney two years earlier.

'Before I left,' he'd told us, 'I was a sales rep doing city and country territories with a shiny new red Holden, selling leather and sundries - tacks, soles, tingles and the like - to boot repairers and shoe factories, and toys to toy shops and major department stores. Man, I was flash as a rat with a gold tooth.'

He had since taken his time in South East Asia. He had taken his further time in India, spending long months on the Sandysudhanlaya Ashram outside Bombay where, under the tutelage of the now long passed-on Swami Chinmayanda, he delved into the mysteries of Hinduism and a stand on your head class of yoga not at all in Harry's quiver. This yoga strain would provide an enduringly unsettling image of an upside down man, often smoking an upside down cigarette, while engaging myself or others in deep upside down philosophical thought. Draped in beads and earrings, with a drooping black moustache and long thick waving hair that looked starched, he padded about (when not on his head) in an Indian shirt, trousers, sandals and a brown, heavily embroidered sheepskin coat from the back streets of Kabul. Smoking a perrenial cigarette held high between ring-encrusted fingers he helped us endure the rattling corrugations that passed for the road from Herat to Ipsam Qala by holding court on India and its ideologies. And he carried in his pack a Tibetan dagger from Nepal that made my hunting knife from Cork look like a toothpick.

At the Afghan post of Ipsam Qala after a delay of two hours while the officials had lunch, Tony had briefly shed a little of the peace and love veneer of India when a short powerful man with a cropped moustache and crew cut, who looked not unlike Oddjob in *Goldfinger*, had begun to rip our bags apart.

'You have drugs?' he asked each of us in turn. 'Or maybe you have pornography?'

'Where the fuck are we supposed to get pornography in Afghanistan?' Tony wanted to know.

'Hippie very smart,' Oddjob said. Georgio's three rifles caused him nil concern.

In time, Tony would become a lifelong friend and would remain a friend of Viktor's until the day the great München man faded from both of our lives.

'Hospital,' Georgio told the taxi driver. 'You must go very fast.'

The taxi raced through the streets of Tehran and skidded to the entrance of the Shafa Hospital. My friends - two of whom I would

## Chapter 17

never see again - paid the driver, grabbed my arms and legs and carried me to A&E.

The doctor on duty, a thin man in his late twenties with shiny black hair swept back from his forehead and a stethoscope hanging from his neck, looked at me in horror and for want of something better introduced himself as Ciyah Push. He then filled a syringe with morhine and jabbed it into my arm.

'To kill the pain,' he said. 'Now tell me what is wrong.'

As best they could, Harry, Viktor and Georgio described the symptoms.

'Ah,' Ciyah Push said in what sounded to me like a jolly voice. 'You haf cholera.'

He then asked for my vaccination certificate. *If I don't show it*, I thought, *that diagnosis will go away*. But the man persisted.

'There,' he said, pointing a thin finger at the cholera entry. 'You haf no protection. We must make some tests.'

'Cholera is bad?' I croaked, knowing full well the answer.

'Cholera is ver' bad,' he assured me - with a smile. 'You can die ver' soon.'

'Ah,' Georgio said. 'We must not speak until we have the tests.'

Head swimming, I was whisked off by wheelchair to see the duty nurse.

I've never waited with more trepidation. As the morphine took hold of my head I wondered how I'd get home if I was dead. I imagined what people would say. Some might say, *What a buck fuckin' eejit!* Others might say, *Poor fuckin' eejit*. I was picturing the hearse going down Evergreen Road, the Carrigaline Pipe Band playing a lament, the guy with the drum wearing his leopard skin, when the nurse reappeared with an unnerving smile on her face. It was the smile Doctor Push had worn when he diagnosed my demise. She led me back to where Viktor, Georgio and Harry were locked in animated discussion with the doctor about the pros and cons of dying of cholera. The doctor read the results and paused.

'Mr. Ciarán,' he said, 'you are ver' lucky. You haf amoebic dysentery. You must know that there are many kinds of amoeba, but this one - the name ees entamoeba histolytica - ees the most dangerous. Eet comes from bad food and bad water. This amoeba, eet forms cysts weet strong walls that protect the amoebas from the acid een your stomach. When the cysts go to the intestines, the amoebas come free and you get ver' sick like you. These amoebas can eat through your intestines and go in your blood to your lungs and your brain and your liver. Ver' dangerous. You can die from this. You must stay three, four days so we can control the fever.'

*And, remind me again why I'm very lucky*, I felt like saying.

'But I can't stay,' I said with Plato logic. 'I've bought a 150-rial ticket for this evening's bus to Tabriz. I can't afford not to use it.'

'Eef you feel better at four o'clock,' the doctor conceded, 'you can go. But eef you wish you can stay three days, four days, one week. All free.' He put a comforting hand on my shoulder.

'I will come for you at 4.45pm,' Viktor promised.

Over the next eight hours the staff at the Shafa Hospital did their utmost to get me back on my feet. They gave me regular drinks, fed me masses of pills, pumped me with injections of Vitamin C, morphine and Streptomycin Sulphate, and helped me to and from the bathroom. At quarter past four they sent in their secret weapon, a beautiful young nurse named Mozayan who spoke fluent English through hazel eyes that would've melted stone.

'You have a fever,' she said. 'The doctor thinks you should stay for some days.'

When Viktor came at quarter to five I told him I wasn't leaving. Then, stoked up on morphine and the thought of losing my 150 rials, I changed my mind and discharged myself. Mozayan shook her head. Back at the hotel, the others were amazed.

'My god! It's the fightin' Irish!' Tony Lee howled. It was in my view a howl of awe and admiration. He would later claim it was a howl of angst.

'We are brothers,' Georgio said. 'We will help you back to Europe.' He gave me a big hug. That did it. The gallopers were back.

A few minutes later another taxi was called and I was carried out again.

'We are sorry,' Georgio said. 'This time we cannot go. The bus leaves.'

'No problem,' I croaked. Three quarters of an hour after leaving the hospital I was back again. Mozayan was still at the door.

'I thought you would come back,' she said as I fell from the taxi. 'I waited here.'

In the coming days Mozayan became a good friend, calling two or three times a day, staying for as long as she could, and getting more beautiful by the hour. No matter how bad I felt, she brought a sparkle to the ward. She also introduced me to Nikou Karr, another

## Chapter 17

young doctor who spoke English and called occasionally to help me pass the time between bouts of blood letting and shivering. Nikou was interested in Ireland and its customs and the differences between the lifestyles of the young of both countries. He would like to visit Ireland, he said. My notes of the time record that we spoke of '...*travelling, doctoring, religion, differences between Irish and Iranian customs (dating etc), and the effects of hashish.*' Poor Nikou's brain must've been fried. Each day Mozayan introduced me to new people and I was overcome by the kindness of everyone around me - staff and patients - as the fever fluctuated and the pills and injections rained down.

After two days without food Doctor Push insisted I eat some plain yoghurt.

'I don't like yoghurt,' I said.

'But, ees ver' goot for you,' he said. 'Ees made from meelk. Eet make you ver' strong. Eef you eat I geef you cheeken for deener.'

I forced it down. It ran straight through me. Later I wobbled to the bathroom and had a shave and a shower, both of which I badly needed. In the bathroom mirror a shockingly gaunt figure, with skin the colour of peat ash, stared back at me from deep black circles.

'The doctors think you should take the aeroplane back to Ireland,' Mozayan said that evening. 'It is not good to travel when you are sick like this.' I didn't want to shatter any illusions by telling her that there was only £10 and 300 Iranian rials ($3) left in the kitty.

'Perhaps they are right,' I said, looking thoughtfully towards my toes.

Across from me in the ward, a young boy from rural Iran looked downhearted. To cheer him up, I gave him one of two pocket flick knives I'd bought in Afghanistan. He was ecstatic. He sat up in bed like Jack the Ripper, flicking the blade and slashing wildly at passing staff and imaginary foes. The staff gave wan smiles in my direction. I was becoming a bit of an institution.

But in the end, I was anxious to get going again. It was a Monday night, the beginning of a new week, and I felt suddenly cured. When Mozayan called I told her.

'I'm planning to leave in the morning,' I said. 'My friend will be waiting for me in England.' She looked surprised.

'So you think you are better?'

'I feel great,' I lied.

'I think you are a little crazy,' she said.

We talked for an hour and laughed a lot and in the end she told me that she didn't work on Tuesdays and wouldn't see me again if I left the next day. Later that evening I wrote her a note of thanks and realised that I would miss her. Had Cora not been back in Cork, who knows what end there might have been?

On the morning of Tuesday, April 7th, I rose and packed. Then I thought about it, and decided to wait until afternoon. That way I'd get a few extra hours of proper treatment, which made sense as I was still bleeding from the nose and felt weak and knotted. A few more injections wouldn't go astray. Not to mention the free dinner.

\* \* \*

Far from well was I. The very effort of shouldering my pack made me whoozy; every footstep drove spikes of pain through my stomach. But pride wouldn't let me go back again. Having no money for a taxi, I plodded in a daze to the bus station and arrived drawn and listless. With no real choice, I bought a ticket for Tabriz and began the long limp back to Istanbul. At four in the afternoon I was joined in the station by a thin, 34-year-old, short-haired, shaggy-bearded German named Werner. He wore a bush hat and looked like some kind of eccentric Middle Earth archaeologist. We sat together on the Tabriz bus.

'I got out of Cambodia just in time,' Werner told me. 'Two days after I left, fighting broke out between the Americans and the Communists. Officially, the Americans are not in Cambodia, but they have had thousands of troops there for some time.'

'You were lucky,' I said, trying to sound alert.

'Very lucky. I have also been lucky in Jerusalem. I left two days before the Six Day War broke out. Before the war, all of the Arabs used to tell me and my friends that, if there was a war, the Arabs would win. One day, I said that I thought the Jews were too strong for the Arabs. We had to run for our lives from a storm of stones...'

Werner had almost been married back in his home town of Regensburg. But the road was too strong.

'Travelling is good,' he said. 'But sometimes I think it is possible to lose the game.'

'Dunno,' I said, struggling to show some spark of interest.

In Tabriz we got off the bus at two in the morning and, in the middle of the city, I introduced Werner to sleeping in building sites. At 5.30am we took a taxi to the city outskirts and boarded a bus to Bazargan and the Turkish frontier. When we arrived, we found the

## Chapter 17

border buzzing with travellers - English, German, Swiss, American, Canadian, Australian, French, Malaysian and a man from Nepal.

'But no Irish,' Werner said. 'Never any Irish.'

We travelled to Dogubayazit in a bouncing wreck of a bus, the effect dire on my stomach. It wasn't helped by regular jarring halts to pick up dozens of people and monstrous loads to be stacked to the roof inside the back door. The weight increased a terrifying crashing of the wrecked suspensions on the rough road.

Werner lightened the journey with his objective view of India.

'You will like it but it is a crazy place. There are many things about it that the Western mind cannot understand. Take for example, the Hindu religion. It is a complete barrier to progress. The caste system makes so the Indian must accept his lot and make no attempt to improve his situation as everything is decided by the gods. And there are many, many gods. In a country where so many people are dying of hunger, people build houses for sick cows and feed the rats, which eat twice as much corn every year as India imports. But the cow is a god and a man cannot sleep in the god's house, or else he might return in the next life as a tree or a rock. For the same reason, a man dares not eat the food being given to the holy animals - the rats. And, if during the night, a rat eats off the finger of a child, the woman of the house, instead of killing the rat, will carry it outside and let it loose. Snakes and monkeys are also sacred.'

'Is that a fact?' I said.

'Another great barrier to progress is the attitude of the Indian towards modern methods and modern ideas. The Indian will always refer to the fact that India had a great civilisation when Europe was living in the Stone Age, so why should they change anything now...?'

I had a problem with much of this, but I was too weak to argue. I adopted a somewhat neutral gaze.

At Dogubayazit, we had lunch in a small lokanta. At one of the communal tables we were joined by another bearded German called Bernd whose well put together frame had been greatly thinned by his months on the road. A dozen noisy men in overcoats, baggy trousers and wool hats who were in from the snows of the Kurdish mountains waved and shouted from the other tables.

'Marco Polo came here in 1270,' Werner said, 'and had a good look for Noah's Ark up there on Mount Ararat.' He pointed towards the twin peaks that towered white and brilliant behind the rooftops of the town. 'And today we must visit the Palace and mosque of Ishak Pasha.'

Despite not feeling up to the five-kilometre uphill hike I trudged along that evening behind Werner and Bernd.

Ruins have never held my breath. Still, you could see why an 18th century Ottoman chieftain, wanting to control the valley below on this desolate stretch of the Silk Road, might plant a fortress here. We wandered the deserted complex and Bernd took photos of the calligraphy on the interior walls. One verse, we later learned, translated into '*Ishak, upon whose will, made the whole world a place of benevolence and the date to witness this was one thousand one hundred and ninety-nine*' (1784 AD). It failed to mention that Ishak's benevolence didn't extend to the Armenian who designed the complex. To ensure he couldn't create a duplicate for any rival, Ishak had his hands chopped off.

Just before dark we climbed into the mosque's minaret. Instantly the complex came to life in the form of a roaring looper in a turban and white beard. Apart from recognising the words Allah and Mohammad, we had no idea what he was saying; but when we came down he attacked us with a walking stick.

'Mind yourself,' I told him, conjuring up an atrocious look.

This seemed to calm him down. None the less, he followed us down the track, yelling apparent curses until we were lost in the dark.

We bedded down that night on the floor of the tiny bus office and slept in fits and starts as people clambered over us.

On the road again at 4.00am, we'd covered quite a distance before the sun rose to scatter pink petals over the snowcaps. Storks and eagles filled the sky and I rallied a little. *This was the life,* I thought. *How great to be still in it.*

At Erzurum railway station there was pandemonium as people fought to get on the eight o'clock evening train to Istanbul which arrived at quarter to nine. With people shouting, piling luggage in through windows and climbing over one another, I became separated from Werner and Bernd and lost them in the crush. Eventually I fought my way onto the train, but hadn't the strength or energy to face two days standing in the crowded corridor. I booked a sleeper in second class and lay there like warmed-up death for the journey back to Üsküdar.

# Chapter 18
## Lorna

---

By the time I reached Istanbul I was pretty much broke. Had I been feeling stronger, I would have made a run for Viktor's place in Munich. Instead I decided I needed money. As waiting for a round of letters wasn't an option and the nearest Irish embassy was in Rome, I went to the British Consulate.

'Hello,' I said to the official at the desk. 'I was wondering if the Consulate could loan me, say £40?' [The equivalent of about $95 at the time.] 'I'll send it back when I get home and get a job.'

'Are you being funny?' the official asked in a rude tone. He was a man in his thirties, dressed in a loose grey suit, white shirt and red tie. His face shone with the signs of good eating and he eyed me with disdain. I was probably cluttering up the office. I on the other hand didn't like his tone and thought he looked like a goose.

'No,' I assured him stoutly. 'I can give you my passport details.' He grinned the grin of the sardonic. 'Look,' I added. 'If there was an Irish embassy anywhere close, I wouldn't be here, I'd be asking them for the loan; but there isn't.'

'Wait a moment,' he said and off he went to confer with his colleagues. *Money coming*, I said to myself. *Yahoo!* But no.

'The only way we can help you,' he chirped when he returned, 'is to contact your family through the Irish Department of Foreign Affairs.'

'But that's going to panic them,' I said. 'There must be another way.'

'There's no other way,' he insisted. 'We'll need to get Foreign Affairs to arrange for your family to deposit the money for you, but it will take several days. In the meantime I suggest that you get your hands on a Bulgarian visa.'

'I was planning to do that anyway,' I said trying to salvage some dignity from the situation.

'Please wait,' he said. 'We'll see if we can send the telegram now to the Irish government in Dublin.' Half an hour later he called me back to the desk.

'The telegram has been sent,' he told me. 'That will be five US dollars.'

'You're having me on,' I said, but he wasn't the having-on type.

Two days later, as I finally began to recover my strength, the money came through. But the Consulate wouldn't hand it over. Instead they gave me $30 in travellers' cheques and 585 Turkish lira - useless outside Turkey. A note confirmed that the money had been changed at the legal rate as opposed to the black market.

'You can go to the train station and buy a ticket to London with that,' the Consulate official said.

'What are you talking about?' I said. 'I don't want a [I felt like saying 'fucking'] ticket to London!'

'The best thing for a sick person,' the official said. 'You can show the note at the station.'

'But I'm better now,' I insisted.

'I'm glad to hear that,' he said. 'But we don't think that people like you, who come without sufficient funds, should be here in the first place.'

'Not your business.' I said. 'This is *my* money. You have no right to do this to *my* money.' But he wouldn't budge. It was, I concluded, another example of British colonialism downtrodding the hapless.

I left the Consulate and went straight to the Osmanli Bankasi to see if they would change the lira back to the dollars or traveller's cheques that I needed for the journey north. But without the proper bank receipt they refused and sent me back to the British. At the Consulate, I kicked up a row, telling them that I recognised robbery when I saw it. But they were as determined that I was going to take the train as I was determined that I wasn't. I was now forced to seek out the black market money changers among the cobbled alleys and wooden houses of old Istanbul. And settle for crap black market rates. I lost $25 of my $95 without an honest mugger in sight. I was furious, but determined to defeat the oppressor.

*I'll make it to Viktor's place*, I swore, *and that'll sock it to the British Consulate and all belonging to them*. Each day I didn't go down or get sick or run broke, I'd be wiping their gobs in manure.

Meanwhile, Lorna from Toronto had graced the scene, adding more steam to the engine.

On arrival in Istanbul, Werner, Bernd and I had booked into the Hotel Gulp before picking up our mail at the Poste Restante. (Along with two letters from Cora, there was one from Tony, writing from Frankfurt to say that he was doing well.) We spent the remainder of the day wandering the alcoves of the Grand Bazaar before concluding with a nighttime mystery tour led by Werner.

## Chapter 18

'This is a special place in Istanbul,' he told myself and Bernd. 'Special for Islamic Turkey too.' He led us through some back streets at the far side of the Galata Bridge to a winding alley crowded with Turkish men.

'The Street of the Prostitutes,' he announced like it was the mines of King Solomon. I had never seen or imagined the likes of a place like this. Women of all ages, shapes and sizes, were on full, semi-naked display behind long windows and glass-fronted doors. Modesty was an occasional bra. Some big rough girls at the bottom of the street were a holy fright.

'I come here,' Werner said, 'every time I go to Asia. It puts me off women for the next six months.'

I hurried out of that place.

The following day Werner and Bernd took their beards off to Munich on the Orient Express. I booked into the Sultan Ahmet Hotel where Tony and I had stayed aeons ago. Sharing the room were Tsutomo Takahashi from Tokyo, early twenties, long-haired, bespectacled student, with a great sense of humour but little English; and clean-cut to a polish, thirty-something Shyam Mohan Shrestha, Inspector at the Casino Nepal, the Boaltee Hotel, Kathmandu, whom I'd already briefly met at the Iranian border. Despite staying in a shared room in one of Istanbul's hippie hotels, Shyam never looked anything other than immaculate. Like a guy about to get married, he made us all feel good.

'You come to Kathmandu,' he said, giving us his card, 'you stay with me.'

When he left after a couple of days, someone else's pack was planted in our room. The owner was a tall, muscle-bulked American with fugitive eyes, a jaw built for gnashing Brazil nuts, and a stubble that equally covered head and face. In short, he looked like a homicidal maniac fresh out of Vietnam, and didn't take too kindly to having his gear moved about 'for the third fucking time in four fucking days'. He went berserk

'This is not fucking on!' he yelled. 'Make no fucking mistake about it.' He swept the pack from the floor, stormed the lobby, demanded his money back, and kicked over a table on his way out. That left me and Tsutomo with a room to ourselves for the night.

Next morning we were both at the Bulgarian Consulate applying for visas when Lorna walked in. A second generation Japanese Canadian student, she was nineteen, long-haired, petite and pretty.

She was also, it transpired, made of rubber. She could double over backwards and stick her head between her legs, which made her look like a giant four-legged spider. Dressed in denims, T-shirt and white Afghan jacket, Lorna was on her way to France. As we'd be covering much of the same ground, we agreed to travel together as far as the middle of Germany. I was delighted. *Giorraíonn beirt bóthar*,' I said to myself.[20] Lorna would brighten the days and the hitchhiking prospects. She in turn was happy to have the protection of a male companion, even if he was an emaciated wreck.

'Just one thing,' I said. 'I'm very short of money and need to get to Munich as fast as I can.'

'Suits me fine,' Lorna said. 'I'm also in a hurry.'

It would transpire that we had different definitions of a hurry.

When we arrived back at the Sultan Ahmet Hotel, Tsutomo stood at the entrance, Lorna went to buy some nuts and I went off to change the last fiver of my traveller's cheques.

'Tsutomo,' I said in slow separate words, 'when-she-comes-back-tell-her-to-wait-for-me-so-we-can-make-plans. Do-you-understand?'

Tsutomo grinned and nodded. But when I got back Lorna was gone and I couldn't for the life of me get from him what the bloody hell he'd said to her. Dejected, I went back to the hotel to find that a blond, bearded, beer-sculling Swedish giant named Olaf had moved into our room. He was on his way to South America through Asia.

'Don't vurry,' he laughed. 'The girl vill come back. Now, haf one beer.'

At seven o'clock the hotel reception brought me a note: '*It's the Japanese girl*,' it read. '*Could you ask the Irish boy if he is going tomorrow to call at the Yucel Hostel by Ayasofya before 8.00. My room is 34. Lorna Sakagami.*'

I was there at 7.30pm. Over the course of the next twenty-four hours, during which we visited Topkapi Palace, Lorna and I were only apart during the hours of sleep. We got on so well that people began to mistake us for a long-established item.

At some point Lorna mentioned that she didn't have a rucksack. She travelled with a suitcase on wheels. I suppressed a terrible prejudice. Was Lorna a *tourist*?

*   *   *

---

[20] 'Two shorten a road' - old Irish proverb.

## Chapter 18

The Orient Express[21] left Istanbul at 9.30pm on April 16th in a mighty black deluge. Using tactics I'd learned from Ismet and Suleyman on the way east, we secured us a compartment.

'Boots to the door,' I advised. 'We'll have a bench each for the night.'

It was a struggle to hold the ground but Lorna was so impressed she said I should come visit her in Canada.

'You'd like Toronto. It's got lots of parks, a beautiful bay on the shores of Lake Ontario - it means "the Lake of Shining Waters" in the Huron language - and heaps of wildlife. Right around the city, there's a load of ravines and wetlands where, on a good day you can see raccoons, coyotes, muskrat, deer, beaver, squirrels, chipmunks, groundhogs, skunks, even turtles, and we have about 150 species of bird. And then you have the rest of Canada at your feet. And there's the Irish connection. After your big famine of the 1840s, we had a lot of Irish immigrants. By 1851, the biggest ethnic group in Toronto was Irish-born.'

'And the other Irish connection,' I said. 'We invaded Canada.' (I couldn't resist.)

'What?' Lorna said.

'In 1866 Irish American Fenians invaded Canada from the States.'

'Never heard that,' Lorna said.

'They wanted to occupy part of Canada and hold it to ransom to force the British out of Ireland. So they got together all these Irish veterans of the American Civil War and invaded across the Niagara River. It was a bit of a disaster, but they tried. Ever heard of the Battle of Ridgeway in Ontario?'

'No,' Lorna said.

'There you go. Ireland won.'[22]

'That,' Lorna said, tilting her head to one side, 'sounds like a load of what comes out of a bull's arse. You didn't happen to have a seizure trying to hold that door?'

'It's true,' I insisted. 'I'll get you the book when I get home.'

Twelve hours on, the Battle of Ridgeway still unresolved, we arrived red-eyed in Edirne. After a quick bite in the station, someone gave us a lift into town and we caught a bus to the Bulgarian border.

---

[21] The original Orient Express was a normal international railway service connecting Paris to Istanbul. It ceased to function in 1977.
[22] 650 Fenians and 850 Canadians fought at Ridgeway. After a two-hour battle the Fenians routed the Canadian force.

Out of sight of the border post we set down our bags and began to hitchhike. Lorna took out a small mirror and stared into it.

'I look like shit,' she said.

'No, you don't,' I assured her. 'You look like Benzaiten, Japanese Goddess of Love and Beauty.' This was a handy bit of cultural knowledge gleaned from Tsutomo back at the Sultan Ahmet. It did the trick. Lorna was appreciative.

'Where the hell did you pick up that fucking baloney?' she said.

That first day wasn't too bad. Fifteen minutes and we were on our way, picked up by a young German in a minibus who drove us the 250 kilometres to Sofia. Exhausted, we slept much of the way. But during bouts of waking we noted roads that had little traffic, and towns and villages dangerously populated by bullock carts, goats, pigs, chickens and ducks while, to the south, the Rodope Mountains with their vast coniferous forests provided spectacular vistas. Twice the cops stopped us on narrow switchbacks as we closed in on Sofia. They wanted to see our passports. Ireland, Germany and Canada were OK.

In Sofia, a city of dreary Soviet-style highrise and a charming old centre of beautiful Orthodox churches and café-lined streets, Lenin was a hundred and they were celebrating his birthday. The city was festooned in hammers and sickles. Eight-storey billboards showed the old warrior as a steely-eyed, fiery god figure in an overcoat, towering above iconoclastic depictions of marching workers and triumphant armies. But, despite the celebratory trappings, the city seemed solemn and unnaturally quiet, and the grey cops who shadowed us to a café close to the gold-domed Alexander Nevski Cathedral didn't like us at all. We tried to change money at the tourist office but couldn't. Instead we were sent around to the Hotel Sofia, one of the city's Intourist hotels open to foreigners as part of the overall control mechanisms in operation. We'd have to stay there, we were told: building sites weren't an option. At the hotel we changed money but the rooms were too expensive. However, the staff booked us in at the much cheaper Hotel Hemus and gave us directions that included a free tram ride that probably wasn't.

Expecting a dive, we arrived at a 20-storey luxury tower looming into the communist sky. It had a big neon sign and cops outside to keep an eye on the likes of us. We braced ourselves: we may have looked like tramps, but that didn't mean we had to feel like tramps.

'Would this meet with your approval sir?' Lorna asked.

## Chapter 18

'Indeed it might madam,' I said. 'After you.'

'Thanking you sir,' Lorna said. Swishing her hair like a thoroughbred's tail, she sashayed her Levis into the lobby like Marilyn Munroe turned out for an audition. I followed in tatty jeans, scuffed boots and faded combats, like an extra down on his luck.

After the initial bewildered stares of staff, glaringly unused to hippie-type visitations, everyone warmly fell over us and treated us like the celebrities we clearly were. They then led us to a room, high above the Sofia skyline and looking across at the vast dome of Mount Vitosha. The sprawling bed, with its soft plump pillows, palatial by hobo standards, was something that had faded from dreams. Lorna saw the wonder on my face.

'In the beginning,' she said, 'human beings slept on the ground. Then they made beds from leaves, straw and twigs. Next step was to put animal skins on top to make things more comfortable. Then they made blankets from the skins. Later came the concept of the mattress, when skins were stitched together and filled with hair, wool and the like. Next innovation was raising the mattress off the floor on wooden frames and ropes. Are you with me?'

'So far.'

'So where along this evolutionary trajectory did you fall off?'

'I'll have you know,' I enlightened her, 'that the ancient Fianna of Ireland could sleep on the tips of their spears. We don't place great value on beds.' This was a bit of an exaggeration but how was Lorna to know?

We showered, changed and washed clothes. Lorna put on some make-up and in that confined space it was hard not to really see that Japanese Goddess of Love and Beauty. Later, we went back into the old city just to annoy the cops again and get ourselves reported to Leonid Brezhnev back in Moscow. It was then time to share that big sumptuous double bed.

'You Irish are very *Catholic*,' Lorna observed in the morning after a night that would've done a monk and a nun proud. I think the adjective she wanted to use was either *wholesome* or *dumb*.

From Sofia we travelled by train to Dimitrovgrad in what was then Yugoslavia where we picked up visas and waited for the cheap local night train to Belgrade. In town, people shied away from us when we asked questions, and seemed to think us funny. Cops with communist-grey uniforms and big black belts crossing their chests wanted to know when we were leaving.

It being Saturday we were unable to change money and boarded the night train hoping to pay in dollars. When the conductor refused to accept dollars, an enterprising passenger described in my notes as 'a sly-looking chap' offerd us ten dinar to the dollar instead of twelve. 'But,' the notes tell me, 'it didn't take us very long to put him in his proper place.' When we reached Nis, some officials changed our money and we paid the fare before switching to a more comfortable train on which Lorna and I managed again to secure a compartment.

'You're nothing short of a hero,' Lorna said. (Or maybe I just thought it myself.)

After a night of torrential rain and little sleep, our train rolled in to a flooded Belgrade at half five in the morning.

'I need sleep,' Lorna said. 'That thing where you shut your eyes when it's dark. That thing we haven't had for two of the last three nights. Yesterday I looked like shit. Today I feel like shit.'

'Once the sun comes up you'll feel better,' I consoled. 'And we should get to a pension or something tonight.' Lorna smiled but it was a wan smile.

Despite the hour, the station was already crowded, and we were welcomed on the platform by a group of students, keen to practice English.

'How is this?' one guy asked. 'How do you have one Irish and one Japanese coming from Istanbul?'

'We're lost,' Lorna said. 'How do we get to France?' I laughed encouragingly. *Lorna me girl, that was a good one.*

Then calamity! After buying some food at a nearby shop and sitting down to consume same at the table of an outdoor restaurant I realised that I'd left my Italian sleeping bag on the train. I ran back to the station but the train had gone.

'Not good,' Lorna said. 'Now you'll have to sleep on the tip of that spear.'

'Very bad,' I said. 'This means that once I run out of money I'll only be able to sleep during the day when it's warm.' Lorna's eyes bulged.

'It may sound odd,' she said (that wan smile again), 'but I could never imagine myself making a statement like that. It's like saying "I broke my cup so I'll never be able to drink again" when you could actually buy another cup.'

'No, it's not,' I said but if I looked sideways I could see the logic.

## Chapter 18

We caught a bus to the city outskirts; but at this early hour motorised traffic was so slow that I suggested we catch up on sleep. Putting my pack and Lorna's wheelie-case beside me, I lay down on the side of the road. Lorna gaped down at me.

'You can't be serious...!'

'What's wrong?' I asked. I was genuinely puzzled. 'I thought you might like a bit of a rest...'

'You want to sleep *here?* On the road?'

Reminded me of the guy in the digs who gets a bowl of milk and, just as he goes to drink it he spots a dead mouse at the bottom. When he complains, the landlady scoops out the mouse and hands him back the bowl of milk. And he complains again.

Anyway, I managed to persuade Lorna of the virtues of a roadside kip and she bedded down on the far side of the bags. An hour later we were woken by the hooting of a car. Someone had stopped to give us a lift.

Over the next seventeen hours we travelled west, then north west, through the villages and towns of rural Yugoslavia in a series of short lifts and long waits, using transport cafés as stepping stones. At one in the morning we arrived in Zagreb and slept in a dosshouse run by the Red Cross. 'Lorna has been very irritable today,' my diary puzzled. 'We've only been roughing it for three days and it's beginning to get the better of her.'

In a better world, we should've stopped, booked into a nice place, slept all day and had dinner and wine. We didn't. A quick breakfast six hours after arriving at the dosshouse and we were away again, taking a (free) tram to the city outskirts, from where an immediate lift brought us to Varazdin, a small town some twenty kilometres from the Hungarian border.

'It's strange being so close to Hungary,' Lorna said, 'seeing as we actually want to go to Austria.'

It had been my suggestion to take this road as it was a primary road. But it was a puzzle to Lorna, perhaps where her faith in me began to waver.

'As we're not going to Hungary,' she pointed out, 'we now have to take this very small, secondary road with no traffic to get back on the road we should be on.' She was looking down the road that pointed towards a village called Ormoz and whatever lay beyond.

As luck would have it, progress at that point came to a standstill with traffic reduced for the most part to crude ox-drawn carts. We walked, ate nothing, walked more and waited long hours by the side of the road.

'Isn't that lovely,' I said as evening settled over a countryside fetchingly dappled in slanting sunlight, 'watching the peasants dawdle home in their carts as if they haven't got a care in the world.'

No sooner was it out than I knew that the brain wasn't supplying filters to the mouth. I was probably lucky I didn't get a hatchet in the head.

'Ciarán,' Lorna said with gimlet eye and unnerving calm, 'it's going to be dark soon. We're out in the middle of goddamn *nowhere*. We haven't eaten since goddamn breakfast and we've had nothing to drink all goddamn day.' Did I detect a doleful wobble in those last few words?

'Someone will pick us up,' I said.

'Who!' Lorna snapped. 'The next fucking extra-terrestrials!'

*Lorna*, I felt like saying, *there's no need for that*.

It then began to rain: small irregular drops at first, gradually swelling to a steady maleficent deadfall of big dopey blobs. In the background I could swear I heard Lorna say terrible words to some man up in the sky.

Finally, well after dark when silence had filled the space between us, two Dutchmen in a truck gave us a lift to the border.

We completed Austrian border formalities shortly after midnight, then sheltered from the rain in the Customs post where we could ask each passing driver for a lift. However, there was such a long interval between vehicles that we eventually dozed off. At two o'clock the cops secured us a lift to Leibnitz. And there in Leibnitz, when one of the wheels fell off her telescopic-handled case, an exhausted Lorna lost it.

'Maybe you don't mind travelling all day and all night,' she sobbed. 'Not eating. Not drinking. Not sleeping. But I do-o-o...' I went to put my arm around her but quickly pulled back as she bared her teeth.

Next day, after sleeping until noon in the Lions' Touring Club, we both felt better and headed off across the eastern Alps, bound for Salzburg, with goodness between us again. It was *look at this* and *look at that*. Quaint *Sound of Music* men in knee-britches, coloured socks, short-sleeved shirts and feathered hats worked the spring fields. Deer crossed the road. Snow glistened on the forest trees, the shark-fin peaks and the mountain slopes. In the evening we travelled along the shores of Wolfgangsee and Fuschlsee, two tranquil lakes

## Chapter 18

separated by a long winding road and locked in between towering peaks, many too vertical to hold snow. In the twilight, the lakes and snow-wreathed conifers glittered silver, adding to a serenity with which I was so taken that I hitchhiked back two days later to retrace on foot a 17-kilometre stretch of the road.

Twenty minutes beyond the lakes, we rounded a bend and saw before us the twinking eventide lights of Salzburg.

'Look!' Lorna said. 'Civilisation! Hostels exist there. And food. And all the trappings of the modern world. Things so many people take for granted. Soon we'll be there. Soon I can sleep. Sleep, sleep, sleep.'

She sounded like an imbecile just rescued from Elephant Island by Ernest Shackleton.

Although Lorna and I had planned to travel together as far as the middle of Germany, we parted in Salzburg after two days of doing the sights: the Mönchsberg Mountain for a panorama of the city; the water gardens of Hellbrunn Palace; cafés where we stuffed our faces; and night ambles along the banks of the Salzach River, overlooked by onion-domed churches and the great white floodlit mass of the Hohensalzburg Castle. Occasionally Lorna livened up the lives of Salzburg's citizens with her remarkable rubber manoeuvres. Then we'd swing one another about, laugh out loud and fall about the place. But, on the eve of the second day, running broke and in a bigger hurry than before, I told her that I needed to push on to Munich no matter what it took.

'If Viktor isn't there,' I added, 'the urgency will multiply.'

To Lorna this had a homicidal ring.

'You know what?' she said with a big genuine smile, 'I might just hang here. But we mustn't forget to swap addresses before you leave. The invite to Toronto still stands. And you promised me proof of that Battle of Ridgeway that I think you made up just to win me over whereas all you really had to do was drag me by the hair from Istanbul to Salzburg.'

On the third day I rose again in pouring rain and bade farewell to the two others with whom I'd shared the male dorm in the city's hostel. One was a man from Amsterdam who, on my arrival, had popped a tab of acid and was talking in riddles.

'The toxins, man,' he told me. 'They are all around you. Like a big aura. You must kill the toxins.'

The second was a Moroccan who spent the night cursing the

German cops who'd fined him 10 marks for hitchhiking on the autobahn.

'They are fucking *nothing* people,' he said.

'It is a new category,' the Amsterdam man explained. 'Full of fucking toxins.'

When I left for Munich Lorna was still sleeping so we never did get to swap addresses. I sometimes wonder where life took her.

# Chapter 19
Munich

Soaked to the skin, I arrived three hours later in Marienplatz in the heart of Munich just as the city's Glockenspiel chimed.

During the Middle Ages, markets and tournaments flourished in this square, named after the Mariensäule, a Marian column dating from 1638 and celebrating the end of Swedish occupation. Dominating the northern side of Marienplatz lay the 100-metre-long Gothic facade of the New City Hall, crowded with images of the Guelph Duke, Henry the Lion, and the entire line of the Bavarian Wittelsbach dynasty - the largest princely cycle to be found on any German town hall. The Glockenspiel, built into the 85-metre tower, was an oddity that was added in 1908.

Every day this collection of forty-three bells and thirty-two life-sized figures chimed out a reenactment of the marriage of Duke Wilhelm V (who founded the world famous Hofbräuhaus in 1589) to Renata of Lorraine. An accompanying joust with life-sized knights on horseback showed the Bavarian knight defeating the Lothringen knight every time. This was followed by the Schäfflertanz (the coopers' dance). According to myth, the coopers were said to have danced through the streets of Munich during a year of plague in 1517 to 'bring fresh vitality to fearful dispositions'. The dance came to symbolize perseverance and loyalty through difficult times.

Show over, I walked to where Viktor lived, and found to my surprise that his abode lay on the ground floor of a smart three-storey apartment block, three kilometres north of the city centre in an area called Schwabing. Once the bohemian quarter of the city, this attractive leafy suburb was now a centre of student accommodation, close to the Ludwigs-Maximilians University and the Technical University of Munich. Within a stone's throw was the entrance to Englishgarten, an enormous park made famous in the 1960s by a decision to allow nude sunbathing in its 'Schönfeld meadow'.

To my greater surprise, the door of Viktor's bedsit was opened by Tony Lee.

'Well, Jesus Christ mate,' he said. 'It's the wild Irish. [Reputation problem again.] Come in mate. Viktor is at university studying his psychology - or he may be one of the exhibits - but he should be back any time. We were wondering just last night how you'd fared in Tehran. How're you feeling mate?'

'Hungry,' I said. 'And what the hell are *you* doing here?'

'Arrived a week ago,' he told me. 'Need work so I can save money before going to London.'

'Money is a bad word,' I said. 'I'm down to my last twenty-two dollars.'

'Come on in,' he said. 'Have some bread and salami.'

I followed him through the hall to a bedsit that had Viktor all over it in staggering proportions. The walls, splashed in a multitude of colours, were plastered with psychedelic posters of rock groups, maps of Europe and Asia, and a huge face of eyes, nose and lips. Cushions littered the floor. Rows of coloured bulbs were attached to a switchboard by the bed. A stove occupied one corner and a record player another. Joss sticks sat on every flat surface, all appearing to smell of hash and sandalwood.

'The lights are for the nightly shows,' Tony explained. 'When the lad gets ripped, we have the light shows.'

At half past six, the great Viktor appeared in the doorway, still in the white sheepskin from Kabul, and now growing a reddish beard to meet the blond hair.

'Hey Irish!' he roared. 'You made it!' He grabbed me in a bear hug. 'But there is only bones,' he added.

'I'm picking up,' I assured him.

'Here,' he said, dropping a supermarket bag on the floor. 'I have bread and four kinds of cheeses. How did you get here?'

He put on some music and we sat on the floor to a bottle of cheap red wine while I described the trip from Tehran and refrained from upending the grocery bag.

'What do you think of my place, man?' he asked. 'You have seen my lights?'

'Oh Jesus,' Tony said. 'Not the light-show again.'

Eventually hunger got the better of me.

'What's this?' I said, whipping from the grocery bag a black sticky slab.

'*Schwarzbrot*,' Tony said. 'Black rye bread. They have 600 types of bread in this country. You can get *schwarzbrot, toastbrot, weizenmischbrot, zwiebelbrot* and 596 other kinds of *brot*.'

'How-do-you-like-my-Ger-man?' I said in an exaggerated accent.

## Chapter 19

'Shaddup!' Viktor said.

I tucked in, safe at last in the bosom of Viktor's flat. It was the first time I'd been able to relax since Tehran and starvation mode set in after weeks of shrivelling illness. I ate and ate but couldn't douse the hunger.

'He's a shrew mate,' Tony said. 'Has to eat his own weight twice a day.'

'How long can you stay?' Viktor asked.

'Maybe a week,' I said.

'H-m-m-m,' Viktor said as his loaf of *schwarzbrot* and four kinds of cheeses vanished.

There then followed a night of reminiscing that would've cleared the decks of any old persons' home.

The next day was Saturday, the last Saturday in April, a lovely spring day of sweet-smelling blossoms that encouraged us to sit outside. Viktor rolled joints while Tony, still in sandals and Afghan coat, recounted his time on the Sandysudhanlaya Ashram with Swami Chinmayanda. He then moved on to the stuff of campfires, the yarns that had marked the made in India ones as the Brahmins of Istanbul's Pudding Shop.

'I came across this guy down in Bangalore, called Sai-Baba, who can materialise things out of thin air, like gold bracelets and the like. He gave me a small carving of himself that he created right there in front of my eyes.'

'We will go back there,' Viktor said. 'He can make for me a new car.'

'I'm not sure that's the full spirit of this mate,' Tony said. 'But, to continue... There's another old swami who's been locked away in a cave for eighteen years and hasn't eaten a thing in all that time. The only person with a key to the cave is the local mayor who comes along once a year to let the old swami out for the day.'

'Maybe we should send Irish there,' Viktor said. 'It would cure his eating.'

In full fettle, Tony now settled into the lotus position and gave us the benefit of his year-long course in Hindu philosophy and associated snippets of wisdom as were to be found on ashrams. On the strength of this, I would spend the coming days immersed in such tomes as *The Tibetan Book of the Dead, The Bhhagavadgita* and *The Universe and Doctor Einstein* while Tony stood on his head in the middle of the floor, Viktor played The Rolling Stones, Jethro

Thull and Jimi Hendriz's *Voodoo Child* at a thousand decibels, and smoke billowed from mighty conical creations. In the meantime Viktor ran us ragged.

On the Saturday night we drove a hundred kilometres to his parents' place in the town of Abensberg with a dishwasher in the back seat of his Volkswagon Beetle and the three of us crushed into the two front seats.

Viktor introduced us to his parents who looked aghast at his choice of newfound friends. And while the mother made us dinner the father asked questions through Viktor as to what Tony and I planned to do with our lives. I got the feeling from the way he grimaced that he wasn't holding out too much hope.

On the way back we stopped off at Haystack Disco in a village north of Munich where we met many of Viktor's friends. Viktor drank a lot and, on the way home, ran us off the minor road twice with the zest of a cliff-bound lemming. From there on, the days pretty much ran into one another.

Sunday was a day of rest, listening to music over a big bong that Viktor had constructed from a lemonade bottle.

Monday night was concert night with Ten Years After at the Circus Krone-Bau after Viktor sold half his stash to buy the tickets. There, we joined the general stampede for the expensive front seats once the lights went out and watched Alvin Lee bring the house down with his guitar work in a haze of hash so thick that you could've sliced it with a hatchet and passed it around.

Back at Schwabing, Viktor went into one of his Afghan deliriums and discovered in his room the Queen of Sheeba. She was under the bed, being attacked by Frankenstein. Tony managed to ignore this and divert back onto his Indian times and his head.

'So much becomes clearer,' he said from upside down. 'Like there's a period in Christ's life that we know nothing about. But according to the Hindu writings, a fair-haired man with a fair complexion came to India about that time, achieved a very high state in the Yoga of Knowledge and became a god-realised man. Some people say that Christ is buried in Kashmir.'

I wrote it all down. Facts were important.

The coming week melded into one long party where neither day nor night mattered. The only noticeable interruptions were Viktor's brief excursions to university, or runs up to Leopoldstrasse for groceries or pizzas or good old German beer. Then May Day arrived

## Chapter 19

and we celebrated in a neighbour's flat, sixty people hip-deep in balls of polystyrene, doing hash, beer and mescaline until they crashed to the floor in a synchronised wave as dawn leaked from the rooftops and the birds heralded another lost sunrise. I'm not recommending any of this, but that's how things were in the early seventies in flats all over Munich.

On the second Saturday in Schwabing, I peered out the window to find that it was snowing. Soft fluffy flakes were settling on everything in sight. For no connecting reason, they reminded me of the wild mountain men who hunted the Yukon in the days of the Klondike gold rush. They then reminded me that I was demolishing a disproportionate amount of food while contributing little in the line of cash. In the spirit of the Klondike men, I decided to compensate. A spot of duck hunting wouldn't go amiss. To the alarm of Viktor and Tony, I armed myself with a plastic bag and two empty beer bottles, pulled my beret from the bottom of my pack and set off for the nearest wilderness, which happened to be in Englishgarten.

'They will not like you in the park,' Viktor warned.

'You'll end up in Munich jail!' Tony shouted.

With the bottles hidden in the bag that would, I hoped, double up as a duck-bag on the way home, I strolled into the trees of the park, then skirted around to a more treeless part of the lake where I stood beside a giant willow. As anticipated, I was shortly mobbed by a flapping flock of public nuisances, convinced that I was carrying swag. However, despite the snow, there were people about so I had to wait my chance until nobody was looking.

When the coast was clear, I fixed on a big, fat juicy mallard. *Ready*, I said to myself, *aim*...

'Squawk! Squawk!' the mallard went.

I let fly. But the duck took off in a spray of feathers and crap and I missed by a mile. I fired the second bottle, but missed again.

The duck came back. Squawk! Squawk! Trust to the point of lunacy.

I scooped up my missiles for another try. But as I did, my ears became attuned to a sound not unlike the shrieking one might find emanating from a dance hall brawl in some place like Ballybahoo. I turned in amazement. Heading my way was the local chapter of Save the Ducks, waving fists and making untoward ecological gestures that were irrational.

'*Du bastard!*' one of them shouted which didn't need much translating. I also recognised the word *polizei*.

'Sorry lads,' I said when I crashed through the door of Viktor's bedsit and slammed home the bolt. 'It's spaghetti and tomato sauce for dinner.'

Back at Haystack Disco that night, Tony convinced myself and Viktor that we should go and live in Auroville. It was down near Pondicherry on the south coast of India.

'It was the brainchild of a French artist, Mirra 'The Mother' Alfassa, a close disciple of a Bengali mystic called Sri Aurobindo Ghose who founded an ashram in French-ruled Pondicherry in 1926. After he died in 1950 Mirra Alfassa assumed spiritual leadership of the ashram, attracting 2,000 devotees from all over the world. A vision of Alfassa's in which she saw a crystalline sanctum where the ultimate states of meditation could be achieved gave life to Auroville. Its founding stone was an urn filled with soil from 126 different countries which was put in place at the 1968 opening ceremony. Since then hundreds of families have moved in. They're living in a hotch-potch of dwellings and still building towards a population that they hope will reach 50,000.'

I imagined myself and Cora in a grass and bamboo hut.

'The freaks are building it mate,' Tony yelled above the music, 'for people with new ideas who want to get out of the rat race and back to nature. They're talking about a community where everyone lives peacefully together in a town built by themselves, where they can be self-supporting and not ruled by the greed that gives us such a twisted society in the west. I might head back there after London.'

He reached into the pocket of his Afghan jacket and pulled out a folded sheet of Auroville's headed notepaper and handed it to me. '*Shanti*' (peace), it said at the top. I have it to this day. But neither Tony, Viktor nor I ever went to live in Auroville.

Three years later, in 1973, Mirra Alfassa died in Pondicherry. By then Cora and I were living in Belfast; Viktor was on his way to climb Kilmanjaro (after which he was mugged); and Tony, minus the long hair, earrings and beads, was back in Sydney, the purchasing manager of a toy company. Who knows the turn of the wind?

Some time after Tony passed me the Auroville notepaper I was laughing so hard at some joke that I knocked over a glass of beer. The ensuing row between Viktor and the Haystack manager cost him his membership of the club. No more Viktor the disc jockey.

'We will leave!' Viktor announced. 'We will go to Pondicherry. We will build a house with the freaks. We will grow cabbage!' But he

## Chapter 19

was too out of it to drive.

A second attempt at 2.15am had us abandon Pondicherry and go back to the flat of a guy called Dagwood in some place that I could never find again. After food and wine, we took off for Munich at 4.00am with myself and Tony in the front passenger seat of Viktor's Volkswagon and five others in the back. On the 35-kilometre journey to Munich we dropped off the five passengers, then ran out of petrol.

'Night, night,' Tony said, bedding down in the back seat.

'We will find petrol,' Viktor vowed. He rolled sideways out of the car and stood on the road, wild bloodshot eyes, dishevelled beard, fluttering Afghan coat, and tried to flag down passing cars.

Luckily, a friend of his, rather than the cops, came along and gave us fuel.

On the final night a bunch of Viktor's friends turned up for a goodbye party. Viktor's light show blinded us all until morning.

Any longer and Munich would've been the death of me.

On May 4th Tony Lee started work in Munich and I left for England to meet Tony O'Connor in Maidenhead. Viktor dropped me at the autobahn to Nuremberg.

'You need some money?' he asked.

'No thanks,' I said, determined to get to Maidenhead on my last ten dollars and really thrash that British Consulate back in Istanbul.

'OK Foreign Legion man,' he grinned. 'Maybe I will see you in Cork some time.'

I didn't expect it. But in mid August, he and Tony Lee did in fact turn up, Viktor wearing a self-made, multi-coloured patchwork trousers which made him look like Coco the Clown, Tony in his Indian trousers and long Afghan jacket. Out in our hall my mother was astonished one morning to find the München man standing on his hands, feet against the wall. 'It helps me digest my food,' he explained.

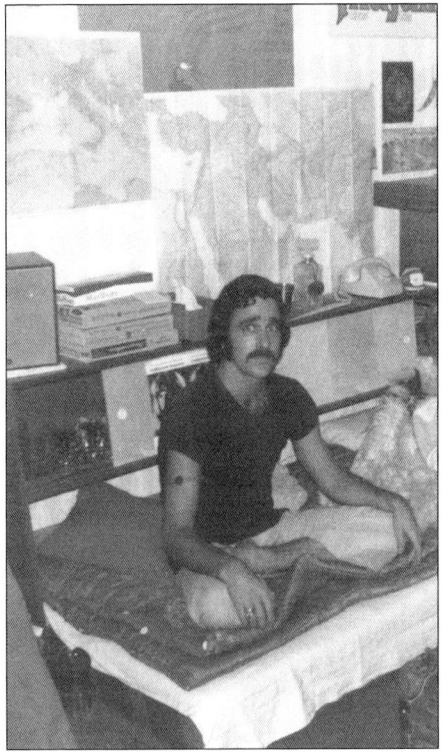

*Tony Lee in Munich, May 1970.*

# Chapter 20
## The End Of The Beginning

Soon I was travelling north. Through the hop-growing area of Bavaria. Through flat farmland and forest. Through the urban sprawl of Frankfurt where I was almost run over by a tram. Progress then came to an abrupt halt. The road out of the city was lined with hitchhikers and I had to join the back of the queue. That was the unwritten code. When my turn finally came I got a lift to within a hundred kilometres of Cologne, and another to the centre of Rotterdam where I landed at half two in the morning. Without sleeping bag or money there was no question of sleep so I kept going. As I walked across town towards the entrance to the Maastunnel the only sounds were the fall of my boots and the lapping of canal water against barges and houseboats.

At half past five on the morning of Tuesday, May 5th 1970, the day the Netherlands celebrated twenty-five years of liberation from the Nazis, I was dropped off on the coast road to Vlissingen. Joining the islands of the south western Netherlands in a series of dykes, the road ran through small picturesque villages of brick, wooden beams and terracotta, where flags and streamers fluttered in a free wind. The sun had just risen. From the hazy distance, the call of a cuckoo welcomed the morning. In the fields there were flocks of wild geese and gulls. A single invisible lark sang high in the crisp air. I walked and sang, the words carried off in little puffs of foggy breath as I passed along the dykes between windmills and flower-filled gardens and no scarcity of tulips. The sun rose higher and swept away the morning chill. I walked long distances and enjoyed every minute. Eventually, I arrived in Vlissingen shortly after ten o'clock and noticed a gap in the road: they called it the sea.

With my ten-dollar note this was a problem. A ferry made the crossing possible but the banks were closed due to the holiday and I wasn't about to cash my entire fortune into Dutch guilders. Begging the ferry fare seemed the only option.

'Excuse me,' I said to the first long-haired guy I saw (everyone in the Netherlands spoke English), 'maybe you can help me...'

'But,' he said when I'd finished my woeful tale to which I'd added a bit about my grandfather having fought the Germans in the First World War, 'the bank in the terminal is open.'

Sure enough I was able to cash enough for the ferry and get my change back in dollars. At Breskens on the far side progress slowed again but I finally reached the Ostende ferry terminal in mid afternoon. I felt a tremendous surge of pride as I bought a ticket to Dover with my last seven dollars. I was home and dry. Nothing could stop me now.

On the boat, however, I was thirst personified. But never let it be said that a man who had travelled to Afghanistan and back, with a North African side trip, on £190 could now be found wanting. I looked around and spotted a silly man with a large beading glass of cold beer rudely ogling a young woman to his left.

Justice was done. I sculled the criminal's beer.

In Dover at five the next morning I got a lucky lift that brought me straight to the Maidenhead roundabout at Thicket Corner, one and a half miles from where half of Tony O'Connor's extended family lived. I walked on air from the roundabout along streets full of spring. Yellow-green leaves twinkled in the sun. Squirrels raced up and down tree trunks. A riot of cherry blossom, apple blossom and birdsong filled the gardens.

Nobody was at home at either of the two addresses Tony had given me but I didn't care. I slept a few hours in a park and called again to his grandmother's flat. A thin, grey-haired Granny Delaney welcomed me with open arms.

'You can only be Ciarán,' she said. 'Come in and have a fry.'

Out came the china and the tea cosy.

'Tony has a job,' she told me. 'He's building England's roads.'

After a badly needed bath, I slept again on Granny Delaney's settee. At nine o'clock Tony walked in and a great slapping of backs was followed by a feed at Kum Sam's and a large swallow at The Bell where a big fat man, wearing a wig, dress and make-up, was singing and stripping off.

'If you're looking for a job,' Tony said, 'I can get you a start with the lads. They're all from home and the craic is great.'

'When could I start? I haven't a bean.'

'Monday.'

Next morning I wrote to Cora, asking her to meet me in Swansea at the end of the month.

I started work on the Monday with a gang of Irish navvies out in a place called Londwick, forty-five minutes by van from Maidenhead.

## Chapter 20

It was blue woeful murder. In sweltering heat I found myself slaughtered with the spreading of tarmac and the digging of useless holes. Over the next few days, energy levels sagged until Kevin the ganger, a decent guy at heart, spotted my predicament. It was early morning and a truck had just dumped several tons of foul steaming tarmac in our midst so we could build the English a path.

'Ciarán,' he said, 'any chance of a bit more on the shovel?'

Eventually he found me a job more in keeping with an artistic nature - pointing the kerbstones that bordered the path. This meant sitting on the roadside with a trowel and a shovel of mortar and expertly filling the gaps between each two kerbstones while getting a suntan. The job ran out two convenient weeks later, just as my navvying career came to an end.

While engaged in this landscaping task, Tony and I took the opportunity of an overnight to London's West End. We travelled on Friday evening by train to the big city where, this time around, I felt none of the breath of old Bishop Lucey. Instead it was heads up as, taller than Big Ben, we trod the avenues around Nelson's Column and loped the lanes of Soho. We even included a trip to Cricklewood so we could savour a pint of the black stuff in the Crown.

Built in 1900 on the site of an earlier coaching tavern, the Crown, crafted by an architect called Henry Rising (I jest not), consisted of three floors of beautifully carved red sandstone. For much of the 20th century it was an iconic spit-and-sawdust watering hole for London's Irish community, centred on Kilburn and Cricklewood. A home from home for those who embraced mayhem. Its forecourt had also hosted the daily 'call-on', when contractors would arrive in vans and trucks to recruit Irish tradesmen and labourers for casual work.

We went there in honour of a *Dubliners'* song, penned by Dominic Behan. *McAlpine's Fusiliers* concerned a bunch of Irish navvies - close kin by now to me and Tony - who worked for the builder, McAlpine, and had among their mythical ranks The Bear O'Shea and the ganger, Horseface O'Toole. The relevant lines:

*'The craic was good in Cricklewood, we wouldn't leave the Crown*
*There were glasses flyin' and Biddies cryin'; the Paddies were*
*goin' to town.'*

'Over in the Murphy [building] ranks,' Tony reminded me as we swilled the black at the bar of the Crown in the rough and tumble of pay day madness, 'they have Elephant John from Cahirciveen.' 'And by the way,' he added, 'don't take off yer coat in case someone thinks you're pickin' a fight.' We left when the clientele began to divide into those who wanted to wreck the joint and those who were comatose.

To cap the night we wrapped ourselves in newspapers and settled down on deck chairs in a quiet corner of St. James' Park. But this met not with the approval of London's bobbies, a full carload of whom rudely awakened us in the middle of the night with stupid questions such as, *What 'ave we got 'ere then?*

\* \* \*

At four o'clock in the morning on the last day of May, I left the building of England to Tony, Kevin and the boys and hitchhiked off to Swansea to meet Cora. In Moroccan sandals, jeans and my bright, blue, embroidered Moroccan shirt that came to my knees, I made a ferry terminal cop suspicious.

'Have you any drugs?' he asked.

'My god,' I said. 'You don't look like a man who does drugs.'

'Very funny,' he said and let me through. When Cora came down the gangway I picked her up and twirled her around the quay. I ignored the people giving her sympathetic looks. We kissed and I almost fell over with the swimming in my head.

'I will never leave without you again,' I promised.

We raced off to a B&B and didn't surface again for sixteen hours. I told her all about the trip, about Morocco, Istanbul, Kandahar, Kabul, about the people I'd met along the way. She looked at me as if I'd come from the moon. I tried harder. She looked harder. This was bad. I wanted so much to share the big adventure, really share it. But we were on different sides of a glass wall. With growing alarm, I began to realise that the only person who could understand what I was saying was someone who had been there too. The trip had done something terrible: we had lost one another.

I said nothing. But late in the night while Cora slept, I stared at the dark ceiling. Then, out of the ceiling it came.

Everything that made sense at that moment deemed that the travels were over. But not everything always makes sense.

'Cora,' I whispered, shaking her awake, 'there's only one way of fixing this.'

'What? Fixing what? What are you talking about?'

'Me and you, we have to go to India.'

## Chapter 20

'You're not right in the head,' she said. 'Aren't you going to university? Go back to sleep.'

The following day we hitchhiked back to Maidenhead where I picked up my blanket-poncho and borrowed Tony's sleeping bag. One of Tony's uncles - big Colin Graham who had personally demolished the side of his house to add an extension (while still living in it with his family) - then drove us to the edge of town and dropped us at Thicket Corner at half ten at night.

'You're both bonkers,' he said (a bit rich, I thought), 'leaving for London this time of night.' But we had plans.

Once Colin had left, we crawled in among the trees and snuggled down on the half blanket with the sleeping bag on top. In the morning we woke up cold, happy and surrounded by sunlight, squirrels, birds and highwayman lore.

'At one time in the 18th century,' I told Cora (a story I'd heard from Granny Delaney) 'when Maidenhead was the busiest coaching stop in England, the landlord of the Sun Inn on Castle Hill used to rob coaches right here after telling the drivers that the area was safe. Dick Turpin used to hang out here too, terrorising the old Bath Road right where we are now, before heading to his aunt's house over in Sonning for a feed.'

Cora eyed me suspiciously.

'Your money or your life!' I howled and we rolled in the leaves.

'This is beautiful,' Cora said, picking grass, leaves and earth from her crumpled clothes. 'Who'd want to sleep anywhere else?' (At nineteen Cora was already pleasantly off the beam. On our very first romantic weekend away, back in Ireland when we were seventeen, she'd been quite relaxed sleeping in a turf shed on the Friday night and a graveyard on the Saturday. She had then happily progressed to old buildings, the undersides of bridges, fields, bushes, bales of hay and other people's gardens.)

Oblivious to the now redundant Cork rumours of murder and lost souls, we left for London to burn a hole in that nefarious town, catch up with Cora's father who worked in Dagenham, and blow every last penny I'd earned in Londwick.

In Leicester Square we went to see the newly released *Easy Rider*; and as Billy the Kid and Captain America fried their brains on acid in a cemetery in New Orleans, I was overcome by a powerful feeling.

India. With Cora.

# THE ROAD AGAIN

*'Only the road and the dawn, the sun, the wind, and the rain,
And the watch fire under stars, and sleep, and the road again.'*

John Masefield (1978-1967)

The author's partner, Cora, beside the Blue Mosque, Istanbul, November 1971.

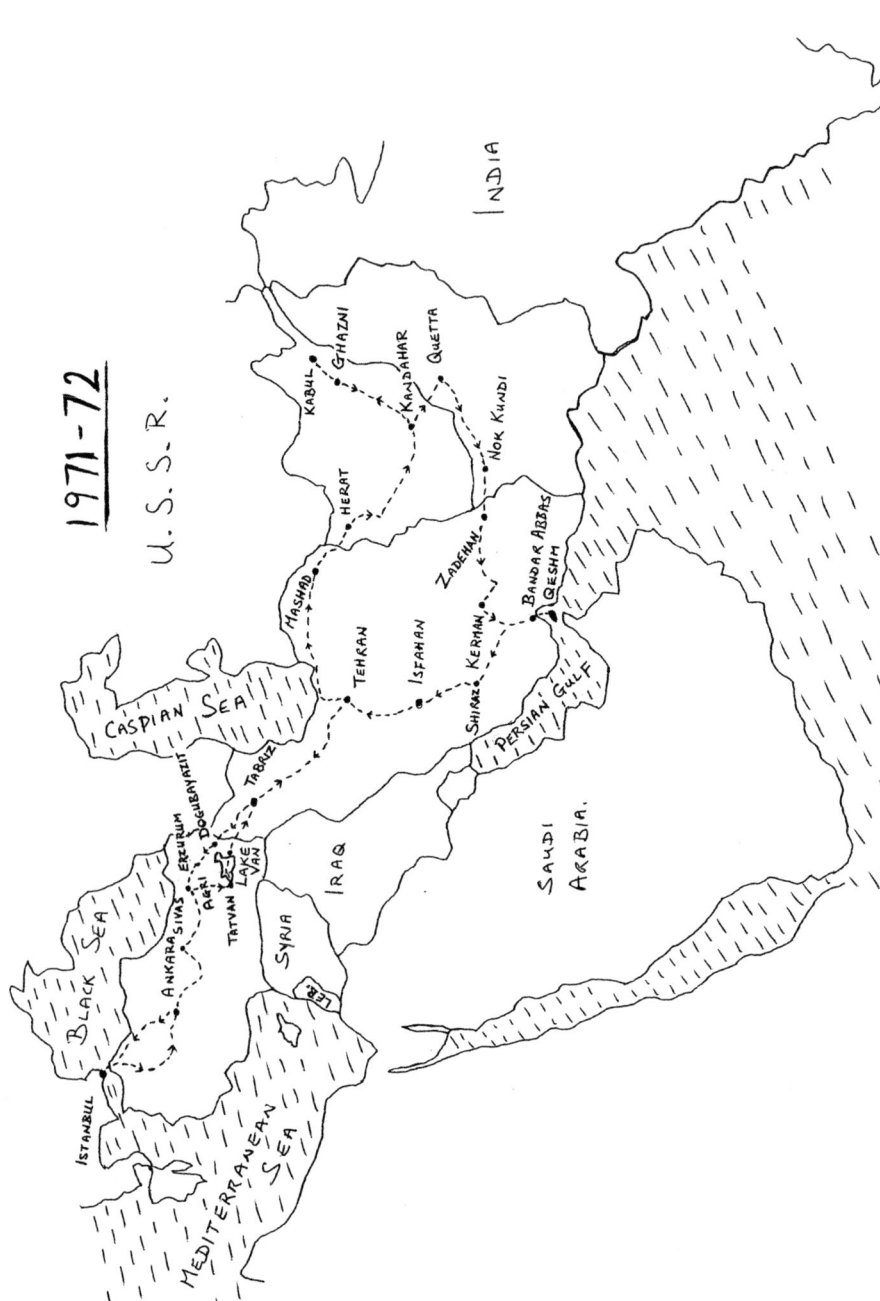

# Chapter 21
'Gone to Afghanistan'

Imagine you're a slightly impetuous lad of twenty. Then put a trip to India with your girlfriend on one side of the scales. Put three years at university on the other. Now, stand clear of the end with the trip in case you get flattened. My university career was a flop.

To begin with, the planning was poor. I enrolled for a degree in Commerce and spent three weeks slowly dying before switching to botany and zoology, which almost finished me off. Secondly, my cousin Seán was a fellow student and Seán and I shared an anxiety about the state of the world. In the early weeks of the first term we spent long hours down in the cafeteria, sorting out Franco, Vietnam and the growing conflict in the North of Ireland. On all fronts I was of a mind to impose sanctions. Seán was of a mind to send in the Russians. And always in the background the scales were tipping.

Gradually the missed lectures outnumbered those attended until I walked into a lecture theatre one morning in December to find scrawled across the blackboard: *de Baróid gone to Afghanistan*.

Fate had come to the rescue. When Cora arrived home from work that night I was waiting with the week's proposition.

'Do you want to go to India?'

She had to sit down and light a cigarette.

'What about university? Your future? Just because you walk into a room and some eejit has written something on the blackboard doesn't mean you have to do it. Supposing they had written *de Baróid set himself on fire in Patrick Street?*'

I thought about this for a few seconds.

'No way would I have set myself on fire in Patrick Street,' I assured her. Nothing to worry about there.

'Maybe you'd like a cup of tea?' Cora's mother said.

When the news came to Evergreen Road, my parents were horrified. The son was heading for a dead end. I had a free shot at university as my father worked there, and I was flushing it down the john.

Tony O'Connor, now back home and studying for the Irish Leaving Certificate - which eventually landed him a carreer as a telephone engineer - could see my side.

## Chapter 21

'India might have vanished in three years' time,' he said. 'If you don't go now, you might regret it. And Cora would be raging.'

Two weeks later I was employed in the paintshop of Verholme shipyard in Cobh, using the morning train journeys to read the writers relevant to life: Jack Kerouac, Che Guevara, Charles Darwin, and Eric von Däniken who reckoned that God was an extraterristrial visitation. Much better than cutting up leaves to stick under a microscope, or dissecting dead rabbits that stank of formaldehyde.

I was also, I might add, elevated within a month to the position of assistant naval architect, working to a pleasant Dutchman named Van Luipan. And when Van Luipan became ill and was off work for some months, I sort of deputised for him, calculating the centres of gravity and buoyancy of the ballast tanks of the ships on which we were working. Given the exhausting social life of the time, I can only hope that none of them are at the bottom of the sea.

When Easter weekend arrived, Cora and I, now fully committed to India, hitchhiked to Killarney for a bit more practice. We cooked on a fire down by Lough Leane and slept in the cloister of Muckross Abbey's ruins, waking up Sunday morning to the voice of an American woman calling: 'Gee Molly, come and take a look at what I've found.'

Six more months and we were on our way.

On Monday, October 4th 1971, we sailed off down the River Lee on another cold and windy night. In our pockets we had our tickets to Swansea and a combined fortune of £450. In our heads we had a plan that had greatly expanded. We would, as talked of back in Swansea, travel to India. We would then continue down through South East Asia to Indonesia and hopefully pick up a working passage on a boat to Australia.

'That might just be possible,' Cora reminded me, 'provided India and Pakistan don't go to war.'

\* \* \*

In October 1971 civil war was raging in Pakistan, then composed of modern-day Pakistan and Bangladesh. Back in March, rising political discontent and a wave of cultural nationalism in East Pakistan was met by a violent crackdown by West Pakistani forces. As a result East Pakistan's Awami League leader, Sheikh Mujibar Rahman, declared independence for the East, choosing the name Bangladesh for the proposed new state. On March 26th Pakistani President, Agha Mohammad Yahya, ordered the West Pakistani military to restore the government's authority, triggering the civil war. Since then an estimated ten million refugees had fled to India as some 60,000 West Pakistani troops carried out appalling atrocities against the civilian population of East Pakistan while India supported the East Pakistani rebels. The question on our minds as we landed in Swansea was how long before all-out war broke out between India and Pakistan.

After a short stay in London with Tony Lee and his new girlfriend, tall blonde Colette Tobin from County Clare, we crossed the English Channel to Ostende on a night of freezing fog such as had welcomed me last time to mainland Europe. Cora had just celebrated her 21st birthday in a Spanish restaurant in Chelsea, thanks to Tony and Colette. (The day after the birthday the bad news came that Tony's father had died suddenly in Sydney. He left for Australia the next day and Colette followed him soon afterwards.)

To escape the fog, we hunkered down in an Ostende phone box until morning before turning south. Over the next few days we hitchhiked to Munich where we landed a great surprise on Viktor and his new (also) blonde girlfriend Gisela. Over a feed of pizza Viktor was careful to explain - in case we thought it a trick of the ears - that Gisela called him Boo-boo. He called Gisela Bo-bo. They were a secure item.

'There will be two babies,' he said. 'They will be called Bo-boo and Boo-bo.'

Nothing much had changed in Munich.

Over the coming days, we were back on the hamster wheel of Viktor's parties, one held in a block of flats being completed for the Munich Olympic City of 1972. Little did we then know that, by the time the Games were over, the complex would be synonymous in the eyes of the world with a televised attack by the Palestinian Black September group in which two Israelis would be killed. In a subsequent firefight between the Palestinians and German cops at Fürstenfeldbruck airbase, another nine Israelis, five Palestinians and a German cop would also be shot dead.

The only significant difference this time was that Viktor, now long in beard, had taken on the role of Cultural Minister for Bavaria. In four days he ran us around the Bavarian Alps and up and down the Danube Gorge like Japanese tourists. We visited the Befreiungshelle of Kelheim, built by Mad King Ludwig to celebrate victories against Napoleon. At Weltenburg monastery, the oldest

## Chapter 21

monastery brewery in the world where Benedictine monks had been making beer since 1050, we drank malty Doppelbock beer. We drove to Neuschwanstein, a white castle with turrets and spires also built by Mad King Ludwig and perched on a rocky Alpine outcrop high over the Pöllat River gorge. And we met Viktor's macrobiotic grandfather, a scowling man of seventy-nine years and slight build whose patterns in life included camping in the Alps; going for 30-kilometre walks; making his own sauerkraut, jams and yoghurts; growing vegetables and fruit in the garden; going to the forest to collect mushrooms, berries and wild herbs; and hating hair, beards and 'hippies'.

Finally, we had an afternoon at Hofbräuhaus, most famous of Munich's beer halls and the source of unsettling news.

We were waving stoneware steins of beer to the thump-thump of an oompah band when Larry from Manchester walked in. He spotted us and headed our way. Cora and I had already met him outside Frankfurt where he'd helped us and the cops clear the autobahn after a beer lorry had tipped its load. Lank and cadaverous, with a droopy face, Larry reckoned that he too was on his way to Australia. At that point he had £50 in his pocket, had neglected to check on vaccination requirements, had a blanket for a bed and was dressed in crumpled sports jacket and trousers.

'I'm a bit disorganised sometimes,' he'd admitted. 'Yesterday I left Frankfurt for Nuremberg, but ended up in Cologne. That's somewhere in fuckin' Belgium.' (It was of course in Germany, but back in the wrong direction.)

'You should go home and get a job,' Cora had advised him. 'Try again when you have more money. And a map.'

'Don't need money, man,' was the answer. 'Jesus will provide.'

'Look,' Cora said when he walked in to Hofbräuhaus. 'He must've mugged Jesus after all. He's still with us.'

But, while the crowd filling the beer hall swayed left and right to the 'Hofbräuhaus Song', led by a fat man in woollen socks, black shorts, white shirt and black hat with a feather to one side, Larry emerged from that world that provides the news that nobody wants to hear.

'*In München steht ein Hofbräuhaus, eins, zwei, g'suffa!*' the band leader sang and then switched to English. 'There's a Hofbräuhaus in Munich - one, two, drink!' Steins of beer clashed in mid-air. But Larry wasn't swaying or singing.

'Heavy vibes from the east,' he said after planting himself beside Viktor. 'The border between India and Pakistan is closed. Looks pretty bad, man. India is cranking up for war. I'm going back to Manchester. Life's a shit, man. If potatoes were invented today, they'd be fuckin'-well banned.'

'What is this potatoes thing?' Viktor wanted to know.

'I don't know man,' Larry said. 'But the border is fuckin'-well closed.'

Potatoes aside, that put a big damper on Hofbräuhaus. If what Larry said was true, our journey was kaputed there and then.

Dark clouds bunched over Munich and trailed us back to Viktor's place where he and Gisela filled a bong, opened a flagon of wine and turned up the volume on Jethro Thull. Eventually Viktor, red of eye and off his rocker, phoned the Indian Consulate.

'Hey man,' he began in English. 'what is happening to the border?'

He then burped into the phone, the prelude to a long debate with the Indian side about good manners.

'The frontier is still open,' he said after finally putting down the receiver. 'Crazy fucking people in that Consulate.'

Viktor then became a little morose.

'Things are changing,' he said, eyes verging on water. 'Now every kind of person is having long hair and a beard and going to India. Soon it will not be possible to tell any more the real genuine freaks from the impostors.'

Whatever he meant, he was right. In a few years the 'heads' who wandered east in the early seventies would be subsumed in the growing wave of young backpackers who would fill the byways of the world and gradually swallow them up. The trail to India would be gone, but Viktor and I never would get around to discussing that.

I invited him to Belfast a few years later but he wrote back saying he wouldn't go anywhere to visit anyone who 'has bombs exploding under his arse'. I got a card from him some time afterwards. He was in Tanzania and had just been robbed after climbing Kilmanjaro. Viktor then slipped off the pages of history.

Sometimes I have visions of him living in the middle of German suburbia, his house painted ice cream pink with yellow polkadot doors, the light show still evolving to the thumping pulse of Jethro Thull.

Viktor, wherever you are, there must be medals for the likes of you.

\* \* \*

# Chapter 21

We hitchhiked across Austria in two days, spending the intervening night in a building site south of Salzburg before crossing the Alps to Graz on a minor road. Mostly it was tireless rain, turning to sleet on the high passes; but despite the cheerlessness of wet travel, the mountain scenery kept our spirits high. In Graz, influenced by bouts of severe shivering, we decided to take the Orient Express to Istanbul but had to scrap the plan as we didn't have Bulgarian visas. Instead, we bought train tickets to Thessaloniki in Greece and sat down to while away the ten-hour wait to half one in the morning.

We almost missed the train.

'There it goes!' I shouted to Cora after being roused from a doze by the whistle. 'Grab your pack! Run!'

Tearing down the platform after the last of the accelerating carriages, I managed to pull open a door and jump aboard.

'Quick!' I shouted to Cora. 'Jump!'

'I can't!' she shouted back. 'It's going too fast!'

'Gimme your hand!' I roared, hanging from the door of the train, pack still on my back, thinking *I'm going to lose her!* She reached out and just about grabbed my hand and I hauled. Seconds later, the platform was gone.

'Jesus, Mary and St. Joseph!' Cora squealed. 'I could've been killed!' Cora was prone to religious outbursts.

After fourteen sleepless hours in the corridor, we finally managed to squeeze into a compartment when we reached Belgrade the following afternoon. By the time we disembarked in Thessaloniki our brains were scrambled eggs. We crawled into the station waiting room and threw down our sleeping bags. Cora on a bench. Me beside her on the floor.

A local train brought us to Alexandroupolis, a ten-hour journey across the cotton and maize fields of northern Greece. We checked into a cheap hotel, washed clothes, had a shower, cooked a meal and slept. In the morning, in bright sunshine we walked to the edge of town aiming to hitchhike to Turkey. After a couple of hours of plentiful donkeys and mules we took a bus to the border. We walked the eight kilometres from the frontier post to Ipsala, the first village inside Turkey, and took a minibus to Keysan. The driver tried to charge us double but we held out. He then dropped us two kilometres outside Keysan so that our triumphant entry to the town took place astride the mudguards of a battered old tractor. From Keysan we took another bus to Topkapi Gate in Istanbul.

# Chapter 22
## Yener and the Golden Rules

_____

The bazaars of Istanbul were as attractive to Cora as Black-eye Friday is to a pugilist since she shared with all women that love of shopping.

Now let me elaborate. Men and women shop. but there are two kinds of shopping. A man will need a pair of shoes. He'll put the money he needs in his pocket, go into a shoe shop, try on a pair that fits, and buy them. A woman, on the other hand, in need of nothing in particular, will go out with a pocket full of money, and come back broke, having saved – you heard me right, saved - a fortune. That's one of the mysteries, the vagaries of the female, that bedazzle us men.

Every morning we found the bazaars. We could not, of course, add to our baggage. We could, however, indulge in imaginary shopping. That's the next best thing to actual shopping - trying things on and, if you're around long enough, buying them and returning them tomorrow.

We could then relax into the afternoon, wander the steep cobbles of the old city, gather information for the trip east, or swap yarns and horror stories in the Pudding Shop. In those afternoons, I was the Istanbul expert. I even threw in a night viewing of the extraordinary shop windows in the Street of the Prostitutes.

'The only thing,' I explained, 'is that you'll have to disguise yourself as a man.'

Now, anyone who has known Cora down through the years will realise how far-fetched a notion that would have been. In combat jacket, boots and jeans and hair rather poorly stuffed up under a bush hat, she looked exactly like a slim young woman in combat jacket, boots and jeans with her hair stuffed up under a bush hat. From both sides of the windows and glass-fronted doors, the stares she copped were vicious.

'I'm not sure,' she said at the end of it, 'if I should laugh, cry or kick someone up the arse.'

To this day I'm certain it would've gone much better had she taken my advice on the false moustache.

The most notable events of Istanbul, however, occurred on the

## Chapter 22

morning of Tuesday, November 16th, beginning in the Grand Bazaar. It's unlikely that, as way leads on to way, either would have happened without Cora.

By now we'd been down to the bazaar twice, and had been particularly taken by the Turkish puzzle rings in the alley of the goldsmiths. Made of interlocking hoops of gold that came apart to form a small chain, the assembled rings looked like gleaming knots. One of the traders, a tall funny man called Mustafa, who wore a wool hat and grinned incessantly through a broad moustache that put a black bar across his face, told us they were traditional wedding rings.

'Very old,' he said. 'Very complicate. They make like this.' He took one of the rings, a cluster of four separate bands, and pulled it apart. 'So, if man or woman pretend not married and take ring from finger, maybe cannot make back again.' He handed the ring to me. 'You like try fix?' he said. Try as I might, I couldn't. 'Now,' he said, 'the woman, she know.'

Mustafa was waiting for us on the morning of the 16th.

'Ah my friends!' he beamed. 'You come back to get marry. Come! Come!'

He led us inside the little shop, glittering with illuminated gold, and pulled out again the two rings in which we'd shown interest. Woven of red gold, they were identical in shape, one fitting each of us perfectly.

'Made in the Heaven,' he assured us. 'Here,' he said, handing the largest of the rings to Cora. 'You must put on his finger.'

'Here,' Cora said to me and did as she was bade.

'Now, you,' Mustafa said and watched me slide the ring over Cora's finger. He then called a young Turkish woman in western dress who was passing by and issued some instructions.

'You must have witness,' he said. The woman gave us a huge smile and stood beside Cora.

'Now,' he said, 'You are husband and wife.'

'All for three pounds,' Cora said. 'God, you are cheap.'

Cheap or not, it nearly became the shortest-lived marriage in history.

Half an hour after we'd exited through the arched Nuruosmaniye Gate of the Grand Bazaar, after a heated debate with a shopkeeper who was selling carved ivory, I had a close encounter with the mad knifeman of Sultanahmet.

We were on a narrow street when two men tumbled out of a shop and crashed to the ground. Three others followed and began to kick one of the guys on the ground, until he managed to get up and run away. When the fracas had died down we went into the shop to buy some cheese. Inside, one of the assailants became the shopkeeper, a bullish-looking guy in his twenties with massive shoulders, a bullet head and a nose that had been broken at least once.

'The cheese?' I asked. 'How much?'

He lifted a heavy carving knife, chopped off a big whack and began to wrap it, quoting an outrageous price.

'No, no, no,' I said. 'Too expensive.'

He stopped dead. He stared. His nostrils flared. Then he was over the counter, knife slicing the air. *A man like that should be ashamed of himself*, I thought, *should get help*. At the same time there was a clammy prickly flood of panic.

I dropped my jacket and jumped back, grabbing a large empty Coca Cola bottle from a crate. A soldier who'd come in behind obligingly stepped aside to allow the joining of battle. Knifeman and Cokeman pranced around the small shop, dodging boxes of fruit and baskets of vegetables that littered the floor. I did my best to avoid being skewered. He did his best to skewer me.

'Jesus, Mary and St. Joseph!' Cora shouted. 'Let's just get outta here!'

Just as I considered firing the bottle into the knifeman's face and making a dash for it, a big woman in black skirts and scarf shot out of a doorway, charged around the counter, and beat the lugs off her wayward son.

'God bless mothers,' Cora said as we scurried off down the street. 'What a town! Married and murdered in the same hour.'

\* \* \*

We retreated to a four-table restaurant close to the Pudding Shop. This establishment, new to me, was owned and run by 40-year-old Sitki Oruç, better known as Yener. With his long dark hair, balding forehead, huge mutton-chop whiskers, bushy sideburns, floral apron and silver neck chain, Yener was an Istanbul institution who had stepped from a Dickons novel. Known to the locals as 'the old Hippie Father' or 'King of the Hippies', he held out to the young travellers a hand of welcome that was warm as cocoa on a winter's night. His restaurant mirrored his love of his clients. A doorway dominated by a sign urgently demanding universal free love led to the cramped interior and a blast of psychedelic paintings and

## Chapter 22

posters. Inside, the tea was free and the food was cheap but good. Those who arrived with no money didn't pay. Sometimes they sent cards when they got home. Sometimes they turned up years later to settle the bill.

I don't know how I'd missed him on the earlier visits.

'Enter,' Yener said.

We went in, nodded hello to a couple seated to one of the tables, sat down and ordered two Nescafés.

'You are shaking,' Yener said as adrenalin rattled the coffee in my cup.

'He was nearly murdered,' Cora said. 'Some psycho attacked him with a knife.'

'Here? In Istanbul?'

'Down the street.'

Yener got the full story.

'In Turkey,' he said, 'we have an old saying: "Sharp vinegar only damages its container". The golden rule is that the man who sows wind will reap the hurricane. This man in the shop, he is a fool. A man is as wise as his head, not his years.'

'Far out man,' the guy at the next table said. He looked a bit like Geronimo, with a red headband and puffy white shirt. His girlfriend looked like Fred Astaire.

'They are Swedish, coming from India,' Yener said. Looking worse for wear, they had finished their meal and were now sitting to a hubble-bubble

'We have no money,' the guy said to Cora. 'We have run on hard times. Yener has been feeding us free of charge.'

'Hey man,' the woman said to Yener. 'You should write those thoughts in your books.'

'Ah,' Yener said. 'Yes. My books...'

He reached in behind the counter and pulled out two large, dog-eared scrapbooks.

'You can see here the writings of many hippies,' he said, handing the books to Cora. They were full of testimonials, poetry, drawings, thank-you cards from people who'd been fed free, and the metaphysical ramblings of lunatics and dreamers. Cora found a contribution that she particularly liked:

> 'Come to me in the morning of my youth,
> For youth slides quickly by to lament for bygone years.'

We wrote it down, folded it and tucked it away in our hearts. Behind us, in the old city, a muezzin in a mosque called the faithful to prayer, his voice broadcasting the *adhān* and rising like a great wave above Yener's and the Pudding Shop.

'The hippies are good people,' Yener said. 'They are like the ancient Sufi dervishes of Turkey. They have beliefs and they have courage. They will change the world.'

I wasn't too sure how the two at the other table were going to manage that, or what the wise old Sufis would've thought.

'Maybe some of them take many drugs,' Yener added as an afterthought. 'But you must blame the millionaire pushers for this.'

'Write,' the Swedish woman ordered. 'In your books.'

'We're looking for people going east,' I said. 'Anybody crossing Turkey or going to Afghanistan or India in a hurry - before war breaks out.'

'I will put up a sign,' Yener said. 'May Allah be your guide.'

He posted a notice on a board already sagging under its weight of notices. We stuck a second on the board in the Pudding Shop. In sharp contrast to the last time I'd sat in Sultanahmet, we had seven responses within the hour.

Down on the rocking Galata Bridge that night, Asia beckoned from across the waters of the Bosphorus. Back at the hotel I lost my only good shirt - the one reserved for crossing borders. I had washed it and hung it in the bathroom to dry. Then some criminal went in, locked the door, climbed out the window - four floors up - crossed the walls like The Fly, and escaped through one of the other windows.

'If anyone needs a shirt that bad,' Cora said after the manager forced open the bathroom door, 'he deserves it.'

To this day I can't understand why the criminal didn't simply come back out through the door.

Yener had his own take on it when we called to say goodbye on the morning we were leaving for Asia.

'We have a golden rule. The man who did this will not have a good life. A white day gives light: a black day gives darkness.'

At that, a Turkish man in his forties walked in. He had the familiar big moustache and was dressed in a loose-fitting, pin-striped suit and wool hat.

'This is my friend,' Yener said. 'His name is Honest Frank. You must tell him what happened to you in the hotel. Also in the bazaar.'

## Chapter 22

After both stories had been recounted for a second time, adopting a little of the style to be found in *The Playboy of the Western World*, Honest Frank advised that we should maybe buy a gun when we went east. 'Bang! Bang! Bang!' he said. 'Bad man is dead.'

'Careful with the life,' Yener said as we left for the Galata Bridge and the Bosphorus ferry. 'We have a golden rule. An ember burns where it falls.'

Yener was a proverbial man.

# Chapter 23
## Run to Kabul
_____

At one o'clock on the afternoon of Saturday, November 20th 1971, nine of us crossed the Bosphorus to Üsküdar. With war looming in the east we were keen to clear the danger zone as soon as possible. We would therefore buy tickets for the new direct route to Tehran, passing through Tatvan and the Kurdish south east of Turkey, closed to outsiders until 1960. It would be a journey of seventy-five hours at the end of which I planned to land a big surprise on Moyazan at the Shafa Hospital. Again, in contrast to 1970, Haydarpasa Station had a fat quota of young travellers.

'Two tickets to Tehran with student discount please,' I said when I reached the ticket desk. I handed the clerk our passports. Passports, for some strange reason, were enough to warrant student rates on Turkish trains. The clerk stroked the moustache that ran thinly across his upper lip.

'You must have student card *Türkiye*,' he said, peering at me over a pair of wire spectacles that sat sideways across an eagle nose.

'Oh no-o-o,' I said. 'We do not. We can get student discounts with passports. I have done it before at this very station.'

'Oh no-o-o,' the clerk mimicked. He leaned forward as if about to share a secret, his neck craning from the padded shoulders of his pin-stripes. 'Not possible,' he said, crinkling up his nose. 'Not this station. Not other station.'

A debate of some merit ensued until Cora intervened.

'Try somewhere in Turkey,' she suggested. I looked at her in astonishment.

'I'm winning this argument,' I said.

'If you were winning this argument,' she said, 'we'd have tickets. Try somewhere in Turkey. Try Tatvan. It's a Turkish train as far as Tatvan. Maybe the international bit is the problem?'

I looked back at the clerk who was poised across the counter like a right angle.

'Two tickets to Tatvan please,' I said slowly, 'with student discounts.' Deflating visibly, he took the passports, briefly flicked them open, took the money and handed me the two discounted tickets.

## Chapter 23

Once again the train across Anatolia was a rough ride: ourselves, three Americans, a Canadian and two Frenchmen packed into a tight compartment; the hot pipes under the wooden seats, no sleep, and a freezing wind if we opened the window. By morning, snow was building on the mountains. As the day progressed and we continued east into the old familiar of barren steppes, stark mountains, mud-brick huts, shepherds, goatherds and bore wells, the snow gradually crept down the slopes. By evening the whole landscape was carpeted in glistening white, turned rose pink by the westering sun, and bestowing on the company an unbelievable sense of wellbeing.

In between bouts of what we all did before leaving home and what we hoped to do when we got back, there was much staring out the window caused by short trips to the corridor to check out the quality of the Pakistani black, picked up by Patrice of Toulon from some pal of Dodgy Ali's back in Istanbul.

At noon the following day we arrived in Tatvan, a small town squeezed between towering mountains and the dark waters of Lake Van, 1,750 metres above sea level. Ringed by 4,000-metre peaks, Turkey's biggest lake was formed when an ancient eruption of Nemrut Dagi created a lava dam. Though several small rivers flowed in, there was no outflow. Evaporation kept the level constant. This gave the lake a highly alkaline content with natural sodas in which the locals laundered their clothes.

Tatvan was as far as the Turkish engine ran. In an astonishing move the cars of our train were shunted onto a waiting ferry to join a number of freight wagons already on board. Each carriage was lashed to the deck-tracks with heavy chains and, after a wait of an hour or so, we were ready to sail. Behind us the mosques of Tatvan stood stark against the snow of the mountains. Extinct Nemrut Dagi rose like a fist behind the town. To the south a ring of brooding crags was mirrored in still water and capped in fluffy banks of cloud. Ninety kilometres away, on the far side of the lake, an Iranian engine was waiting.

'I hope you're writing all this down,' Cora said. 'Maybe one day we'll write a book.'

Some time after dark we stepped from the boat at Van into a freezing night domed in a black bowl of glittering stars, and boarded what had now become an Iranian train. Cora and I bought tickets to the border and shared a compartment with two Londoners, a German, a Pakistani, a Frenchman and Mike Sullivan, a sinewy, big-limbed student from Kettering in Ohio who'd shared our compartment on the train. At the border, the German, Pakistani and Frenchman got off, leaving five of us in the compartment with no tickets and no Iranian money. Big Mike was also without an Iranian visa.

However, any anxiety we might have harboured was without reason.

'I am happy to wait for payment until we reach Tabriz,' the Iranian conductor assured us. 'You can change money in the station.'

'Just like the train from Cork to Dublin for the All-Ireland,' Cora said. Not true, of course.

'You have two days to sort out your visa,' the Immigration officials told Mike.

'Just like the bus from Mexico to San Diego,' Mike said. Even less true, of course.

Twenty-four hours after leaving Van, fifty-two young travellers got off the train in Tehran. A long shot from the ten of us who'd arrived together just twenty months before. In a straggling exhausted, but good-humoured, column we set off in search of the cheap beds of the General Post Office area. Nobody, however, knew that nobody else knew the way. While the front line looked back to ensure they were on the right track, the rear of the column kept following. Up one street. Down the next. A right turn. A left turn. Back to where we began. The sight of the small army of wandering Western half-wits attracted several laughing 'guides', more than eager to lead the fools further.

Eventually Cora and I grabbed Mike and the two Londoners, Roger and Ray, and we took a taxi to Amir Kabir Lane, the shoddy little haunt of thieves and dope dealers that sported the cheapest hotels in town. I'd been there before. I knew the score.

I couldn't, however, have known that on this occasion Amir Kabir Lane would also harbour a suicidal, would-be, Irishwoman molester.

With hindsight it's easy to see that some of the trouble we drew on our own heads. In a conservative Muslim country, young Western women who had burned their bras (it was all the rage), were travelling with boyfriends or unrelated men - sometimes whole groups of unrelated men - unwittingly inviting urban grabbers to see Western women as fair game. (Cora had already been groped in Tabriz railway station.) In crowded streets it would be over in a

## Chapter 23

flash. But in Amir Kabir Lane, stalked by the unluckiest molester in Iran, it would be over before it started.

Cora had been sick a day and was still recovering as we stood at one end of the lane, trying to decide with Roger and Ray whether to get a train or bus to Mashad, and when we should go and see Mozayan. Suddenly, and against all the proscriptions of local culture, Cora raised a fist and smashed it into the chest of a heavily built, scruffy man of mid thirties who was about to pass. A couple of frozen seconds later, the thumped one went ape.

'Fuck you American!' he barked, turning on me who was somehow deemed American and responsible for the awful breaking of his fortunes. Maybe he was in denial that a woman could've given him that beezer. But Cora was back in.

'Are you gonna *do something* about it!' she roared, green eyes spitting flint. He took one look at the slim combative figure before him and decided that would be a big bad idea.

'What in the name of Jaysus did you do that for?' I asked when the scruffy lad had backed off.

'He was about to grab me,' Cora said.

'What do you mean by "*about*" to?'

'ABOUT TO!' petite darling Cora said. 'How many shaggin' kinds of "about to" do you know?'

Henceforth about-to types had better watch out.

Cora decided to go back to bed to recover from assaulting the would-be molester. Unable to contain myself any longer, I rushed off to catch up on Mozayan at the Shafa Hospital and see if Cora and I could meet with her later. But when I got there, my Iranian angel with the beautiful eyes was nowhere to be found. The very hospital was gone. The building had been turned into some kind of rehabilitation centre and nobody knew what had happened to the former staff. Under stern billboards of the Shah and his family I walked back to Amir Kabir Lane, stricken, cheated, and stooped from the weight of it.

'No matter how long life cradles us,' I said to Cora, 'Mozayan will never know that I called.'

'You're being a bit of a drama queen,' Cora said.

\* \* \*

Mike left for western Iran to visit a friend. Roger, Ray, Cora and I left for Mashad on a surprisingly comfortable Mercedes bus with ventilation, curtains, a sink that didn't work and a toilet full of luggage. Our fellow passengers were all Iranians, mainly men, but also some women in chadors. With flasks and baskets of food, everyone looked ready for a long day. North of the city, the day began with a climb into the white-capped Elburz Mountains, bathed in the sunlight of a powder-blue November day.

Mountain roads are seldom fun. Over the coming hours this was confirmed by a terrifying run through gorges, canyons, ravines and tunnels, and countless opportunities to spin around blind bends on the wrong side of the road. Twice, we stopped to clear rock falls. We had a prayer break on one of the passes. Each opportunity to get out onto a firm base that wasn't in danger of hurtling down the bare face of a mountain came as a great, if temporary, relief; but it also made each resumption of the terror more intolerable. On many occasions Cora uttered 'Jesus, Mary and St. Joseph!'

In this barren wonderland that threatened termination on every bend, it was a surprise to find small stone and mud-brick villages clinging to mountainsides, with the apparent primary purpose of providing fodder for some dodgy-looking mines of Old West vintage.

Nothing else stirred.

In the afternoon, we summited the last pass to find before us a lush fertile plain that ran to a broad expanse of black water: the Caspian Sea.

Another twenty minutes of grinding gears and blind bends and we had dropped to the coast, our road veering east to Bandar-e-Shah. But the ordeal wasn't over yet. For the road had to swing back again over the mountains to bring us to the northern reaches of the Great Salt Desert.

By the time we put wheels on the desert, the mountains had miraculously blended into a domain of mirages, dunes, heat hazes and swirling dust devils.

The Great Salt Desert takes its name from the crusts of salt left behind by the extreme evaporation of its short-lived seasonal marshes, lakes and wadis. At first glance it's a vast empty cauldron that you'd never consider capable of supporting significant animal life. But an Iranian zoologist on the bus listed among its wildlife: gazelle, wild sheep, goats, leopards, wolves, foxes, wildcats, lizards, snakes, the Asiatic cheetah, numerous bird species and the Persian onager, a type of wild donkey. This despite summer temperatures that soared to fifty degrees centigrade.

Even now, in a late afternoon in late November, it was hot enough

# Chapter 23

to encourage a halt. The driver's choice was a small settlement that clung precariously to the edge of life. Its mud-brick houses, baked white by the punishing sun, promised little. One, however, had a sign in Farsi, underneath which was scrawled *Restrant*. We went inside. In a shaft of dancing dust a man in a turban was bent over a charcoal blaze.

'I'll go and see what they have,' Cora offered. Five minutes later she was back. 'It's simple. The choice is gristle kebabs, raw onions, bread and tea.'

We ordered and sat cross-legged with other diners on a faded carpet under a solitary tree. From all sides crows and sparrows moved in. To the north, a cluster of goat-hair tents but no sign of people. To the south, a string of camels wound its way down a gully towards a line of black broken hills. A clump of dead brush tumbled across the road. Desolation, beautiful in its absolute integrity.

Some time after nightfall we came over the brow of a hill to find the desert criss-crossed by the lights of vehicles. They were all going in different directions and ploughing through one another's dust, having wandered off the barrel-lined unpaved route that passed as the main Mashad road.

Arriving in the city at one in the morning, the four of us grabbed a taxi.

'Cheap hotel,' Ray said, jumping into the front seat between the bearded driver and his bearded friend. Roger, the bigger of the two Londoners, solid, affable, with long, thick, black hair and the beginnings of a beard, sat in the back with myself and Cora. As we careered through the streets Roger nudged me.

'Check out Ray,' he chuckled.

In the front seat, the slighter Ray, angular face half-hidden by long flowing hair, sat squashed between the driver and his mate. In the dark the mate had mistaken him for a woman and was groping for the breasts.

'A-a-a-ah!' he said eventually, beaming a huge oafish grin at Ray and shaking his head for being a silly boy.

'A-a-a-ah!' Ray said as the mate looked wistfully back at Cora.

'A-a-a-ah!' Cora said. 'Shag away off!'

The taxi dropped us at a cheap but shabby hotel where we managed to sleep well into the next day. The downstairs hallway was home to a resident deer.

\* \* \*

Two days after arriving in Mashad, Roger and Ray took a distant, furtive look at the domes of the Sacred Shrine before joining the general rush aimed at reaching the Indian border before the war closed in. Cora and I had to wait another day for Afghan visas. We therefore changed from a four-bed room to a two-bed room. Whereupon the manager gave us the key to our new room - by extracting it from the lock of our old room. All doors had identical locks! And there was me for the past two days, feeling secure with the key deep in my pocket.

When we went to collect our visas at the Afghan Consulate we were offered a lift to Kandahar in a Volkswagon campervan by a baby-faced American with floppy brown hair who was driving to India. Isaac was in his late twenties and was best remembered for a brightly patterned sweater that looked like something from Lapland - and the fact that he'd hit a horse and cart late at night in eastern Turkey and drove on. He had no idea what happened to the old man on the cart, which left his van faring far better than his conscience and drove any chance of friendship into a dark abyss.

'Hope he wakes up screaming every night,' Cora said.

Nevertheless, just after noon on November 29th, as the war in East Pakistan grew uglier and we picked up reports of thousands of Bengali women being raped by West Pakistani troops, Cora and I set off for Afghanistan in Isaac's van. Sometimes, you can press hard on feelings but it eats you down the road. I still feel somehow responsible for whatever happened to that old man on his cart all those years ago back in eastern Turkey.

\* \* \*

Under the wide sky of that afternoon we crossed the border and skidded to a halt at the first village. Climbing out into sunshine and a thin wind, we made our way to the chai-khana, a dark mud-brick establishment with a low wooden door. Inside, a group of friendly white-bearded men in turbans, flintlock rifles at their feet, faces lined and seamed by desert winds, invited us to share a hookah.

We were in Afghanistan.

'You British?' one of the older men asked.

'American,' Isaac said.

'And two Irish,' Cora said. He had no idea where Ireland was.

'No British,' he said and took another whack on the hookah. 'My grandfather, he fight British in Kabul. Grandfather of my grandfather, *he* also fight British in Kabul.'

## Chapter 23

He paused, sucked in another lungful of smoke and went on to feed us a long tangled story that I later managed to untangle.

In the 19th century, Afghanistan was central to the Great Game between Britain and Russia. This came to a head in 1837 when the Russians supported an Iranian advance on Herat and sent one of their agents, a Captain Vitkevich, to Kabul as a spy.

The British demanded that Afghan Amir, Dost Mohammad, sever all contact with Iran and Russia, kick Vitkevich out off Kabul, and hand over several Afghan territories for good measure. When Dost Mohammad refused, the British invaded and imposed former ruler, Shah Shuja, on the Afghan throne. Dost Mohammad attacked the British and their Afghan puppet but he was beaten and exiled to India in 1840.

By October of the following year, however, Afghan tribes were flocking to the side of his son, Mohammad Akbar Khan. The British, who were now being openly attacked on the streets of Kabul, decided to pull their garrison back to Jalalabad on the far side of the Khyber Pass after an agreement of safe passage by Mohammad Akbar. In early January 1842, almost 17,000 British military personnel and camp followers began a doomed retreat into the snowbound passes to the east. The British, long in the tooth of deceit, were played at their own game by Ghilzai warriors who relentlessly attacked them with long-barrelled, flintlock jezails. In the fifty kilometres of gorges and passes between Kabul and Gandomak all but one were wiped out.

*Remnants of an Army*, Elizabeth Butler's painting of Scotsman, Dr. William Brydon, arriving at the British outpost in Jalalabad on a dying horse, forever fixed Afghanistan as the graveyard of invading armies. Brydon survived apparently because he'd stuffed a copy of *Blackwood's Magazine* into his hat to ward off the cold. It took most of the blow when an Afghan sword sheared off part of his skull.

In response to the slaughter of its garrison the British carried out a brutal campaign of atrocities against Afghan villages and blew up the great Covered Bazaar of Kabul, then kept their distance for three decades. But, in further pursuance of the Great Game, they were back in 1878 with 40,000 soldiers, in the wake of another Russian mission to Kabul.

Despite initial successes, the British quickly realised that defeating Afghan tribes was not the same as controlling them. In a re-run of 1842 they again managed to have their Kabul garrison annihilated, and by 1881 they'd had enough. From then on, generations of British subalterns would rue their postings to the far-flung borders of Afghanistan. However, imperialists never learn: in 2002, the British went back as part of George Dubya's great war on an abstract concept. At the time of writing (February 2013), beyond its phenomenal success at raining death from the air on defenceless people, the campaign doesn't seem to be going too well, with imperialism again in ignominious retreat.

'You have good travel,' our raconteur said when he'd finished. He pushed a small block of hash into Isaac's hand. '*Insha'Allah!*'[23]

Back in the desert, mirages rose from the burnt flats and camel trains drifted over low hills. A converted ambulance with eyes and a mouth came hurtling towards us in the rosy light. Inside, a young couple shared a chillum. They waved and sped by in a blaze of psychedelia. The back of the ambulance read, *Kathmandu or an elephant*.

Two hundred and forty kilometres north west of Kandahar, we pulled off the road beside a lonely desert grave and made camp under a roof of crystalline stars. To the south, we could see the fires of a nomad camp. In a silence so intense that you could hear your heart beat, we imagined the camels, the flocks of sheep, the scattering of black goat-hair tents. The families would be there too, hunkered over the flames to ward off the desert night.

\* \* \*

In the modest Tourist Hotel in Kandahar's central square, showers were not to be: the water was off.

'No water. No shower,' I complained to the manager.

'No water. No shower,' the manager repeated. 'No rain, three year.'

As a result the drinking water was even deadlier than before. The taps were almost continuously dry and the open sewers stank. It was close to impossible to have a wash, never mind a shower. However, Cora and I found an apparently hygienic restaurant on Chowk Shohada and had feeds there of omelette and chips. Outside the door, mule trains and camels were led by men who belonged to desert fantasies of another age. Inside, flies settled on everything in sight.

'Flies carry disease,' Cora mused.

'Don't worry,' I said. 'As long as the food is well cooked, we'll be fine.'

---

[23] 'God willing.'

# Chapter 23

'You're tempting fate,' she said. 'The last time you did that we crashed the motorbike into that ditch down in Belgooley. And you're still owed one for hanging off the cross on top of Mount Brandon, Good Friday before last.'

There was to be some truth in that.

Next day we cashed a traveller's cheque at the DA Afghanistan Bank: it took two hours and the filling of many forms. We then took a bearing from the tent on the hotel's flat roof (normally reserved for the smoking of hash) and set off through the back alleys of Kandahar towards the desert. The sun was shining and the sky was a bright blue, apart from where the vultures circled. Once we'd cleared the last of the mud-brick compounds, we walked a few kilometres and there, in the empy desert, threw down our jackets at the base of a dry fissured hill and stretched out to soak rays. We kissed and knoodled and in a sort of defiant gesture against the Afghan burkah, Cora stripped to the waist.

'Tell me if you see anyone coming,' she said. 'I don't want to be buried to my neck and stoned to death.'

'Don't worry,' I assured her. 'There's not a sinner about.'

'I won't go into detail,' she said. 'But the last time you said that, some guy and his dog walked over the top of us. So keep an eye.'

'Out here?' I said. 'Who the hell's gonna be out here?'

But who the hell was already watching.

Me not being the sunbathing type, I decided after a couple of hours to climb the hill behind. Sitting a hundred metres up, watching for lizards, I could see Cora periodically turning over for an even bake while vulture shadows darkened the ground around her. Then something caught my eye on another of the hills, a brief flash of some kind. I shaded my eyes and there they were: three men sitting still as statues and blending in to the contours and colours of the hill. They were a long way off but I could clearly see them, so presumably they could see us. Thinking of how accurate they could be with their flintlock jezails, and how badly the Brits had fared in the Khyber Pass, I skidded downhill to Cora.

'Pack up!' I said. 'We need to get the hell outta here!'

'What?' Cora said. 'Why? What's up with you now?'

I pointed out the three voyeurs on the far hill.

'You know what?' Cora frowned, grabbing shirt and jacket. 'We need to get further than that.'

\* \* \*

Our windowless ground-floor room was dark as a tomb once the door was shut. In the early hours of the next morning this became an issue when I woke up with violent cramps. A wave of heat passed over me, then a cold sweat and a sudden deep desire to vomit. I jumped out of bed, grappled in the thick darkness for my jeans and fell over my pack. Cora thought she was being murdered.

'What's going on?' she shouted.

'The door! Where's the bloody door?'

'How the hell do I know?'

Three times I ricocheted around the room scratching for the door before Cora found it. A second later, as someone turned on a light, I fell on my face in the corridor outside and threw up with awful sound effects and writhings around the floor. Cora, looking frightened, came behind and knelt beside me like she was ready to give the last rites.

'Will I get a doctor?'

'I'm awright,' I groaned and threw up again. This was followed by an urgent stagger to the loo with Cora holding me up.

'No blood,' I called out to her. 'No blood might mean no dysentery.'

She helped me back to the room, where I took a stomach powder with a little water and was promptly on the floor of the corridor again with Cora, in that wild and woolly place, calling for a doctor. The commotion brought stoned Afghan men running from their rooms.

'Hospital!' Cora shouted. 'Quick!'

'No hospital,' I croaked. 'No fuckin' blood!'

'Nuffikinblod?' The Afghans asked one another with shrugged shoulders and furrowed brows.

They then hoisted me up, carried me back into the room and dropped me on the bed which they must have assumed to be the nuffikinblod.

'Food poisoning,' I said to Cora. 'A 24-hour bug.'

'Wishful thinking,' she said and stood anxious watch for the next three hours. I must admit I was grateful she was there. I knew from experience it could go either way and Cora wouldn't let it get to the Tehran stage. But food poisoning it was and I recovered in two days. By the time I was back on my feet, however, our dreams had crumbled to dust.

Let me rewind. Outside our hotel there was a cop with a big moustache. He stood every day on a blue-domed rostrum in the

## Chapter 23

middle of the junction. There he had clearly found his calling in life. Armed with gun and shrill whistle, it was his job to maintain order in the flow of traffic that generally amounted to donkeys, camels, bicycles, horse-drawn gharries and the occasional car weaving its way around the nut and raisin stalls. From where we sat it was clear to us that cars stirred in this man a desire to blow that whistle hard. Sometimes we'd watch him from the roof of the hotel. Sometimes we'd take up positions in a chai-khana in the square. On the occasion of significance we were in the chai-khana.

'Hello,' a voice said. 'May we join you?' We turned to find two young Afghans standing behind us.

The one who had spoken was 18-year-old Gulam, stocky with a round face and a fringe of black hair across his forehead. In sky-blue Afghan kurta and baggy trousers, he was the boss. His friend, all in black, with a black karakul skullcap, was Aziz, a skinny guy with wiry hair and nervous eyes. When Gulam invited us to his home for dinner, it came as no surprise that Aziz was despatched to fetch the bicycles.

Over in the square, the cop had an accident on his hands: a car had hit a cyclist. The carophile cop flew into a rage. Blowing on the whistle, he charged from the rostrum and kicked the crap out of the unfortunate cyclist.

\* \* \*

The trip to Gulam's house followed a maze of dirt streets, Gulam out front with Aziz on the crossbar, me behind with Cora on the crossbar.

Unannounced as we were, the whole family gathered around and pulled out all the stops. To the Pashtuns, hospitality to guests - milmastia - is a central tenet of their culture. With the mother in her burkah, and three young girls seated across from us, we were set down on faded rugs to a meal of bread, soup, omelette and green vegetables. In preparation, Gulam brought a basin and a jug of hot water and poured from a narrow spout while each of us washed our hands. Aziz then poured for Gulam. The meal was eaten by hand (right hand!) from a central plate and followed by a tray of raisins and nuts and lively Afghan music played on a tape deck. The father, bearded and bare-headed, stood throughout, firing a stream of questions which were translated by Gulam. When it came to describing where Ireland was, I drew a map of Britain and showed that Ireland was next door. The father nodded, but it meant nothing.

'Where do you go, my father ask.' Gulam said.

'India,' I answered. 'Then Australia.'

'Down through South East Asia,' Cora added while passing the father a cigarette.

Gulam translated and the father shook his head. He then spoke to Gulam but looked at us and you could see it wasn't good.

'My father, he say India not possible,' Gulam said. 'Much fighting between India and Pakistan.'

Cora and I looked at one another, then we both deflated with huge creaking sighs.

'You did not know?'

'No,' I said, ready to single-handedly attack Pakistan (I had taken sides). 'This is very bad for us. We wanted to reach India before the frontier closed.'

Gulam spoke again to his father. The father stared at us and spoke again to Gulam.

'My father say it is too late. There is big war.'

The war winds that had filled our ears since Munich had erupted into all-out conflict. With an estimated million Bengalis dead at the hands of West Pakistan's army, the Indian government had sent in its troops. The frontier between the two countries was closed. December 4th 1971 brought the worst news since we'd left home.

'What now?' Cora said. 'Nothing for it but to go back?'

'Maybe we can work something out when we get to Kabul', I said. 'Maybe it's possible to go around the war zone.'

'Or maybe tunnel under it?' Cora said.

'Not possible,' Aziz said. 'Too far.' He looked genuinely concerned that we might consider tunnelling as an option.

When we got back to the hotel, it was almost midnight, the streets were virtually deserted, Kandahar's electricity had failed, and we were locked out. We knocked and shouted, but to no avail. Eventually, as we sat despondently on the empty pavement, an old Afghan man, carrying an oil lantern, appeared. Realising our predicament, he raised a reassuring finger and reached into his kaftan. Without a word, he pulled out a shrill piercing whistle and let rip. Instant results. The manager opened and let us in, yelling torrents of abuse at our benefactor for having dared wake him up.

Next day, Sunday, December 5th, as the people of Kandahar began another day - setting up stalls, brewing tea in the street, taking the first smoke of the day - we took a bus to Kabul to find out more

# Chapter 23

about the war. It was bad. At the Farah Hotel, we learned from other travellers that cities had been bombed on both sides, airports and railway lines had been zapped, and travel across the war zone was out of the question. There was just one last chance: Afghan Airlines was considering a final flight to Delhi the next day.

At the Khyber Restaurant we sat with a number of people we'd met on the way from Istanbul. They had all bottlenecked into Kabul, and were now as stuck as we were. But I had a plan that had been formulating since Gulam had dropped the clanger. I should, I suppose, have mentioned it to Cora.

'We could walk across the Thar Desert between India and Pakistan at night. It's worth a try.'

Cora looked at me as if I'd burst into flames.

'The only thing more daft than that,' she said, 'is nothing. Send me a card if you get there. I'm not going.'

Shocked, I tried to sell the merits of the plan.

'But we have no other way of getting to Australia except overland through Pakistan and India.'

'Funny thing when you think about it,' she said. 'You might have fallen off a lorry onto your head when you were six; but I didn't.'

'I take it you didn't know about this plan,' one of the other guys said.

'That isn't a plan,' Cora smiled. 'That's a medical condition.'

It was a lost cause. I don't know if any of the others tried, but just as we were about to leave, Roger and Ray walked in.

'Fucking 'ell!' Roger said. 'Walk across the desert! Have you seen the file on the window?' We had. It was a three-inch thick folder from the British embassy - of British nationals missing between Istanbul and Kathmandu, each report with a picture and a 'last seen' annotation.

'Three Americans in a campervan had their throats slit outside Kabul last week,' Roger added. 'Another guy was shot just up the street and somebody else was stabbed to death the other night. I wouldn't go walking about in any deserts around here if I was you. In fact I'd hardly walk down the bloody street!'

We left Roger and Ray and went back to our hotel roof, overlooking the Kabul River, now reduced to a winter trickle.

'Stand there for a photo,' I said to Cora. I handed her a Roches Stores bag from Cork and had her look down on the riverside carpet sellers and the gun bazaar where they made flintlock rifles for young Afghans.

'If nothing else,' I said, 'we can sell the picture to Roches Stores when we get home. We'll make a shaggin' fortune.'

'That's two great ideas in one day,' Cora said. 'Careful you don't have another.' But she stood there none the less. We never made a penny from that picture.

Overhead, children's kites fluttered in shafts of sunlight that filtered through a sky of broken cloud. In the background the peaks of the Hindu Kush were already blanketed in winter snow. Inside, we were sinking.

'It's still a beautiful place to be,' Cora said trying to cheer us up.

'India would be beautiful too,' I said, chin on knuckles like the Thinker in Residence.

In the morning Afghan Airlines cancelled all flights to Delhi, along with our last hope. As we didn't have enough money to return to Iran and then fly over the war zone we had no choice but to turn back. For a while we sat despondent in the Khyber Restaurant with all the other despondent, fagged-out freaks. In the heavy sorrowful atmosphere things looked bleak on every front. Then little by little, over buffalo steak and chips, a new plan began to form.

'I know what we could do,' I blurted. 'We could cycle home through Egypt and North Africa.'

Cora looked up at me as if I'd burst into flames again .

But, by the time our old friend, Mike Sullivan of Ohio, unexpectedly walked in with a 'Well fuck me, look who's here!' we had drawn up a list of everything we'd need.

'Down to the large knife to beat off the wolves and leopards we might run into along the way,' Cora told Mike.

She was throwing her eyes up to Heaven.

Outside, the wail of the muezzins filled the city with hope.

'Cycle to Egypt?' Mike said, 'What a damn fine idea.'

'You think so?' Cora said. 'You wanna come...?'

# Chapter 24

## The Bicycle Ride

'Just think of what George Bernard Shaw said,' I suggested to Cora. *'The reasonable man adapts himself to the world; the unreasonable man persists in trying to adapt the world to himself. Therefore all progress depends on the unreasonable man.'*

'Was George Bernard Shaw an eejit?' Cora wanted to know.

At 11.00am on Friday, December 10th, after a breakfast of steak, eggs and chips at the Khyber Restaurant, Cora and I left the Farah Hotel on our new bicycles. They were solid heavy yokes of the old 'high Nelly' genre, thick-tyred and hard to push. Especially over mountain roads in the heat that bloomed in the middle of the day. Although we'd posted home six kilos of gear, we'd replaced it with an equivalent weight of cooking equipment, food, water, and a deadly petrol stove, the lot carried in our packs and strapped to the carriers, which gave us a top-heavy wobble. From my waist hung my wolf and leopard knife, a crudely crafted affair with a wooden handle, leather scabbard and 16 inches of blade. As we passed through the outskirts of the city people stared and waved.

'I get the feeling that this isn't a common sight,' Cora said.

'Dervla Murphy came through here on a bicycle a lot of years ago,' I assured her. (I later learned that the Afghan cops wouldn't allow her to cycle across much of Afghanistan.)

Soon we were out on the open road. Fuelled by the new adventure, we climbed into dry barren hills and set off for Egypt. To the north, the snowy crags of the Hindu Kush stood in bold relief against a tall and far sky, blue to a fault.

'It's less than 4,000 kilometres away,' I promised Cora.

At first we talked and laughed and cycled at a steady leisurely pace. Then the talking and laughing died down as the sun climbed and muscles, that had long forgotten bicycles, began to buckle. After an hour or so, I noticed with some trepidation that Cora was lagging behind.

'We should be in Ghazni tomorrow,' I called back with all the encouragement I could muster. 'This should be an unforgettable trip.'

'Yeah,' she agreed, nodding, smiling and grimacing all at the same time.

As it turned out, it took two long days to cycle the 140 kilometres to Ghazni. It was indeed an unforgettable trip, but for all the wrong reasons.

To begin with, the enervating combination of heavy overloaded bikes, parched mountainous semi-desert, and scorching midday heat slowed us down considerably. Fifteen kilometres out of Kabul, we had to pull off the road, park the bikes on their stands, and sling two light prayer blankets between them so we could hide from the midday sun. That night we had the other extreme - when it got so cold that our drinking water froze as we slept in the open, wrapped in all our clothes and listening to the howling of wolves, driven down from the mountains by winter snow.

Secondly there was our Afghan petrol stove.

Based on the principle of the Primus, this was one of the most frightening of inventions. To light it, we had to pump the petrol until jets of spray hissed from the burner. A match was then applied, causing a spectacular burst of flame, especially at night when we were trying to stay inconspicuous to roving bandits. Driven back by the heat, we could then no longer control the pressure, so we'd cut to a safe distance as the inferno blazed, hoping the shrapnel of any explosion would pass overhead. When the flames began to die back, we'd sidle over to the red-hot tank full of vaporised petrol, and pump again. Sometimes it would burst back into flame; sometimes it would work.

Thirdly there was the food miscalculation.

On the morning of the second day we decided to lighten our load by dumping our sandals and giving most of our food to a passing Afghan who found our presence in the desert at 6.00am a trifle baffling. Our largesse was based on a prediction of being in Ghazni that night. The miscalculation meant that we had no food for twenty-four hours, from midday of the second day until we arrived in Ghazni at midday of the third.

Then there were the village children.

On the second day we discovered one of rural Afghanistan's favourite juvenile pastimes: as we neared villages, groups of delighted delinquents would rush to the road, gather up any large rocks that happened to be handy, and pelt us with them as we passed. This being unpleasant, we devised a strategy. On seeing the assembling assailants, I would peddle on ahead, jump from the bike and engage in a pre-emptive charge, screaming and holding

## Chapter 24

my hands in the air, ghost-fashion. The children would gape, then scatter in blind panic, allowing Cora a chance to run the village in safety. When I deduced her to be reasonaby out of reach, I'd race back to my bike and flee the ambush scene before the terrorists had a chance to regroup. (A few decades later, and nice Mr. Bush might've been able to help me out with a few cluster bombs.)

But, most arresting of all were the men with the guns.

There's nothing more unnerving when you're cycling down a remote stretch of mountainous desert in the early morning than some fellow in kurta, baggy trousers and turban who drops what he's doing, picks up a flintlock rifle and aims it straight at your head for no reason other than that he appears intent on killing you, nice guy that you may be. A moment of disbelief gives way to a realisation that the past was infinitely more reassuring than the present. You look away, go into denial, look back again. The black hole of the barrel is still there. Still pointing at your head. You hope it stays black. You hope it's a sick joke.

But as you come closer and the rifle follows, you realise shockingly that this could be very serious. The squeeze of a stranger's finger might now be all that divides a previously nice morning from a calamity. There's nothing you can do and nowhere to run. It's just you and the man with the gun. I remember a numbness around the back of my skull. We could become buzzard pickings. We could finish up in a small desert grave that nobody would ever think of searching. Then the fear of being suddenly dead crumbled into an irrational trough of wellbeing, a stupidly comforting resignation that was brain turning to water. This was no longer fear as you'd normally know it. This was fear out of control.

'Cora,' I said, 'whatever you do, don't go any faster or do anything sudden.'

'Don't worry,' Cora said. 'I couldn't go faster right now if the boody man [a scary figure who lives in Cork] was on my tail.'

With no other option, we cycled on in the full knowledge that one of us might never hear the shot if it came. It was a long, long, lactic acid ride until we were out of range. Even then the dry mouth and headache lingered for an hour, along with a sense of acute vulnerability. Would he follow us? Out here in the middle of nowhere, we were powerless.

In the afternoon it happened a second time, the exact same thing. Once more we could feel the drilling between the shoulders a long way down the road, followed by a singular thought: we could be bumped off in the middle of the night.

'You didn't think of this when you bought that knife,' Cora said. 'Tell you what, if we see a leopard, I'll eat the bike. We should've bought a machinegun.'

That evening's sunset was stunning. But even as the red globe sank into the peaks, and shadows jumped the ravines, and the turquoise sky faded to a calm grey, we couldn't shake the spectres of the day, or the night that faced us. Soon it would be freezing cold and, along with the danger that seemed to lurk behind every rock and escarpment, there would be another battle with the stove. To shorten the future, we cycled on through the dark, stopping only when our legs had staved in. To avoid any threat from the earlier gunmen (who might still be tracking us), we pulled the bikes well away from the road and slept on a high shelf, where the wolf howls were even closer than the night before.

'You should think about setting up a travel company,' Cora said as we shivered on the cold ground in our sleeping bags. 'Seriously! There's bound to be lots of people who'd adore this. You could sell it as The Flight into Egypt.'

I think she was taking the hand.

Soon after sunrise on the third day we broke our drinking water into little chips of ice and turned it into tea. With nothing to eat, we set off again for Ghazni, hungry, tired and tetchy. It was a bad time for a group of Afgans to try and pull us over so we could help them jump-start their bus.

Finally, around midday, exhausted, starving and still unnerved by the rifle episodes, we limped into Ghazni, a small Tajik town of mud brick and concrete on the edge of the desert. Although the sight of orchards and trees, and a proliferation of birdsong, partially raised our spirits, we literally fell off the bikes. It was left to two Afghan men to wheel them along the dirt street as far as the door of the modest Farokhi Hotel where we dropped our gear in our room, staggered downstairs to the restaurant and flopped into two seats.

'*As-Salāmu Alaykum* [Peace be unto you],' the waiter said, pen and paper in hand. 'What you like?' He stared at the massive knife still hanging from my waist.

'Two omelettes please,' I said. 'And bread and tea.'

'Sorreee,' he said, pen and paper still poised. 'Hamelette finish. Iss no good. Iss no cookin. Cookin sleepin.'

## Chapter 24

With real difficulty we dragged ourselves to our feet and staggered off up the street until we found a place that fixed us kebabs, potatoes, bread and tea. After eating and drinking vast quantities, we got up to leave and fell back dizzy into our chairs.

'Do you think this is all wise?' Cora asked.

Cora often gave great weight to my thoughts.

'We'll be alright after a sleep,' I said. 'Just think, we've already knocked 140 kilometres off the journey.'

'Where did the word 'already' come from?' Cora wanted to know.

'I'll tell you later,' I said. It was the best I could do.

We slept well into that afternoon, then went out and bought Cora an embroidered jacket at one of the town's sheepskin-curing 'factories', where they were beating the skins off a tree stump to soften them. Next call was an antique shop in the bazaar. As there was nobody about, we went into the workshop at the rear of the shop where we surprised two young Sikhs who were sitting over a fire, working metal.

'You're *making* the antiques!' I said. The two lads jumped to their feet.

'This all new,' the one with the hammer admitted. 'But this all antique.' He pointed to one of the outer walls, hung with rows of knives and guns. 'You look,' he said and dragged us back outside.

'This,' he said, pulling down a revolver. 'This very antique. This use in Afghan war with British.'

'Sure,' I joked. 'And by Julius Caesar in Rome.'

'You make funny,' he said.

It was an odd-looking gun, with chambers that were open in front and tiny holes above each chamber to take a piece of flint. I concluded that you couldn't actually load the thing but bought it as an oddity and carried it back to Ireland. Decades later, in March 1996, long after the gun had disappeared in house moves, a maniac named Thomas Hamilton slaughtered a class of sixteen primary school children and their teacher in Dunblane in Scotland. The massacre brought about a British ban on the ownership of pistols over .22 calibre. Some years on, an article appeared in *The Guardian* describing a loophole in this legislation: old 'front-loading revolvers' had been overlooked and therefore excluded. The article described a gun that had front-loading chambers that were sealed with wax once the powder and shot were in place. It appeared that the old gun from Ghazni might well have been used in the Afghan

Wars. Had it been detected, I could've been stopped at any of twelve borders carrying an unlicensed weapon!

On our way back from the antique shop we were invited in for tea by a Tajik man in his late thirties with a large hook nose and stubbly beard. He told us that his name was Farrukh, which meant 'happy'. He was dressed in a black kurta and trousers and an incongruous, brightly patterned orange skullcap that he removed to reveal a head of electrified hair, sheared away in front as if he'd been hit by the debris of a cyclone. Farrukh spoke good English in a brightly amplified voice. When he heard that we planned to cycle on across Afghanistan he let out a long thin whistle.

'My friend,' he said, directing his advice at me, 'this not possible. For more than two year, no rain. The people have no food. People, they are kill for twenty afghanis - the same for one omelette and one cup of tea. You have many bandit. Also, between Ghazni and Kandahar is living illiterate people. They not understand European custom - like woman who smoke and not have veil or burkah [Cora, in other words]. In those place, when nobody look, maybe you shot and rob, and maybe they take she. You are bury in desert where nobody find you.'

He went on to explain that, at that time of the year, hunger drove the wolves down from the mountains, and they came into Ghazni and the villages to take domestic animals 'and people'.

'You see skin in bazaar? You see how big? Even if you have gun, they dangerous. So why you cycle? You crazy? You have danger from sun. You have danger from cold. You have danger from man. You have danger from beast. Why you not take bus?'

'Tomorrow,' Cora said to me, 'you're a bicycle salesman.'

## Chapter 24

*Cora during bicycle ride from Kabul, December 1971.*

# Chapter 25
Desert of Death

_____

Beaten again, we decided to revert to the bus. We would turn south from Kandahar to Quetta in Pakistan. Far enough away, we hoped, from the war zones.

'Now,' Farrukh said, 'you must relax in Ghazni. See very famous tomb of Sultan Mahmud.' He insisted on taking us the next day and telling us the story of Mahmud of Ghazna.

Mahmud, the son of a Turkish slave, became king of Ghazna, (ancient Ghazni) in 998 AD at the age of twenty-seven. At the time, the town was the kernel of a small Central Asian kingdom; but Mahmud had big plans and embarked on more than twenty military expeditions during which he conquered an empire that eventually included Kashmir, the Punjab, and a great swathe of Iran.

For some reason, Mahmud vowed to invade India about once a year, beginning with a large-scale campaign against the Punjab in 1001 and finishing with an assault on Somnath on the southern coast of Gujarat twenty-five years later. During the first campaign, he marched on India at the head of 15,000 cavalry, and was confronted near Peshawar by Jaipal, Raja of the Punjab, who rode against him with an army of 12,000 cavalry, 30,000 foot soldiers and 300 elephants. However, the superior Indian army fell back under the Muslim onslaught, leaving 15,000 dead in the field. Jaipal himself was taken prisoner along with many of his relatives and officers. Though eventually released, he had been so humiliated that he abdicated in favour of his son, Anandpal, before climbing onto his own funeral pyre.

Seven years later, Mahmud again came up against a huge Indian army in the Punjab, this time led by Anandpal. After a forty-day standoff, Mahmud drew the Indians into an attack that he very nearly regretted. A force of 30,000 Khokar tribesmen charged both his flanks with such ferocity that the Sultan was about to retreat when providence intervened. Anandpal's elephant panicked and fled the field. His troops, thinking that their leader had cut and run, followed suit. The ensuing victory gave Mahmud northern India. In the years that followed, as he consolidated his empire, the Sultan set about transforming Ghazna into the outstanding cultural base

## Chapter 25

of Central Asia, which he ruled until his death in 1030.

'From that time,' Farrukh said, 'in all wars and fighting, Allah protect tomb of Mahmud.' He then led us from the tomb back to the bazaar. Under the old city walls and the 45-metre-high, half-ruined Citadel of Ghazni, he began negotiations on the sale of our bikes. Without his help, we'd probably never have sold the woman's bike, an unheard-of abomination in the back streets of Ghazni.

That night we had two visitors at the Farokhi Hotel.

Cora and I had joined two Austrian guys, a German couple, a Swedish woman, and a Welsh woman around the oil stove in the Germans' room. Someone had rolled a joint and everyone was in jocular, storytelling mood when the door knocked. Lisa, the German woman, answered. Outside, stood a skinny, grinning, middle-aged Afghan cop, in a loose uniform. He was squinting in through the fog that floated idly around the 20-watt bulb.

'Oh shit!' Lisa croaked. Her boyfriend, who had the joint in his mouth, almost swallowed his tongue.

'Passport,' the cop said, still grinning as he cut a slow, deliberate path through the smoke to sit on one of the beds, shifting his gun to make himself more comfortable. He then went through all passports, smiling broadly at each photo, and shaking hands with everyone. When he'd finished, he got up, said a polite 'Thank you', and left.

Half an hour later the manager arrived to say that Farrukh was outside. I went out into the night to find him wrapped in a blanket against the bitter cold of Ghazni's 2,225-metre elevation. Looking a bit like a hungry dog, he had a proposition: he'd give me 500 afghanis if I could arrange a white woman for him for half an hour, and he'd give her another 500 afghanis.

'Farrukh,' I said. 'Goodnight.'

Four days after our arrival in Ghazni, Cora and I were ready to leave again on the early-morning bus when we were offered a lift to Kandahar by a slick young salesman in a suit who was travelling in a van with a friend. In Kandahar he produced a slick little pistol and - no link, mind you - asked us for seventy afghanis each. Who could refuse such an endearing request?

\* \* \*

Not long after arriving in Kandahar, we again ran into Gulam and Aziz in the bazaar. They were delighted that we hadn't made it to India. Gulam suggested a run to a small village up in the hills for the following day.

'This will be better than India,' he assured us.

In the first grey, chilly light of morning, Gulam and Aziz were at our door. After a quick breakfast, we left for the bus station, little more than an open space, and waited an hour for the bus. The eight-kilometre ride along a rough, dusty track took a further half hour, the bus stopping numerous times to pick up passengers and an assortment of baggage, which included a young camel.

'We stop here,' Gulam said as the bus pulled up on the perimeter of a small collection of mud-brick huts and walled compounds, protected by a ring of barren rugged hills. Sheep, goats, dogs and chickens wandered between the compounds and a couple of horse-drawn carts plodded along the perimeters. At the edge of the tiny bazaar, that probably hadn't changed much in a thousand years, we stopped at an outdoor chai-khana where an old boy was sitting by the fire pressing hashish. As we sipped our tea, the occasional farmer would arrive from the hills, with a horse or camel laden with local produce - wool, cotton, chickens, fruit (especially pomegranates) - for sale or distribution further afield.

'You have hashish in Ireland?' Gulam asked.

'No,' Cora said. 'Only if it comes from places like Afghanistan.'

'You have opium in Ireland?'

'No, only alcohol.'

'Alcohol is bad,' Aziz said. 'Maybe it make you crazy if you drink.'

At that point two older men in flowing white shawls and turbans, with flintlock rifles slung across their shoulders, galloped by on horses, spirals of dust rising in their wake. One of them unslung his rifle and waved it in the air.

Neither hashish nor alcohol could've made that happen.

'You will come to my house this night,' Aziz said. 'You must visit *my* family this time.'

'Thank you very much,' I said and we arranged a time. We then returned to Kandahar on an old fume-filled wreck of a bus. It was the only time I've ever seen the working of an engine from the inside of a vehicle.

At five o'clock, a horse-drawn gharry brought us to Aziz's house. Again, all the stops were pulled out as the family lavished us with a generosity beyond their means. Cushions were spread on the floor and we were given a bowl of water to wash our hands. Plates of rice, vegetables, bread, eggs, nuts and raisins were laid in the middle and the family - father, veiled mother, younger brother and two younger

## Chapter 25

sisters, sat on the floor across from us. They chatted away as Gulam, Aziz, Cora and I ate with our hands.

'Sit on that left hand,' I whispered to Cora as she reached out to pollute the food.

The father, a tall man in traditional attire and hennaed beard, was full of questions.

'My father, he asks why you want to go to India.' Aziz translated.

'Many young people from Europe want to go to India,' I answered. 'We are interested in the life and customs of the people.' Aziz translated again and the father responded.

'My father say, in India, many Muslims also. India before have big problem between Hindu and Muslim. But now is better. Only in Kashmir. In Kashmir, there is big problem between Hindu and Muslim.'

The children gazed up as we answered, the girls in their colourful shalwar-kameezes and bangles, and the little boy a junior version of his father. The father wanted to know all about Ireland, especially where it was, and all about our families. All was going well until …

'My father ask how many children you have.'

'Oh, none,' I said. 'We're not married.'

Aziz translated. There was a moment's incomprehension on the father's face. He then jumped to his feet. Yelling at his wife and grabbing two of the children, he rushed the family from the room and out of the house. 'Maybe it was the wrong answer,' Aziz said. 'My father, he is strict Muslim.'

'In the name of Jaysus Aziz,' I said, 'you could've warned me.' Aziz looked blank and I realised that he was none too happy himself.

'I think we should go,' Cora said. A gharry was called and we left with a laughing Gulam. Aziz went off to make the peace.

\* \* \*

Two days after arriving in Kandahar we were on our way to the Pakistani border on a ramshackle bus with no glass in the windows and benches for seats when we were embroiled in an unholy row.

Earlier in the day we had to go to the cops and update our Afghan visas at the cost of 700 afghanis. This left us eighty afghanis to get us to Pakistan. The bus fare was twenty afghanis each but when we got to the bus station, we were refused passage to the border post of Spin Boldak unless we paid 200 each. We called the cops and were put on the next bus. However, half way to the border, in the empty wastes of the Desert of Death, it started again.

We'd been sharing cigarettes and sweets with our fellow passengers, and generally enjoying the absurdity of the two camels on the roof and the man who disembarked in the middle of nowhere and hiked off into the desert with a wooden door on his back, when fare time came. Everyone paid their twenty afghanis. When it came our turn the fare again jumped tenfold.

'Two hundred you, two hundred she,' the conductor said. He was a man of about fifty, who looked like an unshaven Afghan version of Benny Hill.

'Not on your nanny,' I said. 'Everyone else paid twenty, and we'll pay twenty.'

'Two hundred!' the conductor yelled and hell broke loose.

We were the only non-Afghans on board. Otherwise, the bus was full of tribal Pashtun men, some cradling flintlock rifles, who all now turned on us as one, yelling in Pashto and jostling in support of the conductor's demand. Nevertheless, we held our ground.

'Go to hell!' Cora said.

The conductor shouted to the driver. The bus stopped in the middle of the desert and the conductor pushed open the door.

'You out!' he ordered.

I gave him one of my famous glares.

'OUT!' he roared.

'Bugger off!' I said. (The glare hadn't worked.)

The chap beside me, a small bulky man of about forty, laughed the laugh that isn't funny. He then tore my pack from my grasp, intending to toss it into the desert. It was a wrong thing to do. In those days I was sometimes prone to a slightly tetchy disposition.

'To hell with this!' I roared (part of the disposition), and grabbed my neighbour by the lapels of his waistcoat, twisting them hard into his bearded throat. He began to choke. His eyes popped. His hands tried to pry mine loose. No mission there. Instantly, everything stopped. In a culture that prized machismo and was wary of the lunatic, I had the rapt attention of the bus.

'OK! OK!' the conductor shouted. He closed the door. 'You pay twenty. She pay twenty.'

'We will,' I said, and let go of my neighbour's throat. 'When we get to the border.' The neighbour was coughing violently. I put it down to too much hash.

For the rest of the journey every man in the bench-like rows in front leaned against the back of his seat, rested his chin on his

# Chapter 25

arms and stared at us in a kind of benign silence. We paid when we reached Spin Boldak.

'Yellabellies,' Cora said. She later confided that she thought I was going to get both of us killed in a rather futile last stand.

The border post at Spin Boldak wasn't up to much: little more than a small, fly-blown settlement of mud-brick huts, clinging glumly to life in the middle of the desert, and engulfed by an obliterating sand storm when we arrived. By contrast to the experience of the bus, however, the half dozen cops and Immigration officials at the ragged post were friendly enough. As we were the only people passing through, they processed us quickly, the only delay being the curiosity of an older, stubble-faced Immigration man in Afghan robes with a face like a weasel. He was fascinated by female underwear and very nearly found our revolver as he fished to the bottom of my pack looking for lurking stashes of hashish.

'Border to Pakistan is closed five o'clock,' a big swarthy, pockmarked cop in black shirt and jeans, who seemed to run the show, told us as we re-packed our gear. 'But you sleep here and go tomorrow. We stamp visa in the morning.' The Weasel beamed approval.

Hospitality at the post was phenomenal. After watching the sun go down in a blaze of fire, we all sat down around an oil lamp. We played cards. We listened to Afghan music on a transistor radio. We ate an enormous meal of rice, meat, vegetables and bread. At 9.30pm Cora and I decided to call it a day and were shown to our sleeping quarters by the Weasel.

'Here,' he said, pointing to a mattress on the floor beside somebody's bed in one of two Spartan bedrooms.

We threw down our sleeping bags. The Weasel looked on, arms folded and an eager look on his face. We got into the sleeping bags in the hope that he'd go away. He stayed his ground, the eager look increasing. He then spread his arms and gestured, matter-of-fact, that I should roll over on Cora.

'Ficky-ficky,' he said. When he was told to ficky away off, he pretended to be puzzled and gestured again. When an angry Cora began to raise her voice, he gestured that she should calm down now, don't let the others hear; after all he was only joking. But, anyway, would she give him a kiss. He leaned his face towards her.

'Go away,' Cora said. Undaunted, he turned to me, pursing his lips in a final gesture of hope.

Later, the owner of the bed - a young guy who'd been with us at dinner - came in and it started all over again. I was woken by a yelp from Cora. Our neighbour was pawing her breasts. Fuse burned to carbon, I hauled out the 16-inch blade of our wolf and leopard knife from under the jacket I was using as a pillow.

'Touch her again,' I said, 'and you're history.' It was the kind of thing you do when you've taken leave of your senses.

Now, there's an old saying that goes something like this: *Oh Lord, let me not tread today on the toes that are attached to the rear end I must kiss tomorrow...*

First thing in the morning, we were perched on the roof box of a truck, on our way to the Pakistani border, ten kilometres away. It was Sunday, December 19th, 1971. No-man's land was full of smugglers loading merchandise from camels to trucks and from trucks to camels. Everything looked normal. But what we didn't know was that Zulfikar Ali Bhutto had taken power in Pakistan the previous day while our fellow bus passengers were threatening us with the buzzards of the Desert of Death. Up to that point, Irish nationals didn't need visas for Pakistan. By the time we arrived at the Chaman frontier post, Mr. Bhutto had changed all of that.

'Where is your visa?' the solitary immigration officer asked. A friendly, painfully thin man in shalwar-kameez and skullcap, he was smoking a cigarette and leaning casually against the outside wall of a hut that said *Welcome to Pakistan.*

'What visa?' I asked. 'We're Irish. The Pakistani Consul in Kandahar told us we didn't need a visa.'

'Yesterday, no visa. Today visa. Mr. Bhutto says everyone needs visa now. You must go back to Kandahar.'

'What!' I blurted. 'But this isn't possible. We have left Afghanistan. We have no visas. We can't go back.'

'And you cannot enter Pakistan without visa,' he said. Cora and I stared at one another and at the prospect of a lifetime in no man's land.

'But, we were at the border last night,' I tried. 'And you were closed.'

'Sorry,' he said. 'You cannot enter without a visa.'

'What can we do now?' Cora asked, on the verge of tears. The official softened, sparking a thin ray of hope.

'One moment,' he said, raising a finger and stubbing out his cigarette. 'I will telephone Quetta.'

## Chapter 25

He went inside and we could hear him pleading our case; but when he came back out, we could tell from his face that there was no budging Quetta.

'I am sorry,' he said. 'I can understand your problem, but there is nothing I can do. I'm sure Mr. Bhutto does not mean you any harm, but you must go back. You must explain to the Afghan people at Spin Boldak.'

While we sat around pondering doom, we were joined in the slurry by two others who had just arrived from Kandahar. One was a large, long-haired, bearded American named Ben, who reminded me of Bigfoot. The second was a small, garrulous, curly-haired Englishman named Anto, reduced by Asia to skin and bones.

'You've got to be joking me, man,' Ben told the official. 'There are other people on their way here from Kandahar with no visas. Why the hell didn't someone tell the Afghans down the road so they can stop people from coming over?'

'Yeah,' Anto chirped. 'That would make too much sense, wouldn't it? How do we get out of here now? In a bleethin' spaceship?'

'May I suggest a truck?' the official smiled.

With no other option, the four of us hitched a ride on the back of the next truck and were returned to our friends at the Afghan frontier. Hoping for some residual goodwill from our stay at the post, Cora and I fronted up to the Immigration hut with our story of perfidious Mr. Bhutto.

'Oh no,' Cora said. 'Look who's on Immigration...'

It was the guy who had groped her the night before, the slubberdegullion I'd threatened with history. If he was surprised by our return, he masked it well. As we approached the desk, he fixed me with a thoroughly unwholesome sneer. The rest of our pals at the post had forgotten who we were.

'You must go back to Pakistan,' the groper said. 'You have no visa for Afghanistan. For you, Afghanistan finish.'

Ben, Anto, Cora and I spent the rest of the day on the backs of trucks, going back and forth between Spin Boldak and Chaman in vain attempts to bleat our way into either country. In the end it was baksheesh: we had to bribe our way back into Afghanistan. Cora and I had to watch as our buddies of the night before pocketed a fat wad of our dwindling cash. The bit I hated most, I had to admit, was the smirk on the mug of the groper.

'I'd love to knock his head in with a hurley[24] dipped in rat shit,' I confided to Cora.

'I know love,' she said. 'But first we'd have to find one.' Cora had ever the practical view.

We were about to leave for Kandahar when a young French couple turned up with half a kilo of hash in their bags. Now, where they thought they were going with half a kilo of hash is a question that will never be answered. But, if they'd arrived half an hour earlier, before we'd paid up our baksheesh, we might have been spared. This was much bigger fish. This was, in fact, baksheesh bonanza. There were border officials at Spin Boldak who dreamed all their nights of nothing else but foreigners with kilos and kilos of hash. The black-shirted cop, who appeared last night to be the headman, took control.

'Hashish!' he yelled into the faces of the couple. You could see he'd rehearsed for this. 'Now you go to prison for long time. You understand?'

The Frenchman nodded in shock. The woman burst into floods and sank to the ground like Scarlett O'Hara in *Gone With The Wind*. The cop emptied their packs into the dust, then let them pick up the contents while he yelled orders in Pashto to two other cops who came running, with grave intent all over their faces.

'You think we are stupid?' the chief said to the Frenchman. 'Now, you will see who is stupid.'

The Frenchman reached down and helped his girlfriend to her feet, both of them now in tears, as the junior cops pulled out the handcuffs. Then Blackshirt stepped forward.

'There is one chance,' he said in a more conciliatory tone. 'You can pay fine of twenty-five dollar.'

'*Oh merci! Merci!* Thank you! Thank you!' the Frenchwoman sobbed. You could feel the tension dissolve.

In 1971, on the Afghan border, twenty-five dollars was a lot of money, but twenty-five dollars or an Afghan jail...? With indecent haste, dollars changed hands.

'Very good,' Blackshirt said. 'Now everyone must come.'

Moving over towards the roadside, he rounded us all up, ourselves, the cops, the Immigration people and the bewildered French couple, and sat us in a circle for a quick lesson in frontier

---

[24] Stick with heavy curved end used in Irish field game of hurling.

# Chapter 25

justice. Fifteen minutes later three young boys arrived with troughs of rice, stew and bread - all paid for out of the 'fine'. We all tucked in, the foreigners again sitting on their left hands so they wouldn't mistakenly let them stray to the food and cause another baksheesh crisis. Blackshirt then ordered glasses of tea from the chai-khana and called for a hookah which he placed in the middle of the circle. This he filled with large lumps of the bewildered French couple's hash. The pipe was lit and passed around to everyone - including the stunned former owners of its contents. No hard feelings. Just a dirty job that someone has to do.

Surrounded by bonhomie, we learned from the Frenchman that a ceasefire had been declared in the Indo-Pakistani war.

'There's going to be a Bangladesh,' he said.

Faced with a coordinated onslaught on the eastern and western fronts, the Pakistanis had capitulated in under a fortnight, surrendering in the east three days earlier. The next day Indira Ghandi, had announced a unilateral ceasefire, and both sides had put down their weapons. By then Pakistan had lost half its navy, a quarter of its air force and a third of its army. India had taken 93,000 prisoners of war. But, ceasefire or not, the borders were still closed between India and Pakistan.

# Chapter 26
## Mr. John and Baden-Powell's Cousin

The sun went down and the night settled cold over the desert. Anto, Ben, Cora and I were on our way back to Kandahar by truck. Anto and Cora were in the cab. Ben and I, along with four Afghans, were perched on top of a swaying mountain of Hessian bags stuffed with wool, twice as high and broad as the truck. With an arm and a leg strapped under the holding ropes, I was gripped by the wind chill factor and the dread of being catapulted off at any moment by a bump in the potholed road.

One of the Afghans managed to smoke a joint.

Back in Kandahar once more, we had another raging fare argument. The truck driver wanted double the agreed fare. Eventually, we booked in to the very cheap Pamir Hotel, which we shared with Anna, Mareike and Wilhelm from Germany, and a visiting, 41-year-old, retired bandit with the unlikely name of Mr. John.

The Germans were at reception when we arrived, trying to find out if they could fly from Kabul to Delhi. The two women were devout hippies from Nuremberg, both about twenty, with enormous hooped earrings and long blonde hair that spun the head of every man in Kandahar. Anna, who wore a long Kuchi dress and a million bracelets, and exuded extreme confidence, was clearly the more inspired of the two. Mareike, dressed in a shalwar-kameez, seemed to live in her shadow, limiting her conversation to supportive grunts hitched to Anna's statements. Wilhelm, in grubby singlet and Afghan trousers, was from West Berlin where he'd been a teacher for four years before taking to the road to become an emaciated, unshaven, doped-out wreck. If you'd met him in a train station in Berlin, you'd have taken him for a down-and-out. As soon as we arrived in reception, the three of them turned to us to see if we had any information.

'The only place to go is Pakistan,' Anto told them. 'And make fucking sure you have a visa. We've just been to the border and couldn't get in.'

'Fucking war,' Wilhelm said. 'Always fucking war.'

Wilhelm then invited everyone to join him in his room.

'I would like to hear how things are in Kabul and Pakistan,' he said.

## Chapter 26

'We didn't get to Pakistan,' Cora reminded him.

As it transpired everyone ended up in our room when Cora invited them all to share some biscuits we'd picked up in the bazaar. Ten minutes later there was a knock on the door. I answered to find the manager standing outside with another Afghan who was in his bare feet and had a big clay hookah tucked under his arm.

'I like you meet my friend,' the manager said. 'His name Mr. John. From Khyber Pass.'

He led his friend, a man of medium height and build, past me into the room.

There are some people who barge into your life, say an awful lot, and leave no impression. There are others who slide in quietly, say very little, and leave an imprint the size of Texas. Mr. John was of the latter genus. He was the man in rabbinical black: black pantaloons, black kurta, black sleeveless tunic, black scattered beard, massive black turban, black-hilted dagger, and black bushy brows that almost covered the blackest eyes I've ever seen. Whereas the rest of us occupied the space filled by our bodies, Mr. John occupied what was left of the room. (He came back to me in later years in a recurring dream. I used to see him swinging on a rope, cutlass between his teeth, towards the deck of a merchant schooner on which I was a hapless passenger. At the last moment, he would grab the cutlass, let go the rope and come hurtling at me, and I'd wake a screaming heap.)

'*As-Salāmu Alaykum*,' Mr. John greeted us as, with a slight reverential stoop, he came padding into the room. With slow deliberate movements, he placed his hookah in the middle of the floor, then stood to one side with a skittish smile while the manager, exuding lofty grandeur, gave us the lowdown.

His shy friend had apparently been a somewhat successful bandit for a time in the Khyber Pass, robbing the rich to help the poor, especially those who dressed in black. Along with a couple of other bearded buddies, he had also engaged in smuggling. Anything that would turn a few afghanis in the bazaars of Kabul or a few rupees in Peshawar was driven by truck, camel or mule across the porous border with Pakistan, where baksheesh was the great lubricant. For many years, all went well until one night in the deep defiles of the Khyber, a would-be victim tore up the rules: he pulled a gun and came out shooting. Poor Mr. John was sent bolting into the dark, a hail of hot bullets whizzing around his ears. At that very moment, the burden of the years and the heat of exploding gunpowder coalesced. The venerable Mr. John decided to give banditry a rest and visit his old friend at the Pamir Hotel. When he arrived in Kandahar, he took an instant shine to the spirited renegades of the passing freak trade. He hadn't left since.

'He especially like German people,' the manager told Anna and Mareike. 'His cousin, he work in Dusseldorf.'

After the introduction, the manager left and we all shook hands with Mr. John who touched his heart after each handshake. Call it prejudice, but looking into the black shining eyes of bandit, Mr. John, I found it hard to imagine any of his relatives tripping the boulevards of Dusseldorf.

'Hello,' Cora said when it came her turn. 'Nice to meet you. Back home I hardly ever have a bandit in my room.' Mr. John grinned pitted yellow teeth.

'Would you like to sit?' Anna asked, gesturing towards the only chair in the room.

Mr. John declined, throwing back his head in the Afghan gesture for no.

Although he spoke not a word of English, our new friend managed to convey to us that he indeed loved us all, just as the manager had said. He also loved hashish, and the cross-cultural bonding so enhanced by his own mesmerising displays on the hookah.

To sit on the floor in a circle around the glowing charcoal and shooting flames of the pipe, and watch Mr. John suck in half an ounce of hash and all the air in the room in a single gulp was to witness in privilege the absolute personification of unhindered excess. Then, in a great display of the cubic capacity of his lungs, Mr. John would jump to his feet and hop about the room like a bar-tailed godwit doing physical jerks. Coughing and roaring and belching huge gushes of smoke into every available cranny, he would send the ants, beetles and cockroaches scurrying for their lives.

He would then burst into laughter, rolling about the floor and occasionally kicking his legs in the air with the jerky movements of a goat that had just had its throat slit. He was fiery elation. He was pure happiness. This charming embodiment of concepts entirely alien to the 20th century then pulled from the pockets of his tunic a big lump of opium, a spoon and a silver pipe.

My final memory of the night was of Mr. John tip-toeing towards the door with a couple of furtive backward glances. He seemed to be

## Chapter 26

raising each knee to his chin. Weighed down by a ton of lead, I lay on the bed. The room faded in and out of a dense red fog. I could've been robbed, kissed or murdered. Somehow, the others had hauled themselves to their rooms and the only person left, other than Mr. John, was Cora. Thankfully, she was still sensible and able to say, 'Goodnight Mr. John.' Otherwise, heaven knows what awful ends might have occurred.

\* \* \*

In the morning, Cora, Ben, Anto and I fronted up to the Pakistani Consulate for our visas. We were met by a very distraught Pakistani Consul. A lovely, grey-haired, grandfatherly man in his late fifties, he so refused to believe that British and Irish nationals needed visas for his country that he initially wouldn't even consider giving them to us.

'No my friends, no,' he insisted. 'Britain gave Pakistan to the Pakistani people. It is not possible that British people must have this visa.' When Cora told him of our experiences at the border he reluctantly left the room and phoned through to Quetta. He returned in tears.

'This is the worst day of my life,' he sobbed from deep in the wounded places, 'that British people must take a visa for Pakistan...'

When we left the Consulate, Cora and I probably carried the first ever Irish passports stamped with Pakistani visas. We also had a record of how much money we had left as it had to be entered in our passports when applying for the visas. Cora had £85. I had £80.

Ben, Cora and I then went to the cops and had our visas extended for one more day. Anto, whose visa had also expired, changed the date himself.

'Look at that,' he said. 'A fucking masterpiece!'

'I sure hope so,' Ben said. 'Otherwise, big shit's gonna fly at the border.'

Having now changed what remained of the hundred rupees we'd bought for Pakistan and spent most of it, Cora and I were left with just enough cash to pay for an evening meal and one more night at the Pamir. As we didn't want to change another traveller's cheque and end up with a pocketful of afghanis, we sold our stove to pay for the morning bus back to Spin Boldak.

It was a hassle-free ride to the border, thanks to one of the Spin Boldak cops who was on the same bus. At the border we were spared the bother of the customs house and went directly to the cops to have our visas stamped. With a stare that went away beyond hate, the groper watched as we were ushered through unhindered and bade a fond farewell by the others at the post. They were our friends again. After a fashion, the balance had tipped to the ascending. We left Afghanistan, filled with great warmth towards its people.

'And not once,' Cora said, 'was I groped or grabbed in the whole of Afghanistan.'

The only problem was Anto. His masterpiece wasn't such a masterpiece after all. He was held at Immigration and threatened with being sent back to Kandahar. Baksheesh was in the air again. The cop who had been on the bus advised the other three of us to go on to the Pakistani side and wait. The matter would be resolved: it was just a case of money changing hands. The last time I saw Afghanistan, the Spin Boldak frontier post was receding into a dusty desert landscape and I was on the roof-box of the truck that would take us to Pakistan. I remember thinking how, tucked away in the wilds of central Asia, the friendly, generous, fiercely independent people of this timeless feudal kingdom seemed safe from the outside world. Their culture, art, and remarkable history at the heart of the old Silk Road, would always be there for those who would come in our wake. The sights, sounds and smells of the thriving bazaars and the buzz of the chai-khana would stay forever. When I think back on it, my heart bleeds for Afghanistan.

On the afternoon of Tuesday, December 21st, three days after first arriving at the frontier, Cora and I crossed into Pakistan at Chaman, 100 rupees and one stove lighter. The Pakistani official was delighted to see us back. He wished us a long life and safe journey. Along with Ben and Anto (who caught up with us at the Pakistani post) we then secured four spaces on an overloaded jeep. It was bound for Quetta, 153 kilometres away. Ben, protected I figured by his Bigfoot pelt, was put on the roof. Anto ate a lump of hash that he'd had in his shoe.

Over the next four hours, we swung precariously along a narrow mountain road that twisted up to the 1,952-metre Khojak Pass in the empty Toba-Kakar Mountains, before plunging down in terrifying switchbacks towards Quetta. The views, when fear receded sufficiently to allow some measure of appreciation, were spectacular, but prone to heart-stopping sideslips. With bad brakes, bald tyres, eight inside and Ben and a ton of cargo on the roof, it was always going to be tricky. But, when the first rains in years lashed the heights of the pass, it became an absolute nightmare.

'Oh Jesus, Mary and St. Joseph, we'll never make it,' Cora

## Chapter 26

said when the spraying mud sent us skidding and spinning in all directions. One couldn't openly disagree.

'What a fuckin' drag,' Anto said in a voice that had receded to a whine. 'We're gonna die in a god-forsaken wasteland.'

Artist James Atkinson who served as the official Superintending Surgeon of the British Army of the Indus[25], described in 1839 the terrifying descent through the Khojak Pass as, '...*threatening destruction among the camels, and it was not long before these fears were painfully realized by a great number of the camels falling headlong into the ravines, being unable, from the soft and loose state of the earth, to obtain any secure footing.*'

It hadn't changed a lot.

\* \* \*

Due to the war, Quetta was blacked out and in darkness. None the less we could see in the faint starlight that there were large numbers of soldiers on the streets, and that people were quickly moving about their business. Groping our way along Jinnah Road, we made it to the Regal Café where we ate in the light of an oil lamp. Around us people spoke in whispers as if afraid of being heard by the warplanes in the skies overhead. In the mosques the muezzins were calling the people to prayer, an eerie sound in a sightless city.

Cora and I booked in at the Palace Hotel where we had a clean, basic, candle-lit room for three rupees (15 pence) each per night. Anto and Ben turned up later, having failed to locate a better deal. After spreading our things about to give a feeling of home, Cora climbed into bed with a book and buried herself in her sleeping bag and a pile of blankets as a blast of frigid air swept through Quetta.

No sooner had Cora settled than a thin bearded man in his mid thirties walked into our room. He was dressed in a grey suit and a woollen hat and was wearing a monocle over his right eye.

'Hello,' he said. 'My name is Ali. I am your neighbour.' He was carrying a tray. 'I have brought you some tea and some cakes to eat.' He crossed the room and placed the tray on a small table beside Cora.

'It's the milmastia,' I whispered to Cora, delighted that this charming custom had followed us from Kandahar. Ali told us that he was a car salesman over on business from Karachi. He stayed until we'd finished eating and drinking, then invited us to join him in his room for a beer.

---

[25] A force of British and Indian troops that marched on Kabul during the First Afghan War.

'I am leaving for Karachi tomorrow,' he said. 'I would like to celebrate our friendship.'

'Too tired,' Cora said. 'We've been travelling all day.'

'No problem my friends,' he said and left.

'That was a bit weird,' Cora said. 'Just walking in like that.'

'It's the milmastia,' I assured her.

'Milmastia me arse,' Cora said. 'He was up to no good.'

I was appalled.

In the morning we'd forgotten all about Ali and his drink as we stepped out into the cool streets of Baluchistan's capital to be blown away by the surroundings.

At an elevation of 1,680 metres, Quetta takes its name from the Pashto word 'Kwatta'. It means fort. It was easy to see why. On all sides, we were hemmed in by an encircling wall of copper and russet crests, dusted in light winter powder. Rising from among them were the peaks of Koh-e-Murdar, Chiltan and Zarghun, great forbidding sentinels towering above the city. Closer to eye level, the city itself crept up the slopes and fed away from Jinnah Road in a confusion of back streets and bazaars. Remarkably, despite the peeling buildings, rusted tins, broken pavements and tattered awnings, modern Quetta was less than thirty-seven years old. A city that had perfected instant antiquity. Even the mosques looked ancient.

Old Quetta had been destroyed in the early hours of May 31st 1935 by one of the most devastating earthquakes to ever hit South Asia. Mountains had split asunder and the city had been reduced to a desolate ruin with an estimated 40,000 people buried in its rubble. Yet, the only tell-tale signs of newness were the reinforced single- and double-storey buildings that had replaced the taller buildings of old; and the broad, straight lines of the main streets, bordered with cypress, pine and black locust, and constructed for modern traffic. During the day, the streets were a noisy cacophony of cars, three-wheeled, fume-spewing autorickshaws, bicycles, horse-drawn tongas, camels and carts, donkey trains, rickshaws and brightly coloured buses and trucks. In the narrower concourses all of these competed for space with a choking clutter of cooking stalls, carpet stalls, juice stalls, fruit carts, barbers' chairs, roadside beds and pedestrians. At night they mostly fell silent.

The Pashtuns of Quetta didn't look all that different from the Afghans of Kandahar; but, for the most part, the full-length burkahs of the women were less visible. Instead, the women wore shawls and

## Chapter 26

beautifully embroidered, full-length lehnga dresses, or shalwar-kameezes. Baluchi and Afghan embroidery decorated the clothes of children

Less visible were the hardy nomadic Baluchis, proud men in baggy trousers and big moustaches who came in from the desert, camels in tow, to trade on the edge of town. Even less visible were the Uzbeks, Tajiks, Hazaras, Punjabis and Turkomen who completed Quetta's eclectic mix.

On that first morning, while the war planes flew overhead and soldiers patrolled the city, we joined everyone else in trying to act as if all was normal. In keeping with the new normality, we registered our alien presence with the cops, and were told to come back for an exit visa when we were ready to leave.

When we returned to the hotel in the evening, Cora felt unwell. She took off her jeans, lay on the bed under her sleeping bag, and tried to read in candlelight as the city blacked out again. Two minutes later Ali appeared in the doorway.

'Oh, hello…,' I said. 'I thought you were leaving for Karachi.'

'I have decided to stay one more day in Quetta,' Ali said, 'so that we can all have dinner together.'

'I'm afraid that might not be possible,' I said, looking towards Cora.

'Not well,' Cora said. 'Something I ate.'

'Oh, I am sorry,' Ali said. He sat down on the side of the bed while I sat on a chair on the far side. We then nattered on about nothing in particular.

'Do you think the war in Bangladesh is finished?' I asked at some point.

'There is no such place as Bangladesh!' Ali snapped.

*Oops!* I thought; and dug for another topic. I didn't have to dig far. In fact it jumped out of the bed where Cora had suddenly stiffened.

'Would you mind getting your hands off my legs,' she said.

'What…!' That was me.

'He's running his hand up my leg.'

'He's doing *what?*' I catapulted from the chair with such speed that I toppled onto the bed.

Ali retrieved the offending paw, jumped up, and fled the room. He checked out minutes later.

'What do you call that again?' Cora said. 'Just for the record. The milmastia, is it? If you had brains you'd be dangerous.'

* * *

We were standing under the quiet trees of busy Jinnah Road when down the long dusty boulevard traipsed a wide-eyed, unshaven, plump man in his mid forties, dressed in a khaki boy scout uniform and carrying a long staff. Hopping from the shadow of one tree to the next, he spotted us and came stomping across the road, shouting *Left, right! Left, right!*

'Oh gawd,' Cora said. 'Why do they always pick on us?'

'Good afternoon!' the Scout bellowed. 'You are very welcome in Quetta.' He shook our hands vigorously, smiled and made a peculiar sucking noise with his teeth. 'You will see, British are no more in Quetta. But I am here to greet you. I have long history.' He pulled out a torn jotter on which he had scribbled some kind of dubious family tree. 'Here,' he went on, sucking again, 'you will see. My cousin is Colonel Baden-Powell of Mafikeng. When he was in Africa, he had many boys to fight the Boers. The Boers, they were fat men. They could not run very fast. My cousin won the battle at Mafikeng...'

At that point a ragged little girl who'd appeared from a narrow alley and was begging on the busy street approached us. There was nothing of her, just skin and bones, grubby face and tangled hair. She said something, looked up at Cora with big eyes, and stretched out her hand.

'A-a-a-rgh!' Colonel Baden-Powell's cousin roared. Without warning, he swung around and kicked the little girl full in the stomach. She buckled over and fell in a heap, screaming and curling up to protect herself. Instinctively, I came to a conclusion. *Baden-Powell's cousin is a fuckin' maniac.*

'YOU BASTARD!' I roared for the want of something better to roar.

He went for the little girl again; but this time I managed to grab his arm and spin him sideways. *What do you do now?* I though. *You can't attack a mental case.* But that didn't stop the mental case. He swung his staff at my head with a force that would've landed the head in Saudi Arabia had it connected. On the return swing, I managed to grab the staff and there was a moment when we looked at one another.

'*Be always prepared* is the scout's motto,' the madman said.

A few minutes earlier, this had been a perfectly normal afternoon.

'What the hell are you *doing!*' I shouted. But the eyes were blank. Meanwhile, Cora had jumped in to pick the screaming child from the street and was ushering her to relative safety among the gathering spectators.

## Chapter 26

A short skirmish followed before the crowd chased the attacker, dodging his swinging staff, and aiming kicks at him.

'Thank you,' a short man in a suit said. 'This is not good for Pakistan.'

Shaken by the event and feeling responsible for the assault, we brought the little girl for something to eat, bought her a bag of sweets and gave her a handful of rupees. With her grubby face streaked in tears, she then melted off into the alley from which she had appeared. Baden-Powell's cousin watched from across the street, yelling obscenities until some soldiers dragged him away.

That afternoon we picked up visas for Iran. The Iranian Consul was delighted.

'Do you remember me?' he asked. 'From Istanbul two years ago.' He was the man who had given me the multiple entry visa for Iran, normally not available to Irish nationals. Now he brought us tea and gave us our visas free.

'A gift for you for Christmas,' he said. 'Now, you will have good memories of Quetta.'

With our eighty rupees savings we went to the railway station to buy tickets to Zahedan in Iran - and got a fifty per cent student discount on the third class fares. We'd have the train to ourselves, we were told. Pakistanis weren't allowed to leave the country because of the war. And while the passports of the wealthy families who controlled the economy were impounded, and posters called on people to join the army, the billboards screamed for the head of ousted President, Yahya Khan, who was being blamed for the whole debacle of Bangladesh.

In the evening we took the remnants of our wealth to a cheap restaurant. Cora had sensible food. I had sheep's brains and chips. On my plate was a large green bean which sat in peculiar isolation. Half way through the brains, I stuck my fork into the bean and popped it into my mouth with a crunch.

'Jesus Christ!' I gasped. 'Water!'

For someone who in those days didn't even like pepper, a mouthful of raw green chilli was quite a blast. All caution to the wind, I grabbed the pitcher of dodgy tap water from the table and emptied it down the hatch.

Christmas Eve, 1971.

# Chapter 27
## Christmas

___

On the stinging cold morning of December 25th we left Quetta in the wooden, third class carriage of an old steam train. Slowly, we began to drop from the mountains into the vast expanses and welcome heat of Pakistan's Sandy Desert. Although Zahedan was less than a thousand kilometres away, it would take a day and a half to travel the distance on this, the slowest train on Earth.

Never before and never after had slow been like this.

Whenever the train stopped - as opposed to hardly moved - we'd get off and wander hundreds of metres into the desert, with no fear that it would ever outrun us. It took so long to pick up speed that, once it started, we could stroll back at leisure and still walk alongside for long periods before ever feeling compelled to move in close or hop aboard. This in a place where it wouldn't do to be left behind. At other times we'd climb out the glassless windows up onto the roof while the train was moving, and sit in the sun and the cooling breeze as we lumbered across the flat wastes of northern Baluchistan.

Ours was the second last carriage, trailed by the empty 'Ladies Only' carriage - the only thing that looked even more downbeat than third class. Normally, twenty people sitting, and as many as could fit standing, would've been packed into our two-and-a-half by three-metre space with its four benches and two luggage racks. Today, however, there were only six: me, Cora, Ben (who had turned up unexpectedly and out of his head); two bearded and turbaned young Pakistani men called Hussain and Mohammad who were on their way to Nok Kundi in western Pakistan; and snuff-snorting Bhingy, originally from Dar es Salaam in Tanzania but now living in Kenya. Bhingy, a man of radiantly sunny disposition, was on his way to Italy, Germany or London. He didn't really know. Bhingy would be the making of Christmas Day.

'I have small business in Mombasa,' he told us. 'There I see some young people who travel in Africa. I want to go travel too; so in October I leave to see the life.'

Bhingy was in his late thirties, tall, bony and slightly balding, with light brown skin and a great smile, despite two solid bars of tobacco-

## Chapter 27

stained teeth. He wore oversized sunglasses, off-white trousers, scuffed shoes and a light beige overcoat, and had a passport that caused consternation at borders as he spread it across desks like those concertina postcards you get in Spanish resorts. His backpack, a big, green awkward affair, was loaded with everything that was useless or unnecessary, and little that was practical.

He first broke into our company when he smelled Ben having a sneaky joint in the folds of his beard shortly after we'd left Quetta.

'Ah,' he said. 'You smoking hashish. Good. I smoke too.'

Before Ben could blink, Bhingy had the joint in his mouth. For the rest of the day Bhingy and a reluctant Ben rolled joints to Bhingy's commands. 'Yes my friend,' he'd say, 'we make cigarette now.' Or, 'Now we have tea, then *you* make cigarette.' Or, 'No sleeping now my friend. First we smoke; *then* you sleep.' By the end of the day Ben's nerves were wrecked.

Then there were the regular news bulletins, stridently delivered but invariably wrong. Bhingy would take out a small circular silver box, slowly undo the lid, tip it over on the back of his hand and, with a theatrical sweep of arm to nose, deliver home a large snort of snuff.

'Soon we come to big station,' he'd say, putting away the box. 'We can get tea there, good Pakistani tea with plenty of milk. Very good. And fruit and cigarettes. Everything, you can buy there.'

'Fantastic!' we'd all say. Bhingy's face would light up at having raised our spirits to such a pitch. 'Who has banana?' He'd say after a short interval. 'Give me one banana.'

And the desert would roll on hour after hour with no big station.

When we passed the tangled wreckage of an earlier derailment, he told us it was from a previous war. Hussain though it might have happened during the 1935 earthquake.

But, whatever shortcomings Bhingy had in the clairvoyance stakes, he made up for in generosity. He insisted that we shared everything he had, including a bottle of Dutch perfume that he gave to Cora.

'Here!' he snapped, 'It's for you. Take it.'

Every time the train stopped, at a station or at the desert water tanks from which it topped up its steam-base, he'd trot off up the track to the dining car and demand boiling water in his gigantic chrome cup so he could make a communal cup of coffee.

When night came, we all gave Bhingy our jackets so he could curl up on one of the luggage racks because Bhingy had no sleeping bag. 'Tomorrow,' he said to Ben, always planning ahead, 'you make first cigarette.'

At sunrise on Boxing Day we arrived at the Pakistani border post, minus Hussain and Mohammad who had disembarked during the night. When we'd finished with Immigration and Customs we had breakfast. It was carried down the line to us from the dining car, as our compartment was self-contained and couldn't be entered from the rest of the train. In the afternoon the train reached the Iranian border at Mirjawa, by which point only seven passengers remained: the four of us in third class, and another three in second class. Two of the others - Wild Bill Hickock lookalike, Carlo from the States, and short, olive-skinned José from Colombia - had ridden horses across northern Afghanistan and were still carrying beautifully adorned leather saddles. The third was Lutalo from Uganda: big, burly British citizen and belligerent, globe-trotting merchant of semi-deranged disposition. At the frontier post we were all given antibiotics by the cops. Cholera, they explained, had broken out in Pakistan.

'But we're not *going* to Pakistan,' I tried to reason.

'You will be,' Cora said. 'If you don't take the pills.'

'What this...?' the immigration official asked Bhingy.

'This my passport!' Bhingy snapped. 'You stamp here.'

Almost immediately, Lutalo and Bhingy struck a common chord, bonded by Africa and the fact that Lutalo promised to get Bhingy a visa for Britain.

'I go to London now,' Bhingy announced.

At the customs post Bhingy intercepted a passer-by and swapped his light overcoat for a much heavier one that was ten sizes too big. Though it looked ridiculous, he was quite pleased with the exchange.

'This better,' he said. Then he went outside, rolled a joint from one of the pieces of hash he had hidden all over his person, and lit up.

'Man, you can't do that!' Lutalo said, 'You'll have us fucking arrested.'

'It's OK,' Bhingy assured him. 'When they see you are tourist, police say nothing. Tourists can smoke in Iran.' Clearly a man who sailed through life without trial or effort.

It took all our persuasive powers to convince Bhingy that that was ever so wrong. Despite his tendency towards the reckless, we now found ourselves following Bhingy around with the sort of growing

## Chapter 27

affection you might develop for a ne'er-do-well relative let out of the attic.

At Zahedan, the customs people discovered that Carlo had lost his cholera vaccination certificate so they banged him into quarantine for two days. Lucky for me, they didn't notice that mine was away out of date. We told Carlo we'd wait and not to worry. José was almost in tears with gratitude.

When we got into town, there was no debate about accommodation. 'We stay this one,' Bhingy said, wheeling us all into the Park Hotel which turned out to be quite cosy. He then insisted that the six of us who weren't quarantined should head off to a double movie in Farsi. Half way through the second show, Bhingy lost the head.

'This no good,' he shouted. 'This language no good. We go to hotel, have tea and cigarette, and sleep. Tomorrow, we must go to Kerman.'

Outside, he swapped his coat again for a better fit. He then tried to swap the dregs of several packs of cigarettes of various brands for a single pack of Iranian cigarettes - his first and only failure.

At two o'clock the next day, with Carlo back on board after an early release from quarantine, we left Zahedan for the 11-hour bus ride to Kerman where Cora, Ben and I would be parting company with the others. A rough dirt track led through a landscape of bare mountains that were - along with the Great Salt Desert - one of the last refuges of the Persian leopard. The intervening valleys were broken by great oases of palms where the nomadic Baluchi people camped with their camels, gathering at night in small huddles, their faces white in the glare of fires. It was warm until the sun went down and we began to climb up into the snowpeaks around Mount Hazaran. An hour after dark we stopped in a village to eat and grab some heat around a wood stove. All the non-Iranians were told to pay up front while the Iranians could pay after eating. Bhingy became furious.

'What is this?' he roared, slamming the table. 'You call me thief? Why I pay now? I am businessman from Mombasa. You know Mombasa? You know anything, you bloody bastard?'

'Bloody bastards!' Lutalo added. 'I am a British businessman. We are all businessmen.'

We all became suitably affronted businessmen. Rather than pay up front, we didn't eat and left. It's called cutting off yer nose to spite yer face. Our retreat from the restaurant was aided by one of the cooks who entered the debate with a blood-stained meat cleaver.

Just after midnight we rounded a bend on the mountain road and saw the lights of Kerman, a glittering jewel far off in the dark desert. An hour later we arrived at the bus station where they offered us the floor to sleep.

Sound as a pound.

Lutalo, however, didn't do floors too well. By morning, the ordeal had gotten the better of him and he was determined that someone would pay. I woke up to a shower of expletives being directed at the man who'd given us our free bed.

'Bhingy,' Cora said, 'make him go away.'

Bhingy took Lutalo to one side. 'We go make cigarette,' he said.

The company got up, washed in the station toilets and it was handshakes and hugs all around. Cora and I were going south from here, 350 kilometres across the vast eroded moonscape of the Zagros Mountains to the fishing port of Bandar Abbas on the Persian Gulf. Bhingy was none too pleased.

'After the long run from Quetta,' I explained, 'we need a rest.'

'You can rest in Tehran,' Bhingy argued, but our minds were made up.

Bhingy's eyes welled up. 'You are my good friends,' he said. 'See you in London.'

'How's that gonna happen?' Cora asked. 'There's no address.'

'Like they say in Arabic,' Bhingy said, '*Insha'Allah!*' And off he went.

\* \* \*

Controlling the Strait of Hormoz, Bandar Abbas has long been of strategic importance. As far back as 1520 some of the offshore islands were seized by the Portuguese, intent on protecting their Indian Empire. A hundred years later, after a fierce naval battle, they were evicted by Shah Abbas the Great who founded the mainland port and left it his name. In time it would become the natural maritime outlet for Persia and a major fishing station, its most obvious function on the evening of our arrival.

A few hundred yards offshore, scores of barges and Arab dhows with tall prows and forecastles bobbed on the silver water. Sombre silhouettes in the late light, they were the furrowers of the sea, providing a living for a considerable part of the local population. Additional work was found along a narrow strip of sloping silky sand where the fish were cleaned, gutted, and smoked in drying sheds,

## Chapter 27

a custom pioneered centuries before by Danish fish smokers. The wicker and thatch huts of fishermen were strung along the beach.

On arrival, we took a room in the modest Inn Bolvar where the manager agreed that we could live on credit until Saturday - three days away - when the banks reopened after the New Year holiday. Exhausted from the journey from Quetta and the unexpected sticky heat of the Gulf, we ate and collapsed into bed. Outside, the crickets screamed among the abundant palms. Inside, the humidity would have been the death of us but for the fan in the room.

We woke up in the middle of the night to a strange sound. It was raining. Spectacularly. With the sky gashed by forked lightning that lit the sea to the horizon.

# Chapter 28
## Qeshm

New Year's Day 1972 came in a blaze of sunshine. Cora and I were sitting at a table in the courtyard of the Inn Bolvar, dreamily enjoying the warmth, when a young couple, walked in. They were dressed casually but well. Clearly not travellers. They came directly towards our table, the first non-Iranians we'd seen since our arrival. It felt like Neanderthal Man meets Homo Sapiens.

'They look straight,' Cora warned. 'Don't say anything stupid.'
'Do you mind if we join you for breakfast?' the woman asked.
'Please do,' I said. 'We haven't had anyone to talk to in days.'
'What am I?' Cora said. 'Chopped liver?'
'Irish?' the woman asked.
'From Cork,' Cora said. 'Down in the south.'

They pulled across two chairs from one of the other tables and introduced themselves. Catherine and Thierry. Thierry was French, thick-set with a generous head of brown hair and a heavy beard. Catherine, slim with blonde shoulder-length hair and piercing blue eyes, was a Scot. Rather unconventionally, they were married.

'We're on holidays from our jobs at the Iranian Institute of Nutrition in Tehran,' Thierry explained. 'The work takes us around the country to monitor the health of workers in industry. We were in Bandar Abbas last year and liked it. How about you?'

They got the whole sad story.

'So now we're turning for home,' Cora concluded.

'Maybe it was meant to be,' Catherine said. 'Now you have other choices. You can join us. We're planning to take a ferry out to the island of Qeshm this afternoon. What do you say?'

'We were planning to post a parcel of souvenirs back to Ireland,' I said. 'Our packs are overloaded.'

'Don't worry about that,' Thierry said. 'We can take it back to Tehran. You can post it from there.'

'This is how the best things happen.' Cora said.

'True,' Catherine said. 'And if you're going to choose an alternative to posting a parcel, you could do a lot worse than a day on Qeshm.'

A few hours after meeting, we were down at the harbour, boarding a converted fishing sloop with a deck punched full of holes. It was

## Chapter 28

known - jokingly I presume - as the midday ferry and was lacking the concept of full. The captain simply packed them in until people, baggage and animals spilled out over the gunwales. Breast-feeding women took the mid-deck. Shortly after setting sail we were joined by a school of dolphins that stayed with us, leaping from the water, skimming under the boat, and generally making a show of themselves, all the way to Qeshm.

Now, if you ask me, a dolphin is an animal deserving of respect, reverence even. If you were ever to fall into the sea and there were sharks about, you'd be wishing for a dolphin, given the many documented cases of them defending people from shark attacks, saving them from drowning, and guiding them to safety through fog and mist. These events are mentioned in tales from ancient Greece and Rome, and the legends of Polynesia. And you have more recent incarnations such as 19th century Pelorus Jack of New Zealand and our own 20th century Fungie who would, I've always felt, have made a fine Irish President.

Pelorus Jack was a four-metre Risso's dolphin that accompanied ships travelling between the North and South Islands of New Zealand. He was first seen in 1888 when he surfaced in front of the schooner, Brindle, as the ship approached French Pass, a rock-strewn channel with powerful currents, located between D'Urville Island and the South Island. Over the next twenty-four years Pelorus Jack would meet boats heading for the South Island at the entrance to Pelorus Sound and swim with them as far as the treacherous French Pass. On the return journey, he'd meet the ships coming out of the Pass and stay with them for the eight-kilometre run to Pelorus Sound.

In 1904, some psycho shot at Pelorus Jack from aboard the SS Penguin. Folklore has it that Pelorus Jack continued to escort ships, but never again swam with the Penguin which was subsequently wrecked off Wellington Heads in Cook Strait in 1909 with the loss of seventy-five lives.

Following the shooting incident, Pelorus Jack became a protected individual when, in September 1904, a law was enacted under New Zealand's Sea Fisheries Act to make him the first individual animal to ever receive such protection, a distinction he retained until his final sighting in 1912.

Fungie, our own bottlenose dolphin, arrived in the mouth of Dingle harbour in Co. Kerry in 1984. After settling into a small cave under the cliffs of Burnham, he quickly attracted the attention of the local fishermen. They who gave him his name also spotted the economic potential of a dolphin that regularly swam with their boats, played in the bow waves and launched himself out of the water in startling displays of acrobatics. In no time at all Fungie was the most famous resident in Kerry, with crowds flocking from near and far and tour boats growing into fleets. Normally bottlenose dolphins swim in pods, interacting with their own kind, but Fungie was a people's dolphin from the start. He delighted in swimming with the crowds, playing with the boats, even bringing gifts of living fish to divers. But, in a show of independence, he himself never accepted gifts.

Rarely straying far from the mouth of the harbour, Fungie baffled the scientists. Why wasn't he looking for a mate? However, there may be an explanation. Coinciding with Fungie's arrival, the body of a young female bottlenose was found washed up on a nearby beach. Fungie, local people said, didn't get the death thing. Having mated for life, as dolphins often do, he was waiting for his love to come home. Every summer, schools of dolphins arrived offshore, and now and again Fungie could be seen among them. He even had a much-heralded fling with a young dolphin named Smokey, leading to great fear for the Kerry economy. But Smokey left and Fungie didn't. Eventually, instead of making him President, they erected a bronze sculpture to him down at Dingle quay wall - an honour accorded to no Irish President.

* * *

Two hours after leaving Bandar Abbas we disembarked on a wooden wharf, behind which lay a gentle slope of scrub, scattered palms and sand, and the small flat-roofed town of Qeshm. Two camels were tethered to a post beside the wharf.

On the journey across, Cora had been stricken by a stomach bug bad enough to warrant, on landing, a rush to the nearest bushes (for once it wasn't me) and a dose of antibiotics. Thierry, who spoke Farsi, asked a local man to guide us to the doctor. This was to set in train a remarkable turn of events.

The doctor turned out to be a smiling man of consummate charm who was in his late twenties. Delighted at the opportunity to practice his English, he gave Cora her antibiotics, charged us nothing and filled us in on some local history concerning English explorer, William Baffin.

While best known as discoverer of Canada's Baffin Bay, Baffin was also an accomplished scientific navigator, believed to have been the

## Chapter 28

first to determine longitude by use of the angular distance of the moon from other celestial bodies.

Having spent the years 1612 to 1616 in the exploration of the coast of Greenland, the Hudson Strait and Baffin Bay in search of the Northwest Passage, he finally abandoned his quest in 1616. Convinced that the Passage couldn't be found from the western approaches, he went to work for the British East India Company. In 1622 during his second voyage to the East, the fleet with which he was sailing besieged the Portuguese fortress on Qeshm. During the siege Baffin was shot dead.

'So,' the doctor said, 'you Irish should visit the fort.' Not sure what he meant, but individuals could read all sorts of things into a statement like that.

Outside the doctor's house, our paths crossed those of a group of people who were celebrating. Some thirty people were singing, dancing and drumming their way through the street. Many of the men were dressed in long white robes. I don't know who was the more surprised; but when they saw us, everything came to a standstill. Thierry called a greeting in Farsi and things began to shape up in a fashion most unlikely to be replicated in Patrick Street in Cork. Two of the women, in long colourful dresses and the beak-type masks[26] we'd first seen in Bandar Abbas, waved. There followed a quick discussion where arms swung up and down and points were made. An older bearded man, wearing the white robes and a matching white skullcap then broke from the party and rushed over to speak to Thierry.

'There's a wedding,' Thierry translated. 'This is the third day. He is telling me that today is the religious part. Tonight at nine o'clock it begins - and we are invited.'

That was the bit that would never happen in Patrick Street. Nobody would ever run over and invite you to a wedding just like that. Especially in faded jeans and scuffed boots.

'Are we interested?' Thierry asked.

'Would a bear poo in the woods?' Catherine said. 'It's the kind of thing you dream about.'

---

[26] Wheras the fishermen down on the beach wore a type of sarong adapted to the climate, many of the women wore masks that covered their eyes and cheeks. Adamant that no religious taboo was responsible, some locals claimed these were a leftover from the homeward march of Alexander's columns. Others dismissed this as nonsense and blamed a fashion that originated in the time of the Portuguese. Others still said they were simple sun-screens.

'Wish I had a dress,' Cora said. Women!

The unforeseen change of plan initially threw us - we had no overnight kit - but we rolled with it and booked into a cheap guesthouse. We now had the remainder of the day to see a bit of the island, including the old fort from which William Baffin was shot dead. In the evening we went to the beach to watch the sun go down, and later walked the shoreline in the light of a big moon, leaving trails of phosphorescence in the wet sand: plankton that had come up from the depths.

'They eat whales,' I told Thierry. He thought I was serious.

Some time around seven, we went back into town and were having dinner in a roadside restaurant when the doctor and his lovely wife pulled up in a jeep and invited us to join them at home for drinks and cake.

'It's a great privilege,' the doctor said when he heard about the wedding. 'On Qeshm, wedding ceremonies are very beautiful. The families celebrate for ten days with friends and neighbours. For the first three days, the couple are not married. Then, on the third night, tonight in this case, the marriage takes place. Afterwards there will be another seven days of festivities.

'Tonight the bride and groom will go to the bathrooms of their fathers' houses. Each family will draw a circle on the floor. They will place some eggs, rice and sugar in the circle. Then the bride and groom will break the eggs with their toes. Afterwards, the bride will be dressed and the groom will be prepared for the journey to the bride's house. You are lucky you have come today. You will see the most interesting part, the climax.'

Shortly before nine, the doctor went outside. He came back after a few minutes with an older man with a deeply pitted complexion, wearing a sarong, T-shirt and turban.

'This is Nouri,' he said. 'He will guide you to where the wedding is taking place. Otherwise it is too dark for you to find the way.'

Our destination proved to be a brick house built around a courtyard in a palm-strung back street. At the door, Nouri left us and we were welcomed by relatives of the groom.

We shook hands, which was probably all culturally wrong (not to mention the scruffy jeans), and were told that we would be separating on gender lines. One of the women who'd waved to us earlier in the day brought Cora and Catherine off to join the other women. Thierry and I were shown into a long room, decorated with brilliant

## Chapter 28

fabrics and thick with the smell of flowers and incense, where the men were gathered in a circle. Sitting on carpets and cushions on the floor, and primarily dressed in turbans and the white robes we'd seen earlier, they were chanting responses to two imams who read from the Qur'an. Five wooden drums and something that looked uncannily like an Irish bodhrán[27] sat against the wall. Space was made for us and we joined the circle while our escort explained what was happening in Farsi whispers, translated by Thierry.

'The containers on the floor are called 'tabagh'. They have been loaded with presents to be transported to the bride's home when the prayers are over. The man over in the corner looking glum is the groom. The one wearing the Palestinian scarf. He is twenty and has never met his bride. She is fifteen. The parents have made all the arrangements...'

The prayers stopped abruptly and plates of rice, stew, bread and fruit were served. One by one, the men welcomed us and asked about our families. The groom seemed bewildered by our presence. He seemed bewildered by the whole event, as if he'd stumbled in on a gathering of aliens.

'Ask if grooms always look like that?' I exhorted Thierry.

'The groom is very happy,' Thierry said after getting the reply.

The prayers resumed and went on for another hour, broken once for tea and concluding with cakes and cinnamon coffee. It was now time, our interpreter expained to Thierry, for the climax of the wedding ceremony. Thierry again translated.

'We go now to the bride's home. When we arrive, the groom will go to the hejleh, the place where he will meet the bride and exchange the marriage vows. After that, the relatives of the groom will also go to the hejleh and congratulate the couple.'

We stood up and the groom was led off by the arms. Six of the men grabbed the drums and the bodhrán lookalike. In an instant the house reverberated to the primal pulse of hands and sticks pounding on stretched goatskin. It was the kind of drumming that makes you want to shout yahoo or charge Russian cannon. Ecstatic. Blood-curdling. Bone-rattling. Other men pulled out miniature cymbals and bells. The drumming went up a notch. The bells tinkled. The cymbals clashed. More incense was added. We were ready to storm the town. We were ready to fight the Portuguese. In

---

[27] Single-skinned drum used in traditional Irish music.

the light of the oil lamps the poor groom looked like he was going to the gallows.

Passing the women's room, we were treated to a shriek that didn't sound human.

'One of the older women,' Thierry explained.

Out in the street, under a big yellow moon, we were led away by some twenty men, all in their white robes and turbans. Some carried oil lanterns and burning palm-fronds. Others continued to ring the bells and cymbals and pound the drums. Others still hefted the tabagh on their heads. A long warbling ululation came from the women's room. Chanting and clapping, the men moved off, followed a few minutes later by the women who slipped silently out of the house and took off on an alternative route that would bring them to the bride's house ahead of the men. Every now and again we'd see them, gliding across our path in the dark distance, blazing torches sparking in the night and silhouetting the ululating phantoms.

It's incredible how we take to other people's rituals. A guy who might scoff at the religious beliefs of his home town might also climb 13,000 feet into the Kashmiri Himalayas to watch 50,000 Hindus pay homage to an ice stalagmite at the sacred cave of Amarnath. I've been him. And here we were again, dancing through the streets and alleys of Qeshm, wishing we knew the Qu'ran.

In a crescendo of drumming, bell ringing, chanting and clapping, we reached the bride's home after about twenty minutes. In a small compound beside a massive palm tree, the procession came to a standstill and the tempo grew to a fever. Palm fronds blazed in the moonlight and men went wild with excitement as the poor groom was led through the courtyard to the hejleh under the flames of the men's torches. Then everything stopped like someone had flicked a switch.

'Now, the men must leave,' Thierry explained although it was obvious, as some were already doing just that. 'But first we will be shown into the hejleh - the couple's bedroom - where the marriage vows will be exchanged.'

We were led into a room covered in tapestries, carpets and cushions. The marriage bed, a mass of bright colours, was being nervously eyed by the groom who now sat to one side, ignored by all. It was apparently bad luck for anyone to talk to him at this stage. Tucked away in the corner, he gave the impression that it was bad luck anyway.

## Chapter 28

'The bride is in another room,' Thierry said. 'She must wait until the men have gone before she is led out to her new husband. Unfortunately, we will not get to see that part...'

Thierry and I wished the groom all the best and went back out into the warm congenial night with its moonlight and bats and chirring crickets to wait for Cora and Catherine. But our interpreter was quick on our heels to explain that this was a waste of time. From here on in, it was the women's night. Cora and Catherine would be home when it was over.

'Better you go home,' the man said in *English*. 'It is a mystery.'

Several hours later Cora and Catherine turned up with the best of the wedding story.

The loud ululation we'd heard when leaving the groom's house had been a signal. The most senior of the women was telling the others to lift a box of the bride's clothes and follow her. With their burning palm fronds, they took to the back streets - Cora, Catherine and the veiled and beaked ululating phantoms - dashing from corner to corner, spotting the men's procession and raising the volume of ululation, until they arrived at the bride's house just in time to step over a dead goat that had had its throat slit as a sacrifice.

After a tour of the hejleh similar to ours, the woman were hidden away until the men had safely gone. They then went back to the bedroom and waited for the bride and her entourage, whose arrival Catherine described as having been 'straight out of *Aladdin*'.

'Two women led the way. Then the bride came in - veiled and dressed in flowing green, embroidered with gold thread, and accompanied by two drummers, one man and one woman. The drumming filled the house while another man in white robes chanted prayers. There was incense smoke, and there we were in the middle of it all.'

'I'm not sure if it was deliberate,' Cora added, 'but one of the men was blind and the other was half blind.'

As soon as the bride came into the room, the drums and prayers stopped and she was led over to the husband.

'At this point,' Cora said, 'one of the older women put the couple's two heads together and the place went up. The women were dancing and shrieking and singing and drumming, and pouring flower oil over one another and over us, and waving incense sticks around to cool us all down.

'Then the groom slipped a bag of money to one of the women. We were told that this woman had to stay outside the door until she could certify that the bride was a virgin. If not, the marriage was off.'

'At the heels of the hunt,' Catherine said, 'the women had the best show.'

'At the heels of the hunt,' Cora added, 'nobody in Ballyphehane, where I come from, would ever believe what happened there tonight.'

Cora and I returned to Bandar Abbas the following day and enjoyed a final spectacular Gulf sunset while preparing for the long haul to Tehran. Thierry and Catherine stayed behind on Qeshm.

Later in the year, after we'd returned to Ireland, Cora was in West Cork with my parents on the type of waning summer's evening that brings on the special colours of big Atlantic skies.

'Aren't sunsets lovely on the west of Ireland,' my father said.

'They're lovely too on the Persian Gulf,' Cora said.

The story passed into legend.

# Chapter 29
Return To Tehran

The road from Bandar Abbas to Shiraz was a rutted dirt track pitted with holes. It took us back over the Zagros Mountains through a series of spectacular passes. During one of many military searches, we were stopped on a high pass by a particularly nasty bunch who hauled everyone off the bus while they ripped open people's bags and scattered their belongings in the mud. They then climbed onto the roof and threw the remaining baggage to the ground, making smithereens of anything that was fragile. They stood back and laughed as people gathered up their damaged belongings.

The Shah's gift to the people.

Shiraz was possibly the most beautiful city in Iran. Built 1,500 metres above sea level in a green plain at the foot of the Zagros Mountains, it laid claim to being over 4,000 years old. Ancient cuneiform scripts from the great ceremonial capital of Persepolis showed that it was a significant township when Cyrus the Great founded the Persian Empire under his Achaemenid dynasty around 530 BC. Known as the city of poets, gardens, flowers, nightingales and wine, Shiraz was one of the most important cities in medieval Islamic times and was the Persian capital during the Zand dynasty (1747-79), when many of its most striking buildings were built or restored. The city also claimed the oldest wine stain in the world. Estimated at approximately 7,000 years, it was discovered on clay jars recovered outside Shiraz.

We arrived on a pleasant afternoon to find a relaxed city, with wide tree-lined avenues and enough monuments, gardens and mosques to occupy a lifetime. And an oil heater of dubious health and safety features.

As it was cold again at night, this particular piece of equipment was meant to bring comfort to our room at the Shahsvar Hotel. When the heater (which looked a bit like a coal scuttle with a flame at the bottom) cut out, I lit a match and peered in to see what had gone wrong. Bang! In the explosion that flung me across the room I lost mucho hair and a good part of both eyebrows.

A great deal of our time in Shiraz was spent in the bazaars with the nomadic Qashqai people who rode in on horses and donkeys from the surrounding mountains to trade. The women, in broad, ankle-length dresses of the most incredible colours, fluffed out by several layers of underskirts, and complemented by flash jewellery and headbands or turbans, sat in the streets and breast fed their children or wandered the stalls with the older toddlers strapped to their backs. The men, in domed felt hats, long cloaks, and wide-legged pants, sold carpets, woven in the Qashqai tents by the women. The men's hats, we were told, with ear flaps worn upward, were a symbol of identity and defiance, adopted when the Shah banned their traditional dress in the 1920s.

Our one excursion out of town was to Persepolis, the remains of the Persian capital founded in the Marv Dasht basin by Darius the Great around 518 BC. The ruins, some seventy kilometres north east of the city, lay at the foot of Kouh-e Rahmat, the Mountain of Mercy. They occupied one end of a broad plain, surrounded by crumbling, sharp-edged cliffs that turned a curiously mauve colour in the afternoon. As ruins go, Persepolis was stunning, covering a vast area that included the scattered remnants of numerous halls and palaces and a massive terrace, partly cut from a mountain. Tall pillars and columns marked the former locations of the principal buildings, including the Takht-e Jamshid (the Throne of Jamshid), the Gate of All Nations and the Apadana, once the most glorious palace at Persepolis, completed by Darius' son, Xerxes I in 485 BC.

Reached by symmetrical stairways on the northern and eastern sides, the Apadana had been a marvel of ancient engineering. Used for official audiences by the King of Kings, it was built on a grand scale, sixty metres square, with an enormous ceiling supported by seventy-two stone columns, each nineteen metres tall. Thirteen of the columns still stood on their original plinths, towering up to tops that were once crowned by lions, two-headed bulls and eagles, and connected by massive beams hewn from the oak and cedar forests of far-off Lebanon.

Behind the Throne of Jamshid, lay the tombs of Artaxerxes II and his son, Artaxerxes III, a ratbag who came to power after the removal of his three brothers by execution, 'suicide' and murder. He subsequently killed the rest of the royal family to remove any lingering rivals.

The tombs were cut separately into a cliff face to form flat, richly engraved façades. On the uppermost part, above the entrance, each façade depicted its entombed king, standing on a broad platform

# Chapter 29

supported by representatives of the subject nations of the empire. The king himself towered before the sacred, eternal Zoroastrian fire, and worshipped Ahuramazda, supreme Lord of Wisdom. In the time of the kings the energy of the creator was represented by fire and the sun, both of which were held to be pure, enduring and sustaining of life. Looking at the images, the irony was hard to miss: fire destroyed Persepolis less than 200 years after its foundation.

In 330 BC it was burnt to the ground by Alexander's army in an act of drunken vandalism. The Macedonians are said to have carried away its treasures on 20,000 mules and 5,000 camels.

More recently, over a four-day period in October 1971, Persepolis had been the site of another plunder: a $600 million bash thrown by Shah Mohammad Reza Pahlavi to celebrate the 2,500th anniversary of the establishment of the Persian Empire. To facilitate the occasion, the airport at Shiraz got a makeover, a new highway was built leading up to the old city walls, an ultra-modern hotel with green gardens and trees rose from the dust of the Marv Dasht basin, and the area around Persepolis was cleared of snakes. Catering was undertaken by Maxim's of Paris, which ceased trading for two weeks to provide for the glitterati, and 250 Mercedes limos were deployed to shuffle the guests to and from Shiraz.

When Cora and I got there, the place still reeked of the most offensive self-indulgence. Along with the flags that cracked in the wind, the bash had left behind massive empty car parks and rows of orange bell-shaped tents and marquees that served only to remind visitors of how $600 million of a nation's fortunes was wasted by a single family. While the poor of oil-rich Iran looked on, muzzled by the secret police of SAVAK, the kings and queens and dignitaries of the world had come to hog out on the Shah's benevolence.

On the evening of October 14th 1971 the hogging reached its climax at a grand gala dinner that celebrated the birthday of the Shahbanu (Empress). (The title was conferred in 1967 by the Shah on Farah Diba, his third royal consort.) Sixty heads of state and royal guests were served quails' eggs stuffed with Caspian caviar, mousse of crayfish tails with Nantua sauce, roast rack of lamb with truffles, roast peacock (the national symbol) stuffed with foie gras. Dessert came in the form of glazed ring of figs with raspberry champagne sherbet. The meal took five hours to eat and went down in the *Guinness Book of Records* as the longest and most lavish official banquet in modern history. How the guests might have choked on their rings of figs had they been able to gaze into the shadows. For, that night in the urban sprawls and mountain villages, Iran jerked one step closer to the Islamic revolution of Ayatollah Ruhollah Khomeini. The following day, the Shah treated his guests to a parade of seventeen hundred members of the Iranian armed forces. They were dressed in the period costumes of Persian armies going back two and half millennia.

It would later be noted that the event brought together the rulers of two of the oldest monarchies on Earth, the Shah of Iran and Emperor Haile Selassie of Ethiopia. History would deign it their great swansong: by the end of the decade, both monarchies would have ceased to exist.

\* \* \*

From Shiraz we travelled north into the mountains, going through places with magic names like Abadeh and Semirom. When night fell, it lashed down hail and sleet. We arrived in Isfahan to a festive atmosphere of darkness, city lights, horse-drawn rickshaws and snow on the ground. We walked from the bus station down along the Zayandeh River to Chaharbagh Avenue in the city centre, and had just passed the old theological school when a Volkswagon Beetle pulled up.

'My friends,' came the voice of a low-sized, older man with glasses, 'can I help you?' He had thick shoulders and a bald head, and was wearing a grey suit, blue shirt and red tie,

'We're looking for a cheap hotel,' I said. He shot us a big smile from a round face buffed to brilliance. 'Please sit in,' he said. 'I can take you.' We thanked him and climbed in.

'My name is Zander,' he told us as we drove off. 'I am a retired army colonel. Now I work in a senior position in Iran's largest oil company. Normally, I do not live in Isfahan, but I have come back for Christmas to visit my family. And, please, where are you from?'

'Ireland,' Cora said. 'We were on our way to India but, because of the war, we had to turn back from Kabul. Then we were going to cycle to Egypt...'

'Ah,' Zander said. 'Like Marco Polo. I like the Irish: they are a little crazy.'

Colonel Zander drove us to the Haghighat Hotel on Shahpour Avenue where we got a room with a clean sumptuous bed, tiled floor, rug and curtains for 100 rials ($1). He also offered to pick us up the next day to show us around.

## Chapter 29

An irony in the name of our avenue would surface a few days hence.

Over the next couple of days Zander became a constant companion as he showed us the sights of the city. He was a busy type of man, bursting with energy and fit as a fiddle, with a physique that smacked of pumping iron and wolfing steroids. By contrast, I was back to my old emaciated travelling self.

'Isfahan,' he told us as he showed us the central square, 'was founded by Shah Abbas the Great. He built this square, the Naqsh-e-Jahan, as the heart of the city. It is the biggest square in the world after Tiennemen Square in Peking. And he lived over there, at the Ali Qapu Palace. We will visit and then we will visit the Juma Mosque, which is the oldest mosque in Iran. It has beautiful mosaics that you will see. And we will see the river. And then we will visit my mother. And later you must go to the Grand Bazaar.' It felt great to have such enthusiasm driving our visit to Isfahan.

Propelled through the city in the Beetle, we saw the palace and the Juma Mosque, and the 1650 Pol-e-Khaju, a two-storey bridge over the Zayandeh River, also built by Shah Abbas.

'It has twenty-four arches and it is 123 metres long,' Zander told us. 'Very famous. You will see it in many paintings. Now, we will go and visit my mother for lunch.'

The mother was a grey-haired gentle woman of indeterminate age, but probably in her eighties. She was wearing a full-length purple dress and white shawl, and wore glasses low on her nose. Through Zander, she asked about our families and how come we had no children. We left out the not married bit, lest it cost us our lunch.

'Now, we will eat,' Zander said, and his mother produced food that must have been ordered in for our arrival. We sat on the floor to eat.

'Don't forget the hand thing,' I said sideways to Cora, but the colonel heard.

'Ah,' he said, 'You know the Muslim ways. Sometimes, European people, they do not know and it can make many problems.' His mother beamed, seeming to understand. Zander then spoke in Farsi to his mother as Cora and I ate enough to sustain us for several days.

'Now,' he said when we'd finished eating, 'I will take you to the Grand Bazaar.'

On our third day in Isfahan, he drove us to Ateshkadeh, an ancient

Zoroastrian fire temple dating back four and a half thousand years. This was followed by a visit to the Monar Jonban (Shaking Minarets), attached to a 14th century mosque that covered the grave of the Sufi hermit, Amu Abdollah Soqla. If you climbed a shaky ladder, clutched the windows of one of the minarets and shook, the other shook in unison. This was due to the special ratio between the height and width of the minarets and the width of the mosque's portico. Up there, in the tall minaret, it was hard not to think of minaret fatigue. However, the visible structural damage was locally blamed on British interference.

'And rightly so,' I assured Colonel Zander.

'In two days,' Zander said on the way home, 'my cousin is driving to Tehran. I am going too. There is space in the car if you would like to travel with us.'

'That would be very nice,' I said. 'Thank you very much.'

It turned out not to be so nice at all.

Wednesday, January 12th, we left Isfahan in a carpet of snow and set off in the cousin's battered cream Chevrolet. Before Cora and I sat in, the cousin, a fat friendly man in his forties named Farzan, welcomed us in broken English and introduced us to two others who were also travelling in the car. One was a loud, square-jawed immense brute of a man in his mid thirties named Shahpour (the name of our street). He was wearing black trousers and a black leather jacket that gave him the look of a low-level gangster. The other was a thin, shifty, bearded guy in his late twenties named Huzvak, who was wrapped in a heavy overcoat. The happy smiling Colonel Zander and Shahpour sat in front beside cousin Farzan. Cora and I shared the back seat with Huzvak. Cora sat in the middle. Our first mistake.

Huzvak, you see, had an affliction: he was prone to sudden bouts of dozing. These were accompanied by a slouch to the left, up against Cora, and an inexplicable involuntary movement that projected his right hand straight onto her breasts. Each time this happened, I'd reach across and heave him back into an upright position which would cause him to 'wake up' with a start. Only to fall asleep again within minutes, giving way to the same remarkable hand affliction.

But, whereas Huzvak was a nuisance, one look at Shahpour - all neck and muscle - and you saw bad news. From the beginning he'd been passing obvious encouragement to Sleeping Beauty in the back, while adding his own suggestive comments to Cora in English.

## Chapter 29

It was an awkward situation: we were guests in the car; nobody else seemed to think his behaviour offensive; and the colonel was our friend, wasn't he? But the more we said nothing, the bolder grew Shahpour.

Meanwhile, during an early stop, the colonel was telling us how Shahpour had once been attacked by five men, armed with knives, in Tehran. They left him with the deep ugly scar that dissected his left cheek, and another that crossed his forehead. He left them - all five - lying in the street, battered senseless. Skinny me versus Shahpour? Not great odds.

Cousin Farzan drove for the first hundred kilometres. We then stopped for lunch, accompanied by two half bottles of vodka.

'You drink more,' Shahpour urged me. Laughing and chugging on a vodka bottle, he pushed and jostled. Then, half plastered, he took the wheel. With a half bottle of vodka in one hand, he shot off like a madman. In speeds ranging from 140 to 180 kilometres an hour he tore along the narrow roads, ignoring all warnings signs.

Across mountain and semi-desert, he spun around S-bends and horseshoe bends in swerves and screeches of brakes that defied logic. Mostly, I'm fairly fatalistic when it comes to lunatic drivers, believing that (normally a *he*) doesn't want to kill himself or smash up his car. But, in Shahpour's case, neither applied. The wrecked buses, cars and oil tankers that littered the road gave little succour (the most memorable being a bus that had somehow run straight up a vertical cliff face and was sitting on its rear end in the roadside gully.)

The only relief came when we were twice forced to stop on a desert plain by herds of gazelle crossing the road in front of us. A third stop brought only stress when Shahpour jumped from the car to assault a young woman in tribal dress who seemed to be waiting for a bus. She ran, but he followed, grabbing at her breasts and running his hand under her dress. He then came back to the car, beaming. This was going nowhere good.

'He is only joking,' the colonel told us. This only accelerated the growing sense of foreboding. Finally, it came to a head in a small village in the middle of the afternoon.

We'd stopped for tea and more vodka when the colonel took to arm-wrestling the other three, all together, on the bonnet of the car.

'You want to try?' Shahpour asked me. 'You want to wrestle with me?'

'No, thanks,' I said, deploying elementary rules of self-preservation. 'You are very strong.' This seemed the best way of avoiding having my arm wrenched from its socket.

'Ah,' he said. 'Irishmen are not strong.'

'No,' I agreed. 'Not strong.'

As an alternative to removing my arm, Shahpour began to pelt me with snowballs. I walked away but he followed and grabbed me tightly around the throat from behind. There was a moment of quiet panic, rational enough under the circumstances. Then Shahpour sailed through the air and landed on his back with a horrible clunk. Long-ago judo nights from back in Gurranabraher parish hall.

But one fall doesn't a penitent make. Shahpour looked up in disbelief at skinny emaciated me.

'A-a-a-a-rgh!' he bellowed. 'Fuck you!' He was back on his feet with diabolical speed, fists flailing and a murder light in his eyes. But the colonel and cousin Farzan held him off. I have no doubt that Shahpour could've ploughed through them; but from his face you could tell that he wasn't sure what else was in the bag of tricks. That was probably the saving of me.

'You are one mad bastard,' Cora said, first quiet moment we had. 'You'll have us killed yet.'

None the less, I was her hero for a day.

As you can imagine, the fall of Shahpour fairly coloured the day. From that point on, his driving was even worse than before; his dislike for me was absolute. Huzvak, on the other hand, stayed wide awake. No more flopping hands. Colonel Zander tried to make peace, but the Rubicon had been crossed. We came into Tehran at 120 kms an hour in the dark and maintained that speed until we screeched to a halt outside the Post Office where Cora and I got out. The colonel was about to wish us well but Shahpour took off in a wheelie. We walked to Amir Kabir Lane and booked into the Aria Hotel to be met by Anna, Mareike and Wilhelm whom we'd last seen in Kandahar on our night with the irreducible Mr. John. Anna was still in her Kuchi dress and the million bracelets. Mareike, still in a shalwar-kameez, continued to live in Anna's shadow. Wilhelm remained the emaciated, unshaven, doped-out wreck, although he seemed to have taken a cue from the two women and now also wore hooped earrings similar to theirs.

'Did you have a good journey?' Anna asked.

'Like a dream,' Cora said. 'Hope I wake up soon.' Outside it started

# Chapter 29

to snow again. Wilhelm pulled out a nodule of hash. Cora started on the stories.

'I must ask you both,' Anna said at some point. 'Have either of you ever been struck by lightning?'

'It's his fault,' Cora said. 'Back in Ballyphehane, my part of the world, people go to Yaughal on their holidays.'

After one night at the Aria, we called at the local hamam for a hot bath before contacting Thierry and Catherine to let them know we were in town.

'You should've rung when you arrived!' Catherine howled down the phone. 'Come over now. It's beautiful here in the snow. We live at the foot of the mountains. Near the Hilton. You'll love it.'

\* \* \*

In snow that was ankle-deep, we hailed a taxi and headed for the glittering white wall that soared above the city. An hour later, we were ensconced in a warm bright living room, surrounded by plush carpets, sumptuous cushions and the curious bleating of a white lamb.

'We rescued him from a market in Shiraz,' Catherine explained. 'He looked so helpless. We thought he'd make a lovely pet.'

'Unfortunately,' Thierry added, 'he seems to rebel against being house-trained.'

'He's gorgeous,' Cora said. I wasn't too sure, mindful of the fact that small lambs grow into big sheep.

'You've no garden' I noted. 'Do they not do gerbils in Tehran?'

'Gerbils would be so boring,' Catherine said. At that, Gorgeous dropped an impressive load on one of the carpets.

'I suppose that's where a gerbil would shine,' Cora said.

'Kebabs...?' I added.

Catherine didn't see the joke.

We spent three days with Thierry and Catherine, sleeping in a comfortable bed, being sung to at night by crickets, and occasionally baby-sitting the pet lamb and not making too good a hand of it. The first time it bleated incessantly, Cora fed it milk from its bottle. But the thing let us down badly: it got sick all over the place. Thierry reckoned the temperature of the milk wasn't quite right.

It snowed heavily throughout the second day and the four of us went outside to throw snowballs.

'It's lovely,' Thierry said. 'But it could be bad for travelling to Istanbul.'

In the evening we had visitors, friends of Thierry and Catherine whom they'd invited around for drinks and a (tobacco) waterpipe. Mainly drawn from Tehran's middle class and expat populations, they were all opponents of the Shah's regime. Thierry introduced myself and Cora and the four of us regaled the arrivals with stories of the wedding on Qeshm.

Later, I mentioned my stay in Tabriz during the first journey, and the story of Howard Baskerville.

'Is there any chance of another Constitutional Revolution?' I asked.

Parvis, a young university professor, whose wife Gail worked at the Canadian Embassy, was gloomy about the prospects for change. Prematurely bald, with a Van Dyke beard, he was lying on the floor, his head propped against a cushion.

'SAVAK is everywhere,' he said. 'If you raise your voice, you are arrested. It is dangerous to even have a conversation like this. You could simply disappear. With the terror of SAVAK it is difficult to see how things can change.'

'It has happened in other places,' I said. 'Like Cuba.'

'The conditions are not the same,' Gail said. 'In Iran there is no chance of an armed insurrection, and democracy has been destroyed. With the levels of oppression and surveillance that exist, it is hard to see any options. Any attempt at change would simply bring a violent backlash from the state.'

'There has to be space to organise on a large scale,' Parvis added. 'In Iran that is not possible.'

Reminds me now of Thomas Hardy on the sinking of the Titanic:

> 'And as the smart ship grew
> In stature, grace, and hue,
> In shadowy silent distance grew the Iceberg too.' [28]

If we could've looked six short years into the future, we would've seen an Iran rocked by huge demonstrations. These would indeed prompt state violence on a massive scale, with the Shah's forces reportedly killing hundreds of people in a single demonstration in Tehran's Jhaleh Square in September 1978. President Jimmy Carter would call the Shah to assure him of ongoing American

---

[28] 'The Convergence Of The Twain.'

## Chapter 29

support. But the momentum would prove unstoppable. On January 16th 1979 the Shah and his family would be driven into ignominious exile. Sixteen days later, a tall, white-bearded mullah would step from an Air France plane in Tehran, triumphantly ending fourteen years' exile from his homeland. By then SAVAK and the Shah's entire terror machine would have been swept aside, to be replaced, unfortunately, by the terror machine of Iran's Islamic revolution.

When Thierry and Catherine bade goodbye to their friends that night, Tehran was blowing a ferocious blizzard.

*Cora at the Ali Qapu Palace, built in the 17th century during the reign of Shah Abbas, Isfahan, Iran, January 1972.*

# Chapter 30

## Minus Forty

As winter had now closed in harshly, Cora and I decided to take the train directly back to Üsküdar. But we discovered at the railway station that the line was cut in eastern Turkey by heavy snow. In the hope that things might change, we waited until two o'clock in the afternoon, but no luck. Trains to Turkey were off.

'Seems like snow in Turkey doesn't melt like snow in Ireland,' Cora said.

'We could take a train to Tabriz,' I suggested, 'and see if we can make our way by road from there. The oil run to Europe runs through eastern Turkey; you'd imagine they'd have to keep that road open.'

Two others, who were also at the station, shared that belief and decided to join us. One was a lanky, pale-faced, 23-year-old German with a runny nose, thick black curls and wide sunken eyes. His name was Siegfried and he was dressed in jeans, boots, wool hat and heavy white Afghan jacket. The second was a big 25-year-old Afghan named Abdul, a friendly broad-faced figure with a huge moustache, who wore a full-length heavy overcoat and a wool hat pulled down to his eyes. Carrying two enormous suitcases, Abdul was on his way to Germany to work.

'I am not sure of the Afghan man,' Siegfried confided when Abdul was talking to Cora.

'German man looks crazy man,' Abdul confided in Cora.

The train left Tehran at three o'clock on an afternoon of winter darkness, compressed by a black bulging sky full of snow. Siegfried quickly fell asleep. Abdul was full of questions about Ireland.

'In I-lan, you have snow?' he asked.

'Yes,' Cora said. 'But not like this. Only a little snow.'

'In I-lan you have Muslim?'

'Only a small number.'

'Only *small* Muslim!'

'No, no. Only *not many* Muslim.'

'Oh! In I-lan you have camel?'

'Only in the zoo...' And so it went until Cora got him to talk about himself.

'My family live Kabul,' he said. 'Father, mother, three brother, two

## Chapter 30

sister. One sister die before. My father, he make shoe and bucket from old car, old - how you say - wheel?'

'Tyre?' Cora said.

'Tyre. Yes. Family no have good money. No have good house. I go Deutchland for working. Working München to make place for Olympic. For make money for send family. Now is holiday. Christmas holiday from Deutchland.'

We chatted for an hour while the train rumbled through the dark. As we began to doze, Abdul promised to come to Ireland if he could get a visa.

'No easy,' he said. 'Visa no easy for Afghan man.'

After a journey through a freezing night, we arrived in Tabriz at eight in the morning. On the platform, we were joined by a 28-year-old American named David, dressed in dungarees and sweater, and sporting a beard that was the result of a point-blank refusal to shave in the cold.

'So you guys are gonna make a run for it?' he said. 'Then, OK. Let's give it a go. You got some kinda plan?'

We hailed a taxi.

'Bazargan? Frontier?' I asked. 'How much?' I accompanied the question with the universal twiddling of the thumb and fingers that denotes money.

He showed me two 100-rial notes.

'Two hundred?' I said.

'Two hundred,' he agreed, waving the two notes and pointing to each of us. Two hundred each to take us to the Turkish border.

As soon as we left Tabriz it began to snow again, and snowed most of the way until we were inching along the mountain roads in a shroud of white on snow-chains and adrenalin. The journey of about 160 kilometres took nine hours. In those hours, the price doubled in the driver's head.

'Four hundred rial,' he said when we went to pay at the border.

'No way man!' David yelled. 'In Tabriz, you said 200 rials each and that's what you're getting!'

'Bastard American!' the taxi driver shouted and the row mushroomed, with Siegfried developing an uneasy, *what's-happenin'* look and the border guards joining in on the Iranian side. Next thing we knew, we were all arrested.

'Pay man,' Siegfried said in a fit of panic. 'We just pay and we go.'

We were on the long ride to nowhere as the handcuffs were

produced. We coughed up the extra two dollars each, cursed the taxi man and crossed into Turkey at Iranhududu in a blinding blizzard. Driven by a ferocious ice-wind that swept down from the eastern cone of Ararat, horizontal sheets of snow sent us scurrying for the warmth of the only accommodation we could find, a basic little abode with bare rooms that had seen better days.

'What's going on?' Cora asked when we were shown our room. 'Siegfried's after arranging the accommodation so that Abdul is in a room of his own and the rest of us are in here.'

Apart from a possible racist motive, this made no sense until we'd thrown down our packs and pounded the snow from our boots, at which point Siegfried took off his jacket, rolled up his left sleeve, shot up with morphine, and flopped onto his bed with eyes bulging like golf balls.

'Man,' he moaned. 'For 200 rials we get arrested? You know, I have 4,000 tabs of morphine sewn into my jacket.'

'You have what...?' I said.

'Back in Germany, I am a dealer. I go many times between Munich and India, where I can find the morphine cheap and easy.'

'Nice of you to tell us now, man,' David said, pulling out from his dungarees a nugget of hash that he'd bought in Tehran. 'If you'd got busted back there, the rest of us woulda got busted too, and Iran is not the fuckin' place to get busted.'

'I used to do heroin, man' Siegfried said. 'But I OD'd on it twice - I was dead, man - and had to be brought back to life again. So, now I only take clean morphine that I can know the strength. The problem with the heroin is that you can never know the strength. If it is too pure, it will kill you.'

'Fuck you man,' David said.

In the morning the snow had stopped but it was freezing hard outside. With everything covered in snow and Ararat and its neighbours washed in pale sunlight, a dolmus brought us over the mountains to Dogubayazit. Twenty months before, I'd shared the bus office floor with the Germans, Werner and Bernd. This time round, it was a survival hut, glittering with icicles. Inside, men in heavy coats and blankets stamped their feet and blew on their hands. Veiled women, similarly muffed up, huddled around the wood stove. Outside in the streets, horses and overloaded trucks skidded in all directions. Yet, life went on, with market stalls open and one man selling naturally frozen fish from a handcart.

# Chapter 30

Another dolmus brought us to Agri, now under siege by the weather. On the outskirts, the small, scattered flat-topped houses were half buried in snow; a bitter north easterly, whipping across the steppes, had brought life to a virtual standstill. It was the coldest winter in ten years, they told us, with night temperatures dropping to minus forty centigrade.[29] And the days not much better. The frost was an inch thick on the only street lights in town and half-dead sparrows perched on frozen trees. If you stood outside for any length of time your face would go blotchy, your eyes would sink in grey lined circles to your cheekbones and the blood would race from your ears, fingers and toes to save the vital organs. Yet, the town centre struggled to maintain itself. People stood at corners, selling cigarettes. Others moved around on crude ice-skates on the hard-packed snow. Others still pushed loaded handcarts - some with entire shops attached - up and down the impossibly slippery streets, boots crunching loud on the frozen snow. In an alleyway, the garbage men had arrived to shovel a mound of rubbish - which included discarded cows' heads - onto a cart.

Walking anywhere was deadly, as the ice was often hidden under fresh snow and could land you a terrible fall. Nevertheless, in the central square of single- and two-storey blocks where two-metre icicles hung from buildings, horses trotted along, pulling sleighs without a bother, while the one visible tractor had to resort to snow-chains.

As soon as we'd left the minibus, our entire group fled to the warmth of a back-street restaurant and had kebabs and scalding hot tea. We then crunched our way through the snow to one of Agri's small bus depots and bought tickets for the 5.00pm bus to Istanbul which, we were told, would take twenty-four hours. On our way to the depot we were passing under the eaves of a small hotel when a man leaned out of an upstairs window, whacked at the massive icicles hanging there, and sent several of them crashing down around Cora and Siegfried. If you were hit by one of these, it would be like being hit by a concrete block.

'Fuck you man!' Siegfried yelled whereupon the offender sent a second shower for good measure. We took to walking on the street.

In the afternoon our numbers grew to nine with the arrival in town of a German couple named George - and Cora. And two young

---

[29] The lowest temperature ever recorded in Agri was minus 45.6 degrees centigrade on January 20th 1972.

Iranians, Ahmad and Iraj who had crossed illegally from Iran into Turkey by riding horses over the mountains.

'It was so cold in the snow,' Ahmad said. 'I lose every feeling and fall from my horse two time.' Ahmad and Iraj were on their way back to England, from whence they had recently been deported for dealings linked to the smuggling trade.

'We are on the same bus as you,' George said. 'And we have just come from the bus station. Now the bus is not leaving until seven o'clock tomorrow morning. They are saying that the road is cut off by snow.'

Having double-checked this information back at the bus depot, Abdul and Ahmad went off and found us all a cheap hotel where the bathroom taps were frozen and we spent the evening wrapped around the wood-stove in an attempt to ward off plunging temperatures.

After dark, I went outside to see how minus forty centigrade felt.

Within seconds the condensation from my breath became solid ice on my moustache. A couple of minutes, and my hands, feet, shins and thighs felt buried in permafrost, the ice moved to my sideburns, and the hairs in my nostrils turned to pricking needles. The only way to breathe without having the frozen air catch my lungs, was to take it in slowly through my nose to warm it.

In the weak light escaping from the frosted windows I could see my exhaled breath freeze and drop away. When I opened the door to go back inside the rush of incoming air froze the moisture in the room, sending a small white cloud of ice crystals rolling across the floor like the plagues of Egypt.

That night, away from the wood stove, ice clogged up the window of our bedroom while Cora and I slept in every stitch of clothing we had, wrapped in our sleeping bags and every blanket in the room.

At half six on the morning of Wednesday, January 19th, we stepped out into the dark streets of Agri and were greeted by the coldest morning any of us had ever, ever felt. Cold that can't be imagined. By the time we reached the bus depot through streets of frozen trees, ice had formed again on beards, moustaches and sideburns, noses were prickling and we were frozen solid. At the depot I used an outside loo where everything was ice, and the risk of breaking your neck on the frozen floor was superseded only by the risk of losing forever any bared extremities.

At eight o'clock perfect pandemonium broke out in the vicinity of our bus. It was to do with the width of the door and aisle. Whole

## Chapter 30

families who had finished their on-board goodbyes were battling to get off while other entire families were battling to get on, everybody yelling at everybody else. Then there was the usual mountain of luggage that had to be fitted on somehow. But, eventually it all got sorted and we left Agri at half past eight.

Despite the cold and the treacherous road there was initially a good sense of camaraderie on board. People passed around food and cigarettes; and a sense of shared adventure grew between the passengers and crew. With no concession to conditions, we careered along, overtaking in triumphant sweeps even when the road had completely disappeared in the snow, or visibility was reduced to a few metres by swirling spindrift blown up by the wind. On both sides, the frozen steppes rolled away to distant mountain ranges, covered in snow. Every now and then, the ranges would close in on the road and we'd find ourselves overlooked by towering massifs, with warnings of potential rock falls jutting out of the snow. Omer the driver, a big, dignified man with a three-day stubble and trimmed, greying moustache, sat hunched over the wheel in a heavy overcoat, gloves and woollen hat, his concentration set firmly on keeping the bus on the road. His mate, 20-year-old Ayhan, lean, narrow-jawed and rolled up in sweaters and a heavy blanket, kept him company up front or chatted with the passengers. In spite of the language barrier, I got on well with Ayhan, a finer detail for which Siegfried should be eternally grateful.

From the start it was clear that we had a problem with the heating. The trickle of lukewarm air filtering up from below was totally inadequate, so the bus never warmed up. As the day wore on and we reached the gorge country around the 2,315-metre Sac Pass - narrow defiles cutting through precipitous cliffs midway between Agri and Erzurum - ice had formed on all the windows. Regardless of Ayhan's best efforts with the heating, everyone was shaking with the cold. Cora and I were buried in our sleeping bags, teeth chattering and the cold biting to our marrows. Although the sun had risen in a clear sky, its weak rays gave no comfort. To add to our woes, increasingly deteriorating road conditions meant increasingly less progress. Eventually, nerves began to fray.

A short stop at Erzurum bus station brought temporary relief, allowing us to grab a cup of tea and something to eat, and to thaw out a little over the waiting-room stove. Then it was back to the bus again, and serious mountain country.

At first we rose slightly, topped a pass, and cut into a long narrow gorge where some pines began to appear. Past the village of Tercan the road ran into the valley of the narrow, half-frozen Firat River (known further down as the Euphrates) that meandered between the Keþiþ and Munzur ranges. Here, the pines began to rise in small stark forests from the blanket snow of the slopes, giving the sense of hope that trees so often do. But, as we approached Erzincan, the hope was brushed away by the Mercan Mountains. Looming up to the south, their razorback ridges and vast snowfields looked terrifying in the fading light.

David, who was sitting across from us, muttered out of a frozen stupor.

'It's gonna get worse. Once it gets dark we're gonna be plummeted back into the temperatures we had last night, but no stove this time. They'll have to stop the night in the next town.'

They didn't.

I suppose we could've got off, but numbed to stupidity, none of us did.

At Erzincan bus station, there was a fierce row. A couple turned up with a wagonload of baggage which had to be loaded onto every last crack on the bus. The woman, in full veil and blanket, was clearly yelling, *I told you so*. The man, in several layers of coats, a blanket and a turban, was waving his hennaed hands in the air. He was clearly yelling, *It's all your rubbish*. Once they'd stopped shouting, they boarded the bus. We then left the city and continued through a series of gorges and valleys, rising eventually through the pines of the 2,160-metre Sakaltutan Pass.

Occasionally, small villages with tin-roofed, half-buried houses, lay crouched in the valleys, some looking fresh out of Switzerland, while alpine snow-meadows were criss-crossed by the tracks of numerous small animals. The last light of the day saw us begin the long haul up the Kizildag Pass where the mountain vistas stretched forever. In the frosted pines on both sides of the road, everything that wasn't freezing to death was now surely already dead. We were still hauling our laborious and dangerous way up towards the top of the pass when night fell, making everything even more laborious and dangerous.

In the dark, we passed two trucks that had crashed headlong into one another and were lying at an angle, down off the road on a bank of snow.

## Chapter 30

'Tut! Tut! Tut!' went Omer, despite his own driving.

'Tut! Tut! Tut!' agreed Ayhan.

Some time after dark we were held up for two hours in a blizzard of grim determination while snowploughs cleared a mini-avalanche from the road up ahead. David went outside briefly, came back looking like an ice cream and spoke from the door.

'One of the guys out there told me that a bus broke down and got stuck in the snow last week and everyone on board froze to death.'

While this cheerful news was digested, Omer ran the engine in short bursts to keep whatever semblance of heat we had alive. Then, just as the snow was cleared, the heating went and we all started to really die. The cold that now gripped the bus was of a kind you never want to experience. The windows, already caked in ice, took a second coat, while the whole interior of the bus - the roof, the sides, the floor, even the seats - iced over. In attempts to retain body heat, people resorted to everything: some drew closer together; others sat cross-legged to keep their feet off the frozen floor; some jumped up and down and stamped their feet; some swung from the handrails; but gradually everyone slumped back into their seats. David called it the hide-and-die syndrome.

'Happens just before you pop off,' he said.

Now, the engine fuel line also began to freeze. Every now and again, Ayhan had to get out into the deathly cold with an iron bar wrapped in a flaming petrol-soaked rag, so he could melt the problem. This he did without complaint, although it left him shivering uncontrollably each time. Then, out there in the bleak and frozen wastes of Anatolia, on a bus that was pretty much on its own, Siegfried fell foul of the driver's mate.

Ayhan had been rummaging in the back for something when he put a pack down on Siegfried's overcoat. Siegfried, wearing the coat at the time, gruffly pushed the pack away. It was the straw that broke the donkey's back. Ayhan picked up the pack and hurled it at Siegfried's head. In response, doped-up Siegfried got up and thumped him. Ayhan flew into a rage, lashed out with his fists and flattened Siegfried. He then rushed up the dimly lit bus, grabbed his iron bar and came charging back to finish the job. I was sitting in front of Siegfried; and as he ducked to save himself, I managed to wrestle Ayhan to the floor and get the bar from him as everyone on board got involved along ethnic lines in a yelling match.

'Not good,' I tried to reason with Ayhan.

When we got up from the floor he put his hand, still shaking with rage, on my shoulder.

'*Effendi, effendi,*' he assured me, letting me know I was still his friend. But Siegfried, to whom he'd taken a deep dislike, was most certainly not. Just as we all relaxed, Ayhan swung for him again with the iron bar and we both ended up on the floor a second time. Then Ayhan saw the funny side and he laughed. Siegfried, with his nose bleeding, was shaking from the thumping and the morphine.

By four in the morning, conditions on the bus were serious. It had taken twenty hours to travel less than 450 kilometres and we were just over a third of the way to Istanbul. With temperatures inside the bus not much better than those on the outside, most of us were already in various stages of severe hypothermia. How Omer kept on driving is a mystery to me. Then, just after four, we stopped at a small isolated hotel and the passengers brought the nightmare to an end, stumbling wildly through the snow towards the comforting cracks of light and the warm stove and life-restoring hot tea. Neither hell nor high water would've shifted a soul until the sun was well up in the morrow's sky.

Next day, we crossed another desolate stretch of steppe, its sparse settlements tucked away among the hills, and finally arrived at Sivas bus station. We had now, we were told, left the worst of the snow behind. Our ordeal was over.

Then, while most of us waited around the stove and Ayhan went off to find a mechanic to restore our heating system, Cora went out to buy bread. Ten minutes later, she burst through the door. In her combat jacket, jeans and walking boots, she looked like an unhinged soldier who'd just been ambushed.

'Quick!' she shouted. 'Outside and catch the bastard.'

'What bastard?' I asked.

'The bastard who grabbed me! Two guys came from behind and one of them went for me. I turned and got him by the coat and kicked him around the station - but it was the wrong guy. When I went for the other one, he got away.'

War...

I shot out of the office, followed by Cora, Siegfried and Abdul, still carrying his two suitcases which he'd removed from the bus. We rushed to the tea shop where we found the guy who'd taken the proxy kicking. Abdul dragged him outside and he pointed out the culprit who was mingling with other passengers about to board

## Chapter 30

a bus. When he realised he'd been spotted he took off, running towards a group of buildings at one end of the station. Now joined by Ahmad and Iraj, we scattered our forces. Abdul, still carrying his suitcases, ran towards the exit to cut off any possible escape towards town. Eventually we cornered the quarry. I was for summary justice - let Cora and her boots loose on him - but the poltroon screamed for the cops.

'I think we should let the police take care of the problem,' Siegfried said, mindful of his 4,000 tabs of morphine. 'Otherwise we will be arrested again.'

Very reluctantly we hauled him off to the station cop shop where bureaucracy intervened.

'To have some actions,' the chief told us, 'you must to go to central police station.'

'But we can't,' I said. 'The bus will be gone.'

'I am sorry,' he concluded. 'It is too bad.'

On hearing this I lunged at the defendant but was checked by Siegfried. The culprit backed out of the cop shop with a dirty grin on his face. He was about to escape justice. Then Abdul arrived. Spotting the retreating groper, a great smile split his face. Breaking into a run, suitcases still dangling, he came from behind and landed the enemy an almighty boot up the arse that sent him sprawling, face first, into the mud and filthy snow of one of the bus bays.

'Good shit, old shot,' David said. It was a saying of the time.

At nine o'clock that night, more than thirty-six hours after leaving Agri, we arrived in Ankara, free at last of the deadly cold of eastern Turkey. In the bus station, we celebrated with tea and beers and waited for a replacement bus to take us to Istanbul. At half ten, we were ready to leave again but there was no sign of Siegfried.

'He went to the toilet,' George said.

'That was fifteen minutes ago,' David said.

'Jesus, Mary and St. Joseph,' Cora choked. 'Take a look at what's coming.'

Siegfried looked like he'd had a stroke. Huge bags had inflated under his eyes, which were bulging bottomless out of deep craters. The rest of his face was blood-red and distorted, and his lips were trembling uncontrollably. 'I have shot up in the toilet,' he mumbled. 'The morphine and the beer...'

The ghastly apparition slumped into one of the seats and sunk into what looked like deep death.

'Rest in peace,' David said.

We left Ankara, and as the new bus warmed up, the rest of us gradually dozed off into comas.

In the morning, we arrived on the Asian side of the Bosphorus to a heart-warming sunrise and the bus boarded the ferry for Istanbul. Now, when rejoicing was logical, I found myself sinking into deflation. I had just completed a second failed attempt on India.

'What's meant to be is meant to be,' Cora said. 'It was a great trip anyway.'

'Next time,' I said.

'Next time?' Cora said. 'You are joking...'

On the European side Abdul got off and we never saw him again. The bus took the rest of us to Topkapi Gate and a mini-bus brought us into the city. David, Cora and I had breakfast at the Pudding Shop before booking into the Ayasofya Hotel where David finally took off the boiler suit he'd been wearing since Tehran. After a well-earned shower, Cora and I slept for the afternoon and ate at Yener's that night, where we ran into George and the other Cora. Siegfried also turned up, looking exceptionally despondent.

'There was a letter at the post office from my father,' he told us. 'He says that the police have found out that I am bringing morphine from India to Germany. They are waiting for me at every border.'

'Oh, this is not good for you,' mutton-chops Yener said. 'Maybe they extradite you?'

'The German cops have smashed the circle of people bringing the stuff in,' Siegfried said. 'They believe that this is leaving only two of the big dealers free. They believe that I am one of them.'

'Very bad news for you,' Yener said. 'You must have coffee or some other thing.'

'So, you are back,' Yener said, turning to myself and Cora. 'No India this time. But maybe we will see you again... Another time?'

On Sunday, January 23rd 1972, two days after we arrived in Istanbul, the city was placed under curfew from 3.00am to 6.00pm as the army and cops searched for five escaped political prisoners. All day long, trucks, jeeps and cop cars patrolled the empty streets and helicopters circled the city while 80,000 of the state's forces combed every single street and building, including our hotel room, for the escapees. At six o'clock on the dot, the city burst to life again, with people appearing simultaneously at every doorway. The search, it transpired, had been fruitless. They found nothing.

## Chapter 30

When the search was over, Cora and I went to the train station and bought tickets for the express train to Munich. This left us with £15 in our pockets which meant that we'd have to borrow from Viktor in Munich to enable us to get home. After dinner, Ahmad and Iraj turned up at the Ayasofya to celebrate the escape of the political prisoners.

Two days later Cora, David and I boarded the train for Munich and shared a compartment with a Turkish student who told us that the line from Tehran to Istanbul was still closed because of the snow. The news induced a collective shudder. Then the three of us laughed.

'Never again!' David said. 'Never again will we have to take that awful road, except maybe when we wake up in the middle of the night screaming for our mothers...'

In the not too distant future nobody at all would take that road. Unknown to us, the thunderstorms of history were darkening over the hippie trail. In 1979, after the Islamic revolution in Iran, the mullahs would close it and its day would be done.

# Chapter 31
Later

I went back to Turkey in December 2004. It was to be a two-week, all-inclusive package holiday on the south coast, but I should have known better.

I stayed three days, then packed a small bag and fled east, going from twenty-three degrees centigrade to minus thirty-two in four days and finding myself in a flip-side world. Military saturation, political murder, and sinister stubble-faced secret police who jumped from unmarked vans and refused to believe that a foreigner in Kurdistan could be innocent, were a far cry from the sanitised resorts of the Mediteranean. Over the next ten days I found friendship among the Kurds and again visited Sivas, Erzurum, Agri with its appalling cold (*The coldest place in Turkey*, they told me), and Dogubayazit at the foot of snow-covered Ararat.

Walking along the base of the mountain, I covered several kilometres towards the Iranian border in an area now torn apart in the long war between the Turkish army and Kurdish separatists. Then the name of the border post, Iranhududu, appeared on a signpost and I felt a thump in my chest from a time when young women and men thought they could change the world by being free. For a fleeting moment I could hear their ghosts tramping down the old trail towards the frontier, the turn of a phrase or the way of a laugh lingering on the edge of the wind. I sat by the roadside, a curious figure to the men who stared from the odd truck that rolled by, and I remembered in that freezing afternoon how it was all such a long time ago. I wondered where Viktor was, and what he was thinking. Someday I might go to Munich and look him up.

Almost thirty-three years had passed but the place had changed little. Looking up at the snows where Bill from Leeds had once sworn he could see Noah's Ark, I felt sorry that my old friend and first travelling companion had never made it that far. Tony O'Connor would have loved Asia. He would have loved Turkey and Iran and the desert kingdom to the east. And I would have enjoyed seeing them through the irreverent scrutiny of his eyes. In Istanbul in the spring of 1970, we had put it on hold until the next time, but the future is a silent thief.

# Chapter 31

When Tony left us in January 2008 I was in northern Mauritania. Less than three weeks earlier, on Christmas Day, I'd been walking with a camel through a Sahara dust storm in the company of two desert nomads when I made three calls on my satellite phone, the only time I have ever carried such a device. One was to Tony, catching him as he and Marie, and their grown children, Niall, Rory and Sinéad, sat down to the festive dinner.

'Good luck, boy,' he said at the end of the call. 'See you when you get back.'

That was the last time we spoke. Tony died suddenly on January 12th and left behind a world the poorer for his passing. When the news reached me I was in Dakhla in Western Sahara. After close on fifty years of friendship stretching back to childhood, the keeper of our shared history - who was there on the day back in 1970 when we crossed the Strait of Gibraltar and left behind the familiar world - was gone.

At the time I was already working on this book and was writing it in part for Tony who asked that the first copy I took into my hands would be his. I wish I could have made the deadline. He would have enjoyed the end product and laughed and told me over a jar in Cork's Spailpín Fánach that it was a good yarn.

He was, after all, my most enduring friend.